THE MISSING JFK ASSASSINATION FILM:

THE MYSTERY SURROUNDING THE ORVILLE NIX HOME MOVIE OF NOVEMBER 22, 1963

GAYLE NIX JACKSON

Skyhorse Publishing

First Skyhorse Publishing edition 2016

10 9 8 7 6 5 4 3 2 1

Library of Congress Cataloging-in-Publication Data is available on file.

Cover design by Rain Saukas
JFK image is public domain, camera image courtesy of istock.

Print ISBN: 978-1-5107-0661-3
Ebook ISBN: 978-1-5107-0663-7

Printed in the United States

But they that will be rich fall into... a snare... which drown men in destruction and perdition.

I Timothy 6:9 KJV

It is easier to perceive error than to find truth, for the former lies on the surface and is easily seen, while the latter lies in the depth, where few are willing to search for it.

Johann Wolfgang Von Goethe (1749-1832)

German poet, novelist and dramatist.

When truth is our history, truth buried, even slain, can rise again.

Harold Weisberg

The Founding Fathers gave the free press the protection it must have to bare the secrets of government and inform the people.

Hugo Black

There is a power somewhere so organized, so subtle, so watchful, so interlocked, so complete, so pervasive, that they better not speak above their breath when they speak in condemnation of it.

President Woodrow Wilson

TABLE OF CONTENTS

DEDICATION

To my children, Taylor and Chance; you are the lights of my life and my greatest joy! My wish for you is that you walk in truth, make a difference and be happy with the special people you are.

*To Darryl, my husband, my friend, my conscience and my love.
Thank you for your patience and for your humble support.*

To Dad, Orville Nix Jr., thank you for the lessons you have taught me the memories we have shared and your belief in me.

*To my nephew Adam, I couldn't have done this without you.
You are a man of generosity, honor and understanding.
The world is a better place with you in it.*

To my Mother, who I miss terribly but who I know is looking down on me and comforts me with the knowledge that I am her daughter.

*To my Paw-Paw, Orville Nix and my Granny, Ella Nix.
Without you, this book would have never been written.*

ACKNOWLEDGEMENTS

I've wanted to be a writer since I was a teenager, but it took forty years and a stranger on Twitter asking me if I were Orville Nix's granddaughter to do it. I want to thank that unknown person for giving me the impetus to complete a non-fiction work when I had always fancied myself a fiction writer. My dreams of writing were supplanted by the bigger dream of becoming a mother; who I am privileged to be, to my daughter Taylor and my son Chance. They are my best-sellers!

I would like to thank the inimitable Jones Harris for his weekly phone calls and his sharing of memories with me regarding the research and time he spent in trying to prove the Nix film is much more important than the media and the government wanted people to know. In a metaphysical way, it was like talking to a friend of my grandfather, though they never met. I hope this book gives credit to his tireless efforts to find the truth of what truly happened November 22, 1963. I adore you, Jones!

Chris Calderhead, my book cover designer and friend of many years who I've never met. Thank you for the book cover I saw in my dreams. You made it a reality. Your talent, wit and baseball discussions will never be forgotten.

The countless hours I spent on the JFK Assassination Forum were the grandest hours of discovery I've had since becoming a mother. I am honored to call Duncan MacRae, Rick Needham, Martin Hinrichs, and Robin Unger dear friends, advisors and oftentimes tutors. Their patience, support and hard work are groundbreaking and they deserve exaltation in the JFK Research Community.

Tink Thompson, David Lifton, Jim Marrs, Jefferson Morley, and Mary Ferrell are the Jupiters to my Callisto. I orbited around their knowledge and writings hoping I could shine some gratitude upon them. Thank you kind experts for your patience and sharing. Especially you, Jim!

Thank you, Dr. Larry Sabato, for wanting to know more about my grandfather and his story, and for inviting me to be a part of your book launch. Educators like you set the bar for others.

Thank you Chris Scally, for your tireless Nix film research in trying to help me find the missing camera original film as well as for your kind emails and dear friendship. Thank you, Clint Bradford, for trying to help me locate my grandfather's original film

Thank you to every person who has said, "I can't wait to read your book!" to me. You have no idea how much that means to this writer.

Bruce Marshall holds a special place in the completion of *Orville Nix: The Missing JFK Assassination Film.* He is a brilliant man who took time from his busy schedule to not only share his wisdom with me, but he helped with my manuscript, finding me an attorney, and directing me to the right equipment to purchase in doing telephonic interviews. I was the 'little old lady crossing the JFK research book' road and he was the Eagle Scout that chivalrously accompanied me to the other side safely.

My editor, Ann Westlake should be granted literary sainthood for her patience. My dear friend and website designer Lin Taylor is the sister I always wanted to have and now do. She is talented, supportive and the best part is, *she gets me.* For many years I have known that when you find someone that understands your emotional /intellectual/spiritual roadmap you keep them in your life. Lin is one of these people. Johanna Socha, another one of those 'keep in your life' people, is the most upbeat, positive, creative graphic designers I have ever met. She puts the 'ful' in beautiful.

To one of my best friends, Doug Conn. Meeting you made my life in East Texas bearable and your friendship means the world to me.

I know there are many I am forgetting, so please accept my apologies. Know in your hearts that you were there for me when I floundered. You were there when I doubted. You were there when I needed you.

Thank you

PREFACE

Our country was founded upon conspiracies. Look at our history: The Boston Tea Party, The Continental Congress, even *The Federalist Papers*. These conspiracies were to make our country a better one in which to live *"for the people."* The only ones who questioned those conspiracies at the time were those who were attempting to control our freedom. The JFK conspiracy is the opposite of those colonial conspiracies.

This book will *not* solve the question that was first asked on November 22, 1963, "Who killed John F. Kennedy?" What I hope this book *will* do is underscore the fact that there was and is a conspiracy to withhold the truth as to what happened that dreadful day, not just to my grandfather, but to the world.

For years we have been lured into believing that the obvious must be denied. We have been told by our government, the media and several taxpayer funded committees and commissions that Lee Harvey Oswald was a lone gunman. What we haven't been told is the story of Orville Nix. We haven't been told how many pieces of evidence are missing. We haven't been told of the many stories of intimidation, misinformation and lies.

Our freedom is waning.

Why?

Are the risks too high? Are our choices limited? Have we become the people our government wants us to be rather than our government becoming the people *we* want them to be?

If we choose to allow the media to continue to lie and not ask questions, we risk history repeating itself. If we choose to allow our government to mismanage, mishandle and misinform, we risk being governed by the kind of government we detest. If we choose to not demand truthful answers to pertinent questions, we risk losing our collective intelligence and worse, our collective consciousness.

It is up to us to make a difference. We must demand the truth. There may or may not have been a conspiracy to kill John F. Kennedy. What we do know is that for over fifty years there is and definitely has been a conspiracy to withhold the truth from the people. We deserve the truth to be exposed, studied and dealt with, no matter how sinister or problematic. We fight corruption on foreign shores. We must also fight it on our own shores as well.

We must not lose our freedom to a few when freedom is meant for all.

CHAPTER ONE

FIFTY YEARS OF QUESTIONS

"A nation that is afraid to let its people judge the truth and falsehood in an open market is a nation that is afraid of its people."

John F. Kennedy[1]

Anyone who has taken a history course since November 22, 1963 is well aware of the heinous primary events that took place on that picture-perfect day in Dallas. The 35th president of our sovereign nation was gunned down in front of thousands of people at half past noon on that Friday, in broad daylight. This horrible crime marked the first time television viewers were introduced to reality television. Those who were fortunate enough to own televisions watched the repercussions of the assassination unfold before their eyes for the next four days. Others listened by radio or read newspapers. His suspected murderer, Lee Harvey Oswald, was captured later that day at the Texas Theater after allegedly killing Dallas police officer J.D. Tippit. The crime wasn't hidden by darkness—but much of the evidence has been hidden in its aftermath.

One of those pieces of evidence is the home movie my grandfather, Orville Nix, took on that fateful day. Though there are many extant copies of "the Nix

Film", the camera original has been lost since at least 1978.[2] While researchers combed the files of the Warren Commission, the House Select Committee on Assassinations, the Rockefeller Committee, and the Assassination Records Review Board, obsessing over overlooked clues as to whether or not Oswald acted alone, the whereabouts of the camera-original Nix film remains a mystery.

The better-known Abraham Zapruder film has been analyzed, written about, called a 'time clock' of the assassination, and purchased by the United States taxpayers due to its designation as an official assassination record by the Assassination Records Review Board.[3] But why, thirty-seven years after the assassination, was it finally treated as evidence? Why wasn't it seized by the Secret Service, Federal Bureau of Investigation, or the Dallas Police Department on November 22, 1963? Orville Nix's film was seized by the FBI as soon as it was developed. The first time Orville saw it was in the middle of the night with his son Orville Jr., projected onto a textured white wall at its place of development, Dynacolor Film Processing. Orville, unlike Zapruder, was not allowed to keep a copy for himself and give the first generation copies to law enforcement officials. When is evidence ever handled in such a manner? Were the law enforcement authorities in Dallas so ahead of their time that they could adjudicate between 'evidence' and 'conjecture' during the 1960s?

Furthermore, have other pieces of evidence; like the missing autopsy photos or missing audio files of transmissions between the motorcade cars and Secret Service, garnered the same designation as the Nix Film? Or are they already hidden in some dark, government vault labeled Top Secret. Does the American government's sixteen million dollar purchase of the Zapruder film render it the only important piece of evidence, and put an end to the ongoing conspiracy theories? I suggest it does not. How can it, when the film that shows the area behind Abraham Zapruder is missing, thereby leaving open-ended questions as to the location of a second or third gunman.

That our government should be questioned as to why, in a check and balance system such as ours, we have no checks on this evidence (save a sixteen million dollar one) is abhorrent and reprehensible.[4] The original Nix film could be examined, enhanced, and may even prove that the Zapruder film is worthy of every taxpayer's dime. It could also prove that Lee Harvey Oswald did *not* act alone, and that shots came from the grassy knoll or picket fence area, as my grandfather always adamantly insisted. Should not a film taken from the opposite side of the infamous Zapruder film receive at least equal consideration?

Have we as Americans become so complacent that we do not demand the truth of our government unless it's wrapped in Hollywood trappings? When did we *stop* wanting to know the truth?

The Zapruder film isn't the only film record of that horrific day in Dallas; there are still photos as well. Including the Nix film, there were at least five hundred films and photos taken of that day with new ones being dropped off at the Sixth Floor Museum in Dealey Plaza as recently as 2009.[5] The Sixth Floor Museum, located in the building that was once the Texas School Book Depository, is the City of Dallas's attempt to explain what happened in November, 1963. It houses films, exhibits and artifacts of a time many in Dallas would like to forget, but more in the world want to understand.

Very few of the films and photographs from that day show the fatal headshot, much less the entire assassination sequence, and for many, that seems to be of the most importance. There are some researchers and authors though, who believe the Nix Film is the Holy Grail in writing the final chapter of the fifty-year book of the JFK assassination. Their viewpoints and research are included in this book.

*****

HAVE WE AS AMERICANS BECOME SO COMPLACENT THAT WE DO NOT DEMAND THE TRUTH OF OUR GOVERNMENT UNLESS IT'S WRAPPED IN HOLLYWOOD TRAPPINGS?

WHEN DID WE *STOP* WANTING TO KNOW THE TRUTH?

Orville Nix was not an educated man. He wasn't a perfect man either. He did his best to provide for his only son, Orville Nix, Jr. and his wife Ella. He believed in America and loved his government; but he did not trust it. He worked for the government as an air conditioning repairman for the General Services Administration but he never spoke badly of anything he witnessed, heard or saw, for fear of losing his job. He was proud to be friends with Forrest Sorrels of the Dallas Secret Service, but he did not take advantage of that friendship by asking too many questions. He was insecure about his education, his financial standing and his social stature, but he was proud of his family, his golf prowess, his love of snooker, and his luck at cards.

Then there were the women. His kind eyes and tall stature seemed to attract them and though he had ample opportunity, he remained faithful to his wife. He was a man of juxtapositions. In retrospect, he was the 'everyman' of the 1960s. He was the American the government desperately wanted all its citizens to be: hard-working, unquestioning, and happy with their lot in life.

His film brought him his fifteen minutes of fame, a trip to New York and five thousand dollars. To him, it might just as well have been five million dollars.

He had never had so much money in his lifetime. He was able to take his grandchildren on trips, buy new suits and fedoras, play golf and poker at the country club, and buy all the Kodak film he could use. Through the years though, he often said how he wished he had never been on the corner of Main and Houston on November 22, 1963. After the death threats, strange occurrences, destruction of his Keystone K-810 camera, and humiliation in front of America by the national news media, his life and world view changed drastically. He was no longer the happy man who answered the telephone on the first ring. He no longer spent hours outside his home taking home movies of jet airplanes without worry that he would be accosted. He spent more and more time watching television and midget wrestling late at night because of the recurring nightmares he had of watching the president murdered. One of the last reporters he allowed into his home was the future mayor of Dallas, Wes Wise. He no longer trusted the media or government. He and Ella moved from their rental home on Denley to the Wynnewood Apartments in Oak Cliff and paid extra for an unlisted phone number. He died there, in his favorite Naugahyde armchair in 1972.

His film went missing six years later. I don't think he would have been surprised. He was convinced that his film had been tampered with. He believed that the shots that killed the president came from the stockade fence. He felt that the government kept far too many secrets, but was too afraid to ask if his beliefs were true. He feared our government. Should our government expect us to never question what they do in order to have happy lives? When did the government stop working for us? Is ignorance truly bliss?

Knowing these things about my grandfather bothered me for years. I adored him. I was with him that day in Dallas. I have read letters from government officials and researchers and authors that were sent to him. I watched my mother type letters to the FBI, the Keystone Company, Walter Cronkite, and United Press International. I was with him during his last national televised appearance with CBS. When I think back about my adolescent years and how I laughed at his fear of people wanting to kill him, I chastise myself. He wasn't being paranoid. He had valid reasons to be afraid, but I was too young and immature to understand them. People who weren't from Dallas still don't understand the fear that gripped many witnesses then and now.

Why weren't his viewpoints given the same respect by the government and media as others were? Why wasn't he asked to testify before the Warren Commission? Why did the FBI keep his camera for over five months and finally send it back to him in pieces? Why was his film taken by the FBI, kept for several days, and then sent back to him? Why is his camera original still missing?

Why?

It is my hope that this story of his life and experience with John F. Kennedy's assassination will shed some light onto these questions and the human condition. Through research, interviews, and my own experience in trying to locate the film, I have a much better understanding of our society and human nature. So many people all over the world are still trying to find the same missing puzzle pieces. Some fabricate unsubstantiated scenarios, hoping no one realizes that their theories are no more than fantastical hoaxes created for immediate fame, fortune, and Hollywood. More often than not, these are the theories that garner the most media attention and hurt the JFK research truth-seekers. The educated JFK researcher realizes the photographic evidence never quite fits their scenarios.

The mainstream media is still trying to convince us that Lee Harvey Oswald acted alone and refuses to investigate conspiracy evidence for fear of losing their biggest financial backers: the government. Others still believe that the government doesn't withhold information from its citizens. These are the people who do not realize the media spoon feeds us a pablum of propaganda we can digest, like the Warren Commission. Still others wish these questions of guilt or conspiracy would all go away because the memory and knowledge they have of key information assuages the guilt they have kept for over fifty years.

Even after Orville Nix's death, the inadequacies that haunted him in his life still do the same to his memory, yet the loss of his original film isn't noted. As the Sixth Floor Museum states on their website when describing the "Nix Collection"

> *"Nix unfortunately used Type A film, specifically designed for indoor use, but without the needed filter. As a result, his film appears darker and grainier than others made in Dealey Plaza that day."* [6]

Time will tell. As the great writer Francis Bacon said, "Truth is the daughter of time…"[7] In Orville Nix's case, I hope truth is the granddaughter of time. He deserved so much better than the life he led after taking this historic film. This book is for my grandfather, who we lovingly called "Paw-Paw" and for every American who gets caught up in anything the government deems unfit for public consumption. It is time for United States citizens to ask questions of our government. It is time to stop allowing double standards in our justice system. It is time to recognize that more often than not, the media allows its readers and viewers to know only what the powers that be want them to know. It is time to demand the truth.

This is a call for action.

CHAPTER TWO

CURSED LUCK

"Do not pray for easy lives. Pray to be stronger men."

John. F. Kennedy[8]

The cloudy drive from Riverlakes Country Club was a reflective yet happy one on November 21, 1963 for Orville Nix. Dallas looked cleaner than it normally did and Orville reveled at the transformation. The Fleming and Sons paper processing plant that usually permeated the air with an acrid smell of chemicals seemed to have filtered the normally pungent aroma that engulfed the neighborhoods of Cedar Crest to Trinity Heights in Oak Cliff. The president would be in town the next day and the whole city was gussied up to welcome John F. Kennedy and his beautiful wife Jackie. Even the rain had helped clean the city and air as if God were an invited guest, or maybe just the hired help.

Yessiree, Orville thought, *this was going to be the beginning of a lucky weekend.*

Orville had taken a rare two days off from his regular night shift, and since there was no reason to sleep, he had spent the day at the Country Club. Not only had he won his round of golf in the intermittent rain, he had also won the poker games he played with his friend Forrest Sorrels, who worked for the Secret Service, and a couple of guys who lived in Kessler Park, the place everyone called 'Pill Hill' because the homeowners were mainly physicians. It was always satisfying to win, especially knowing he wouldn't have to ask his wife for lunch money for the next week. But triumphing over these guys made him feel even better.

FORREST SORRELS

Beating accomplished men made him feel smart. It also meant luck was with him and like his daddy always said, "Men with luck don't have to have brains."

"Brains," he said out loud as he walked to the parking lot and got into his car. It was time to pick up his wife Ella.

The smoke from his Lucky Strike cigarette seemed to make the shape of a brain and then dissipate into a million little pieces—just like his dream. He wondered what his daddy would have said about the dreams he kept having. As he turned onto Lancaster Avenue, the scent of magnolias fragranced the air as he dismissed the thought. He didn't want to think of anything bad that might spoil this lucky streak. Like many athletes, Orville firmly believed in keeping the "streak" intact by not changing anything that was right.

> *****
>
> **... AND LIKE HIS DADDY ALWAYS SAID, "MEN WITH LUCK DON'T HAVE TO HAVE BRAINS."**

Funny thing was, at the Country Club he frequented, he never knew if the men he played with were doctors or businessmen. All he knew was that he, an air conditioning repairman for the General Services Administration, was beating these men at golf and poker. Men who had university degrees, fancy cars, and big houses. As he raised the bet on his two pair, aces over fours, he wondered if they could tell that he had only a fourth grade education. He and Forrest were only there for an hour.

"So Forrest," the heavy man with the blue tie said, "Gonna be a busy day for you tomorrow, isn't it? What with that liberal president being in town. Think it will be another Adlai Stevenson type event?"[9] He chortled as he spoke.

"Naaah, not at all," Forrest replied as he looked down at his cards again. "This parade should run smooth as that tie you're wearing."

Orville knew his friend Forrest well, and knew he hardly ever talked about work. He liked that about Forrest. He also knew that Dallas was embarrassed by the Adlai Stevenson "incident" where some silly woman named Cora Lacy Frederickson, an insurance executive's wife, had hit U.N. Ambassador Stevenson with a placard she was carrying and then later blamed it on a Negro hitting her hand.[10] The *Dallas Morning News* would later concur with her by reporting it was an accident, but Forrest had told him she was 'touched.' It was odd to Orville how so many people could walk the earth without using the brains the good Lord gave them.

Orville had a feeling that on his next raise, the business man wearing the blue silk tie would fold. When the bids went around the table and stopped at him, he raised the bet by a dollar. It was a quarter ante game. Not only did 'Smooth Blue Tie' fold, so did the man wearing the shirt with the alligator on it. Orville won! As he opened his wallet to deposit the ten and twenty dollar bills he won from them, he watched their faces. He carried a brown hand-tooled leather billfold with his name branded on it. This was as close to being a "Texas Cowboy" Orville ever became. He didn't like Stetson hats. He didn't have a penchant for cows except to eat, and he didn't own a pair of cowboy boots. All he had was his western billfold. Some would say it looked like something a little kid would own. Orville didn't care. He loved it. His daddy had given it to him.

Forrest winked at him. He noticed Mr. Alligator Shirt smirking. *Was it because he lost or was it because of the wallet?* A wave of insecurity rippled through him and then dissolved. What did they know anyway? It sure wasn't cards. And it didn't sound like it was politics.

They also didn't know that his wife Ella had to work on the serving line at the vegetable station of Wyatt's Cafeteria[11] to help pay the bills for the rental house they lived in on Denley Drive in Trinity Heights. She had worked there for over twenty years, the steam from the Brussels sprouts, green beans, and mushrooms absorbing into her face like a trendy organic spa treatment. These men didn't know that he had saved for almost a year to buy the custom-made suit he was wearing from Turner Brothers, the fancy mens clothier in downtown Dallas. He loved that suit almost as much as his billfold; it was a modern Frank Sinatra-like suit that changed colors in the light. These men didn't know how badly he wished he could live the lives they were living. What they did know was that he had a son, Orville Nix Jr., a pretty young daughter-in-law named Elaine, and three beautiful grandkids, all with blonde hair. They knew this because he bragged about his family anytime he got the chance.

Forrest commented one time, "I've seen those kids so much, I feel like they could be mine."

His oldest granddaughter, Gayle, was too smart for her age, as he had said many times. He told his son Orville Jr. to keep a close watch on her; too much knowledge would lead to trouble in her life. People who knew too much were destined to lead lives of fear and loneliness. Gayle could read business letters when she was four. She could write letters for him when she was five. She wasn't scared of anything or anyone, and he couldn't be prouder. He loved to show the men at Riverlakes Country Club pictures of his grandkids between card games. There was Gayle, three years older than her little sister Cindy, and then there was his grandson David, who he had lovingly nicknamed 'Bubba', born eleven months after Cindy. People often asked if they were twins because Cindy was so petite and David was so active, and they were similar in size. The children in the pictures he showed the wealthy men were of three blonde children with bright smiling faces and fancy clothes. He prayed they would have lives like these men and their families from Kessler Park. *Why shouldn't they?* He asked himself as he walked to the parking lot.

"Orville!" Forrest yelled, "Orville, don't forget where I told you to stand if you want a really good view tomorrow."

"I remember Forrest… the corner of Main and Houston at Dealey Park. I'll be there!"

He and Forrest hadn't been at the Country Club long; just for a few games of poker, and back to work Forrest went. He had told Orville that an associate had come in from Washington, D.C. and he had to meet him. Forrest never stayed in one place too long. In fact he was known to show up in all kinds of places in downtown Dallas.

Orville smiled and shouted to his friend, "Thanks for reminding me, Forrest, I'll wave at you in the parade."

He smiled thinking of the great tip his friend Forrest Sorrels gave him. He had bought a new camera just for this parade and couldn't wait to see how it worked. It was a brand new 8mm Keystone Auto-Zoom Movie Camera[12] he had bought less than a week ago: the newest model, a K-810. It cost him $159.99 on sale at Sage's Department Store. He had wound the spring too tightly on his last camera, and not only had he lost a new roll of film trying to fix it, he had broken it. Ella had been furious.

"Orville, another new camera?" she shouted. "Do you know that is almost two week's pay for me? You go through cameras like I go through nylons, but nylons are cheaper," she ranted.

Orville winced at Ella's reprimands. She was right. But what did it matter? It was just the two of them now, and they had suffered enough financially while Orville Jr. was growing up. Why not indulge in something expensive now and again that was just for their pleasure? When Forrest had told him the President and First Lady would be in town, that made the decision even easier. Orville had bought the fancy camera, where the auto-zoom even had a grip-power mechanism on the handle. It still had to be wound, so he made a mental note to not wind it too tightly this time. Holding the camera's squeeze mechanism was like squeezing a trigger on a gun. *Ha,* he thought, *Forrest may have a real gun, but I have a gun for taking pictures.*

His friendship with Forrest had gone back a long ways. Forrest was the Special Agent in Charge of the Dallas Secret Service and his offices were in the General Services Administration. The GSA had offered to pay for Orville's high school equivalency diploma through courses taken at Southern Methodist University so that he could get promoted, but that wasn't until later. Orville always wondered if Forrest had put a good word in for him. Acquiring this diploma did get him a promotion, and although Orville had recently transferred to the Terminal Annex building[13] in October, he still visited Forrest once or twice a week. Orville remembered the day a week or so earlier that Forrest had told him about

how he changed the parade route.

"Don't you think this route will be better for everyone?" he had queried Orville. "We're headed to the Trade Mart, so this should be a straight shot to the freeway." Orville couldn't tell if his friend was trying to convince Orville, or himself.

"I don't recollect you ever having a bad idea, Forrest," Orville replied. "It looks good to me."

It was true. He respected and truly liked Forrest Sorrels. Forrest had an important, high government security position, but he never let it go to his head. He was close to Orville in age and more often than not, they talked about their personal lives rather than politics. Forrest was a family man and a professional who never jumped to conclusions. He solved problems logically and patiently. Like the time that drifter had found his way into the GSA. Orville had been working near the elevators when a tattered guy had come into the building. Anyone could tell he was lost, but a couple of young Secret Service men pushed the poor guy into a wall. A lady screamed and an elderly couple just getting off the elevator hurriedly rushed out the door. Just then, tall, thin Forrest appeared. Orville watched as he calmly spoke to the drifter, and with nothing more than his eyes, told the two young men to release the poor guy. After speaking with him for a few minutes, Orville saw Forrest reach into his pocket and give the guy what looked like some money. They shook hands and Forrest patted his back as the man left the building and everyone went back to their jobs. Forrest was a good man. He missed seeing him now that he had been transferred to the Terminal Annex building on the south side of Dealey Plaza. The postal inspectors and postal employees weren't nearly as friendly as his friends in the GSA building.

On his drive home from Riverlakes, Orville paused for a moment still thinking of his friend and lit another Lucky Strike, though one was still smoldering in the ashtray. He inhaled deeply and pulled into the Wyatt's parking lot at Cedar Crest where Ella was still at work. His son Orville Jr. worked part-time at the Cedar Crest movie theater just a few stores down.[14] He smiled at the thought of nuzzling against his wife's vegetable-scented face and his stomach growled. It was 6 p.m. and she would be getting off work soon. The rain began to fall lightly again and his thoughts shifted from hunger to the presidential parade tomorrow and he realized he had never been to a presidential parade. Hell, he had never had a birthday party! He never had a formal education. He never had anything to call his own except Ella and Orville Jr. He caught himself tapping the steering wheel with each 'never' and watched the people entering the cafeteria, hoping Ella would come out soon.

The wait allowed Orville more time to reflect upon his hardscrabble life. He seemed to do that often. When Jr. commented on how often his dad thought about his past, Orville would say, "You have to know where you come from to see where you are going." Orville hoped that if he taught his son anything, he taught him that. He wanted his son to have a better life than he had.

His parents were young but old as he remembered them. It had been twenty-five or more years since his mamma had died and for the life of him, he could barely recall her face. At least his daddy had lived long enough to see his son Orville Jr., but then he too died when Jr. was only two. His parents had worked hard and had expected their children to do the same and none of their six kids, except Eva, questioned their chores. As the children made the long walk home from the small schoolhouse, they would see other kids playing baseball or flying kites. Heck, some even had bicycles; but not anyone in his family. They didn't even have a radio. Though all of them worked, even the kids, they could barely afford food and clothing. Orville picked cotton to help his parents. That's what boys from families like his did, even at the age of six. His two older brothers worked the cotton fields right along beside him and they made up games to help them forget how the bolls cut their hands and to make the time go by faster. His sisters had sometimes helped, but they had had other chores. His younger brother Edward had had epilepsy, a disease so scary that Orville was afraid he would get it too. He remembered Mamma's Mama saying one time that having an epileptic child in the family meant the Nixes were cursed, though he didn't really know what 'cursed' meant. He just knew it was bad by the look on her face.

He lit yet another Lucky Strike and inhaled deeply, remembering a day in November, much like today, and his brother Edward. That day he had grown up by about three years. He must have been in second grade and his older sisters and brothers weren't home yet. He had been happy that day because the teacher had to leave early, so all the kids in his class had gotten to leave early too. The fresh fall air had carried a scent of apple cider from the farm next door, a sweet scent that made Orville's always empty stomach growl. He had begun to walk a little faster, hoping there would be an apple left in the kitchen for him to eat. From several yards away, he had heard a rapping noise inside the two bedroom frame house. *Had that ornery Billy goat gotten out again?* he wondered. It had happened before and his daddy had whipped him good for not making sure the goat gate was secure. As he walked faster down the dirt road he had realized the screen door to the house was halfway open. He ran faster hoping the goat wasn't in the house, or worse, hadn't eaten the apple he could almost taste. As he opened the door, he half expected to find the Billy goat charging and tearing up what few pieces of furniture they had, but it *was* worse. His little brother Edward was having a seizure. Orville went white as he watched his little brother's body bouncing up and down on the floor as if manipulated by a mad puppeteer. Orville didn't know what to do. He cried out for his mamma and daddy for what seemed like hours while trying to hold Edward down. He could feel the tears running down his face as thoughts raced through his mind. *Was Edward dying? Would he catch this horrible disease that Eva said caused you to slobber and foam at the mouth like the rabid dog his daddy had shot last week?*

Time passed by slowly as Edward's frail body quaked on the floor. His small legs contracted and relaxed, contracted and relaxed, while his arms did the same. Edward's elbows and heels bled from the uncontrollable spasms his little body had been making, as he lay on the floor. He had urinated in his pants and Orville felt worse about this than the blood he saw on his younger brother's body. He had kept patting his back and crying 'Edward' as he watched his little brother's head banging on the hard wooden floor. *I can't help him, I can't save him, I'm useless!* Orville thought to himself.

"Mamma! Daddy!" Orville screamed. Finally they had both come running into the small house.

"Orville," his daddy's voice had boomed into the small space, "get away from him now, your mamma will take care of him."

"But Daddy, I think he's dying," Orville had screamed.

His mamma had pushed him away and cradled Edward in her arms. His small body went limp. The seizure was finally over. Orville's tears ran freely now. His brother must be dead.

Seeing his next to youngest son cry, his father admonished him, "Don't you ever cry, boy, don't you ever. Nix men don't cry and they don't look back. You did the best you could and you hold your head high. He's not dead, boy, he's just had a seizure. You were there for him which is all family can do for one another. You were there." He hugged his son hard then let him go. That's the only time Orville ever remembered his father hugging him. "Besides, all this excitement has caused a distraction for you. Have you done your chores? Your homework? Hug your brother and thank him for making your life easier today."

He hadn't thought of Edward's epileptic seizure as a distraction. He also hadn't thought Edward had made his life easier by purposefully having a seizure. His daddy seemed to misunderstand. Some things in life happened on purpose. Other things in life happened by someone else's purpose. His only thought had been how to keep his brother from dying.

From that day on, someone had to stay with Edward at all times. This job had usually fallen to his mamma or his older sisters Grace or Eva. Grace was the best at it. She probably could have been a doctor if women could have gone to college, because she was too smart for a girl and truly cared about Edward. Orville had a close relationship with Grace. It had always seemed to him that though Eva was prettier, Grace was the best sister. She showed him how she had begun to keep notes about Edward's behavior, trying to come up with anything that could clue her in as to when he was going to have a seizure. The seizures scared Grace too. She had told Orville that one time, but not because she was scared she'd catch it, but because she couldn't make them stop. Orville watched Grace, who was five years older than he was, care for Edward like her own son…not a brother. She did that until Edward died at the age of twenty-eight; twenty-five years after their mamma had died from pneumonia.

*****

HIS DADDY SEEMED TO MISUNDERSTAND. SOME THINGS IN LIFE HAPPENED ON PURPOSE. OTHER THINGS IN LIFE HAPPENED BY SOMEONE ELSE'S PURPOSE. HIS ONLY THOUGHT HAD BEEN HOW TO KEEP HIS BROTHER FROM DYING.

His sister Eva wasn't like Grace. She hated watching Edward as she too thought she would get epilepsy and if that happened, she would never have a boyfriend.

"Who would want to kiss a woman who foamed at the mouth?" she would ask their mamma. Eva wasn't like her brothers and sister. She hated her life and was very loud about it. Mamma wouldn't let daddy spank her because she was a girl, but Orville could tell their daddy wanted to, and often. Eva had no desire to stay with Edward longer than five minutes at a time and she had soon made a pact with Grace. Eva would do the washing, cleaning and cooking if Grace would handle Edward. It was a pact that worked until the day Eva ran off with the older man two farms over. Orville didn't hear from or see her again until many years later.

Orville and his two older brothers were expected to do Edward's work as well as their own because the medical bills and Edward's medicine costs often times meant there wasn't enough food in the house for the family of eight. He learned to butcher hogs and chicken by the time he was eight and though he dreamed of candy and toys and real presents at Christmas, fate had another plan. For the first four years of school, he didn't think he could ever be more tired. School was hard for him because there wasn't much time to study with all the chores he had to do before and after the long walk to the schoolhouse. But then when his sister Eva had run away, his daddy made him quit school to help with the farm and with Edward because Grace was about to graduate, and since she wasn't very pretty, his daddy said, she needed to put her brains to good use.

The ash of the cigarette he was barely smoking dropped onto his lap and he cursed hoping it hadn't ruined his suit. He stopped thinking about his youth and checked his watch. It was 6:18. Where the heck was Ella?

He looked toward the cafeteria and noticed someone had left a newspaper near the door. He got out and went to get it. *Darn, it's a Dallas Morning News*, he thought to himself. He was hoping it would have been a *Times Herald*.[15] He didn't trust the *Dallas Morning News* as he had heard his Secret Service friends at work talking about big parties the owners of the paper, the Dealeys, gave all the time, and how if you were invited to a Dealey party, you would be getting a promotion soon.

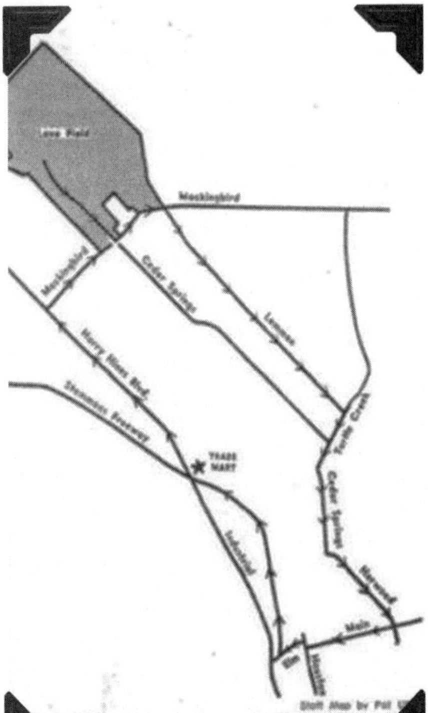

JFK motorcade route in Dallas.

As an air conditioning repairman, he wasn't invited to parties, but his friends in the Secret Service, like Forrest, often talked about them in the lunchroom.

He always felt uncomfortable when those kinds of discussions started, but he didn't let on. He just didn't like the idea of government employees mixing with big businesses. Everyone and everything had their places, and that's where they should stay.

From the corner of his eye, he saw Ella coming out, her face weary and tired, but her eyes excited. He loved that about her. He jumped out of the car and put the half-read newspaper over her head to protect her from the rain.

"Orville, did you call Jr. and remind him to tell Elaine to meet me at the bus stop in the morning to go to the parade?" she asked breathlessly.

"No Ella, I just left Riverlakes, I haven't been home yet. You can call her when we get home." Ella rolled her eyes and smirked at him. "At Riverlakes… so I guess you'll need…"

"No," he interrupted before she could complete her sentence, "I don't need any money from you. I won today. I'll pay for the bus and lunch at Walgreens for us all." He beamed with pride as she looped her arm through his.

Finances were always a bone of contention for the couple, though since their son Orville Jr. had left and married Elaine Walker, it had gotten better. Orville found he had more money to buy fedoras, suits, and play more games of poker and golf. Sometimes, okay, more times than he liked, he lost and had to beg Ella for money. He hated those times. It seemed as if he would have to work hard his entire life. He never seemed to get a break. At least not until he married Ella.

The tall, beautiful Ella had lived a hard life as well. She had to care for her brothers after her parents died. Though she and the boys had moved in with her grandparents, she felt responsible for the brothers' care until she caught her uncle stealing her hard earned money. Her uncle had always thought himself a Clyde Barrow-type and had even had him over for dinner one afternoon at their home in Scurry, Texas. Ella knew at an early age that money was the ticket to freedom, though not by the Bonnie and Clyde way. Luckily, she had met Orville soon after she caught her good-for-nothing uncle. After a whirlwind romance, they fell in love and married quickly. Orville was more a way out of her horrible home life to her than he was a soul mate. But she loved him in her way and he loved her in his... their son Orville Jr. was proof of it.

Now that their son had children, Ella was in her element as Granny. She adored her three grandchildren and spent whatever was leftover from her meager earnings buying them clothes and taking them places. Tomorrow she was taking the grandchildren and her daughter-in-law Elaine to see John F. Kennedy at the presidential parade in downtown Dallas. She had never seen a president in person, and while she was alive, she intended to ensure her grandchildren had many of the things she never had. They would ride the bus to keep from having to pay parking fees and meet Orville at the ten-cent store on Main. The ten-cent store had a soda fountain and the kids would love a sweet treat. The best part of it, though, would be that Gayle could play Elvis Presley records on the booth jukeboxes. She knew how much her little granddaughter loved playing music.

* * * * *

Across town, Abraham Zapruder was closing up late. The luxurious surroundings of his executive office never ceased to make him smile. His life in Texas was a far cry from the one he grew up with in the Ukraine.[16] As he looked out the window of his offices he thought how proud he was to be an American and how many opportunities this country afforded its citizens. He wished there was a way he could thank the government of his beloved country. He had become a Mason; he voted religiously; he donated money to worthy causes. He still didn't feel those things were enough to show his love for America. He knew that the 35th president would be in Dallas tomorrow and he thought about watching it out his window. He had excitedly voted for John F. Kennedy and firmly believed his presidency would change the nation. As he gazed out and glanced at the Texas School Book Depository across the street, he wondered if his friend D. Harold Byrd[17] would like to join him at the parade and he grabbed the phone to call him, but then remembered he was on safari. D. Harold owned the School Book Depository. When he bought it, Abraham was sure he would clean it up and maybe even renovate it. It was a bit of an eyesore and Byrd seemed to allow every bum, race, and jailbird to work there. No renovations had happened yet, save a floor remodeling because, he supposed, D. Harold was busy with his East Texas Oil project. He was jealous that he couldn't expand his own office. He wanted a bigger space in which to impress buyers from large companies and he hoped this would be a good selling season for both his clothing lines: *Chalet* and *Jennifer Juniors*. Few people knew that he had named his company *Jennifer Juniors* after the lovely actress Jennifer Jones.[18]

"Well," he thought, "I can watch it from here myself," as he turned back to his ornate desk.

He changed his mind when he saw all the orders he had to fill for his company. The lovely First Lady had done wonders for his business this year. It was as if every woman in Texas wanted to look and dress like Jackie. He smiled as he thought of the young couple and how their progressive lifestyle was the total opposite of the leaders in his home country of Ukraine. He again thought how lucky he was to now be an American and decided he would definitely take time out to watch the parade. He wasn't sure which way the presidential motorcade would proceed, but he had heard rumors from his friends, the de Mohrenschildts,[19] or was it Neil Mallon, that it might cross right in front of his building at 501 Elm Street. He checked his appointment book for the next day and then had his secretary, Lillian Rogers, check it again. Lillian, as well as all the girls in the office, was excited about seeing the elegant First Lady, Jacqueline Bouvier Kennedy.[20] All they could talk about were her clothes and her handsome husband. Listening to them chatter Abraham wondered if men really understood how much power women had in the world of finance. His father had told him years ago that where the heart's desire lies, there the money will go. Women who wanted to look like Jackie, be married to a dazzling young man like the President, or live an elegant lifestyle like the couple would spend the money to make their dreams come true…and women usually controlled the household budgets, no matter what the *I Love Lucy Show* portrayed. Zapruder knew; he was a dress manufacturer and had a wife of his own. Women were the silent power of the Sixties.

"I'll bet she'll be wearing a beige Chanel," he heard one of his models say.

"No, Cassini is her standby fashion and green is this year's color. She'll be wearing a bold green Cassini," his receptionist Marilyn Sitzman said.

One of the young girls with dreams of having her own clothing line interrupted, "I think she'll be wearing a bright yellow Dior. You know how she loves Dior. She'll have a smart clutch, low pumps and a smart Dior sundress, a bright print with yellow as the key color."

Abraham closed his office door to silence the 'what will Jackie be wearing?' chatter, though the thought of the First Lady's colorful wardrobe gave him a few ideas for his summer line. Yes, bright colors might be the way to go. He wondered what his friend Jeanne de Morhenschildt would be previewing. Maybe he should call her. Jeanne had been his first boss, but at that time her last name had been LeGon.[21] Abraham had cut dress patterns for her at a clothier called Nardis until she married the debonair George de Morhenschildt in 1959. There were rumors that Jeanne's husband had dated the First Lady years ago. But actually, de Morhenschildt had dated Jackie's aunt. *God, I'm beginning to sound like one of my employees,* he thought to himself. *Everyone has Jackie on their mind!* He straightened his desk as his mind went back to his clothing line. No, he wouldn't ask Jeanne, he would ask his wife when

he got home. She's the one who had convinced him to buy the Jackie mannequin[22] that was such a hit with his buyers. His wife had always been his good luck charm, and he had a feeling this was going to be a lucky weekend.

* * * * *

As Abraham Zapruder was leaving his office, Forrest Sorrels and Winston Lawson were meeting the President's advance team at Love Field Airport.[23] An airplane had been sent ahead to transport Secret Service cars for the presidential motorcade. Once Forrest and Win got there, they met with Agents Samuel Kinney and George Hickey. Forrest had arranged for officers from the Dallas Police Department to provide security for the cars overnight in the garage beneath the Main Terminal.

"Great to meet you," Forrest said as he shook hands with both Kinney and Hickey. With the best Texas accent Win could muster, he also greeted the men with, "Howdy ya'll, welcome to Texas."

Of course his accent had a northern tinge because he wasn't from Texas, though after being there over two weeks, he felt he was beginning to develop a Texas twang. They all laughed as they got into the car and drove to the Sheraton Hotel.[24] The Sheraton was the hotel chosen for the president's advance and support team to stay.

Several hours later, at approximately 11:00 pm, Air Force One, the President's official airplane, was landing at Carswell Air Force Base in Fort Worth. Thousands of smiling Fort Worth residents weathered the cold rain to get a glimpse of the President and his fashionable wife on the nine mile route from West Fort Worth to the Hotel Texas[25] at the center of downtown. Fort Worth had worked hard to welcome the couple with the best the city could offer in order to make the glamorous couple's stay a memorable one. The citizens were excited to see the president as the future of their city was intertwined with politics, aviation, the military, and the black gold that supported it all: oil. The oilmen of LBJ's Texas were distinctly different from the oilmen of Rockefeller's New York. The difference was in taxes. Texas oil not only meant large sums of money, it also meant large government tax breaks. Texans paid no state taxes, only federal taxes to Washington and oil people wanted it to stay that way. They also wanted to keep their oil tax break. They knew their 'Big Steel' compatriots had taken quite a hit in profits when President

Kennedy forced them to rescind price hikes, and they weren't about to see that happen to Big Oil.

Not to be outdone by the oil rich oligarchy of Dallas, the leaders of Fort Worth spared no expense. The art on the walls of the suite the president and his wife would occupy were paintings by Franz Kline, Monet, Van Gogh; sculptures by Henry Moore and Picasso[26] and other masterworks borrowed from private owners specifically for the executive couple in order to make their short visit a comfortable and aesthetically pleasing one. The leaders of Fort Worth had even put together a little studio type room especially for the First Lady.

A few days before the presidential couple's arrival in Fort Worth, a description of the presidential suite at the Hotel Texas had been released to the public. Some of the city's art lovers had not been happy with their accommodations: they felt the rooms too 'gauche' for such an elegant couple. Owen Day, the art critic for the *Fort Worth Press* suggested to some of the more prominent art collectors and leaders of Fort Worth that they install a miniature museum for the President and First Lady.[27] With the support of Ruth Carter Johnson, Ted Weiner, Samuel Benton Cantey III, and Mitchell Wilder, a three-part private exhibition was installed in the parlor and bedrooms, each room of the suite outfitted with works of art that befitted such an elegant couple. In the parlor were works by Monet, Lyonel Feininger and Kline. Two sculptures, one by Picasso entitled "Angry Owl" and the other by Henry Moore entitled "Three Points" now seem eerily prophetic. Knowing the affinity Mrs. Kennedy had for impressionistic art, the master bedroom was adorned with a Prendergast painting, a Van Gogh, a watercolor by John Marin, and an oil painting by Raoul Dufy. President Kennedy's room was designated the second bedroom and it featured American art by Thomas Eakins, Marsden Hartley, and Charles Russell among others.[28]

Room 805 at The Hotel Texas would unknowingly be the setting for John F. Kennedy and his lovely wife Jackie's last night together as a couple. Cut crystal vases filled with the First Lady's favorite flower, periwinkle iris[29]and goblets sparkled on the table.

There were L&M cigarettes left surreptitiously for the First Lady because, though she smoked, she didn't want the public to know, and Cuban Petit Upmann cigars (called Demi Tasse in the U.S.)[30] for the president. They were surrounded by art, sculpture and the gilded elephant in the room that whispered, "You're a traitor if you do anything to hurt our oil and military economy. Enjoy yourselves, then mosey on home."

CHAPTER THREE

TIMING IS EVERYTHING

"We're heading into nut country today,"

John F. Kennedy reportedly said to Jackie after reading the Birch Treason Ad in the Dallas Morning News.[31]

The people were everywhere. Screaming, running and then hitting the ground like bombs were going off. He just kept squeezing, squeezing, squeezing. Then everything went shimmery red.

It was the dream again. The same one he had been having for a few weeks. What did it mean? Orville shivered and reached over to the window unit to turn it off. Though it was late November, he couldn't sleep without cold air blowing on him so the window unit ran year round. He ran his palm over his face as he sat on the edge of the bed and listened. Yes, Ella was up; he could hear her in her bedroom. He opened his bedroom door and the smell of freshly brewed coffee made him smile.

"Ella," he shouted, "want a cup of coffee?"

Ella appeared at her bedroom door wearing a long cream-colored silk robe. Her hair was in rollers, but she still looked beautiful.

"No Orville, I better not, you know how it affects me and there are no bathrooms on the bus," she smiled. "Besides, I made it for you. I hope Elaine has the kids ready; we need to be leaving soon. I know downtown will be crowded and we need to get there early if we're going to get a good view of him." She pulled the curtains back and saw it was raining.

"Oh no! Not rain! The weather man said it was going to be a clear and sunny day today. You just can't trust anyone anymore," she said. "Now I'm going to have to take an umbrella and a rain hat for my hair. I wonder if Elaine has raincoats for the kids?" She reached for the phone ready to pepper her daughter-in-law with her worries and questions, but Orville ended the call before Ella had finished dialing.

"Ella, no need to get all riled up this early in the morning, you're supposed to be having fun." He ambled to the window and drew back the curtains again. "See that line of clouds? They're moving towards the east. There's bright sunshine behind them. It's going to be an exciting day." He kissed her on the cheek and patted her shoulder as he sat down to drink his coffee.

"What are you going to wear? Where's your camera? What time are we supposed to meet you?" Ella volleyed him with more questions. She always did this when she was excited or nervous.

"I'm wearing my new dark blue suit I got from Turner Brothers with my dark blue fedora, the one with the black feather and my light blue shirt and black tie with the design in the middle. My camera is on my dresser in my bedroom and I'll be meeting ya'll at noon at the corner of Houston and Main. Any other questions?" He winked at his wife.

ORVILLE NIX

Ella always melted when her tall husband winked. He was such a handsome man, even at fifty-two years old.[32] His eyes were green in the morning, but turned blue when he wore blue. He had the smile of a bad boy but the countenance of a gentleman: it was a deadly combination that few women could ignore and the single women of the neighborhood didn't. They visited the Nix home often. There were plenty of female admirers at the Riverlakes Country Club as well. The visits never bothered Ella, why would they? Orville was her husband not theirs and neither of them believed in divorce, even if most of the women who brought him cakes and cookies had been married more than once and dressed in tight pencil pants and crop tops. She walked back into her bedroom to finish getting ready when the phone rang.

"I'll get it, Ella," Orville said, answering it before it could ring a second time.

"Hi, Paw-Paw." The young voice of his pretty daughter-in-law Elaine made him smile. "Let Granny know I'll be over in an hour to pick her up. We'll take the bus from the Cedar Crest station."

"Will do, Elaine, are the kids excited?"

"Yes they are bouncing off the walls. I'm not bringing Cindy and David, my friend Linda across the street is going to stay with them. It will just be me, Gayle and Granny."

Orville frowned knowing how Ella would receive this news. She liked having all three of her grandchildren together.

"Gayle will be easy enough to handle, that's a good idea. I'll see you at the corner of Main and Houston at noon. Tell Gayle I've got a new letter for her to read. Drive carefully!"

He hung up the phone and walked into Ella's bedroom to tell her of the change of plans. She was brushing out her auburn hair into Greta Garbo waves. She looked beautiful, and he told her so.

"Well," Ella replied to the news, "I won't have to chase after Gayle. She never runs anywhere." She spritzed some *L'air du Temps* on her neck and began putting on her makeup. Orville lingered in her room taking in the sweet fragrance, and then left her to finish getting ready. He looked at the clock over the television.

The Dallas Morning News

Storm of Political Controversy Swirls Around Kennedy on Visit

Yarborough Snubs LBJ

"Ella, did you get the newspaper? I want to make sure the parade time hasn't changed."

"It's on the table," she said.

He felt his coffee cup and decided to warm it up as he thumbed through the *Dallas Morning News.* He hated this paper and since he worked at night, he hardly ever read it. He much preferred the *Dallas Times Herald.* There on the front page[33] of the *Dallas Morning*

News was a picture of the President, his wife Jacqueline and LBJ and Ladybird in San Antonio. That damned LBJ never missed a chance to get his hound dog face in the news. The headline read, "*Storm of Political Controversy Swirls around Kennedy on Visit.*"

"Ella," Orville shouted. "Does controversy mean trouble?

"What?" Ella shouted in return. "Did you say anniversary?"

"No, C-O-N-T-R-O-V-E-R-S-Y" he spelled it out to her.

"Oh, controversy. Yes, that means trouble. What are you reading about?" she asked.

"Just the newspaper," he said.

For a split second his heart caught in his throat and he stopped reading. He shook his head and blamed the strange feeling that had just come over him on too much coffee. He lit a Lucky Strike and continued to read. There was a big article about the feud between Texas State Senator Ralph Yarbrough and the governor, John Connally. Orville hated politics, but loved the Democratic Party. He felt they cared about people like him, and this president, though young, seemed sincere. His son Orville Jr. was a die-hard Republican and couldn't wait to vote for Barry Goldwater in 1964. Jr. said he wasn't going to the parade because he had to work, but Orville guessed he wasn't going because he didn't much care for the current administration. His son felt the Kennedys were more 'Hollywood' than Washington, D.C. and cared more about arts and fashion than about taxes and recessions. It didn't matter. Though he would have liked to have his son there at the parade today, at least he had his son's wife and oldest daughter. Orville smiled at the thought. As he scanned the paper, he noticed in the right hand corner that Nixon was hinting Kennedy would drop LBJ in 1964.[34] *That should stir the political shit-pot even more,* he thought. What with Connally, LBJ, and Ralph Yarbrough all wanting to be in charge, the conversations in the limos had to be volatile. He wondered if their wives would be bickering as well. He also wondered if Forrest's job would be more dangerous than he thought. He slathered some molasses and butter on a piece of toast, wishing he had asked Ella to fry him up some bacon fat. He was hungry.

Reading on made him dislike the *Dallas Morning News* more. They made everything into a 'Soap Opera' like the ones Ella watched on her days off. He looked at the bottom left corner of the front page and saw a map of the parade route.[35] *Wait,* he thought, *was Forrest right? This map wasn't like the one he saw in the Times Herald yesterday, this map says the parade would stay on Main.* The place they would watch the motorcade pass by should be perfect, though Forrest had said the parade would turn right on Houston St to Elm St.

The map in the paper showed the motorcade would stay on Main St. *Well it's too late to ask Forrest about it, I'll just stand where he told me to stand,* Orville thought to himself. As he thumbed through the pages he saw that Sanger-Harris was having a toy sale.

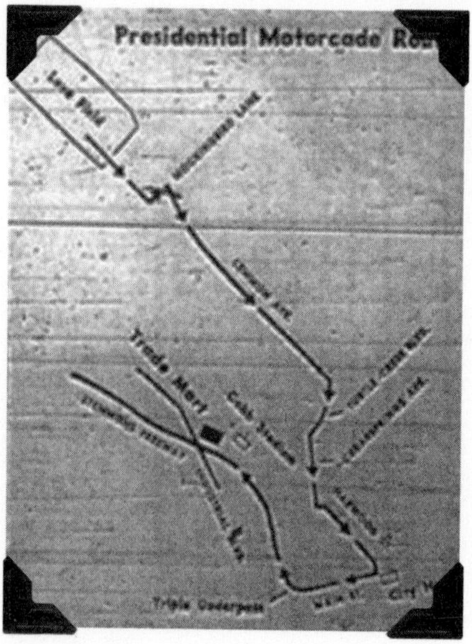

He made a mental note to tell Ella so that after the parade they could do a little Christmas shopping for the grandchildren. He skimmed over the myriad of articles talking about the crowds that had gathered to see the Kennedys in San Antonio and Houston and then worried that they should leave a little earlier to beat the crowds.

As he turned to the editorial pages, he saw a cartoon of JFK with a long rifle shooting at a deer with LBJ laughing and driving a roofless jeep.[36] Texas was the deer and the title read, "BIG GAME." He shook his head. "I guess these newspaper guys think all Texans hunt, and wear Stetson hats and boots," he muttered to himself.

"What did you say, Orville? Quit mumbling to yourself! You better get dressed. Time's a 'wastin," Ella scolded as she walked to the small dining table.

She picked up the paper as Orville trailed off to his bedroom to get ready. As he passed her he winked again. She smirked and moved away. She read the front page as he had, shaking her head at all the political drama. *Why can't grown men just act like grown men instead of bickering like little girls*, she thought to herself. She never liked Lyndon Baines Johnson and she sure didn't like Ralph Yarbrough. They didn't like each other. They were the uppity types of Texans she knew from her younger days; the ones who thought because of their power, money and 'Daddies' they could do anything

they wanted, especially with women. She had met her fair share of them. The smoke from Orville's forgotten, still-lit Lucky Strike was burning her eyes, so she stubbed it out. *Good grief, cigarettes were nasty smelling things!*

As she thumbed through the paper, she paused on page thirteen to read the ad from Skillern's Drug Store. Hershey bars were 2 for 33 cents. She should buy some for the next time the kids came over. Since there was nothing else of interest to buy, she turned the page. There on page fourteen was a huge full page ad welcoming the Kennedys to Dallas.[37] She smiled as she read the headline of the ad, "Welcome Mr. Kennedy" in large black bold letters and in smaller letters, "To Dallas." *Well that's nice*, she thought, *and it must have cost a lot of money.*

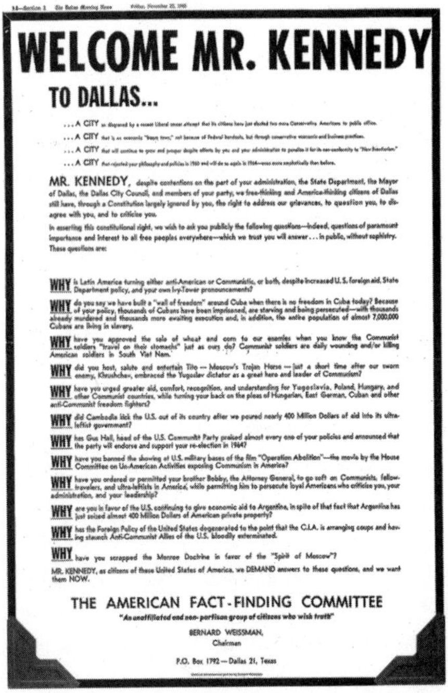

WELCOME MR. KENNEDY

TO DALLAS...

...A CITY so disgraced by a recent Liberal smear attempt that its citizens have just elected two more Conservative Americans to public office.

...A CITY that is an economic "boom town," not because of Federal handouts, but through conservative economic and business practices.

...A CITY that will continue to grow and prosper despite efforts by you and your administration to penalize it for its non-conformity to "New Frontierism."

...A CITY that rejected your philosophy and policies in 1960 and will do so again in 1964—even more emphatically than before.

MR. KENNEDY, despite contentions on the part of your administration, the State Department, the Mayor of Dallas, the Dallas City Council, and members of your party, we free-thinking and America-thinking citizens of Dallas still have, through a Constitution largely ignored by you, the right to address our grievances, to question you, to disagree with you, and to criticize you.

In asserting this constitutional right, we wish to ask you publicly the following questions—indeed, questions of paramount importance and interest to all free peoples everywhere—which we trust you will answer... in public, without sophistry. These questions are:

WHY is Latin America turning either anti-American or Communistic, or both, despite increased U.S. foreign aid, State Department policy, and your own Ivy-Tower pronouncements?

WHY do you say we have built a "wall of freedom" around Cuba when there is no freedom in Cuba today? Because of your policy, thousands of Cubans have been imprisoned, are starving and being persecuted—with thousands already murdered and thousands more awaiting execution and, in addition, the entire population of almost 7,000,000 Cubans are living in slavery.

WHY have you approved the sale of wheat and corn to our enemies when you know the Communist soldiers "travel on their stomachs" just as ours do? Communist soldiers are daily wounding and/or killing American soldiers in South Viet Nam.

WHY did you host, salute and entertain Tito — Moscow's Trojan Horse — just a short time after our sworn enemy, Khrushchev, embraced the Yugoslav dictator as a great hero and leader of Communism?

WHY have you urged greater aid, comfort, recognition, and understanding for Yugoslavia, Poland, Hungary, and other Communist countries, while turning your back on the pleas of Hungarian, East German, Cuban and other anti-Communist freedom fighters?

WHY did Cambodia kick the U.S. out of its country after we poured nearly 400 Million Dollars of aid into its ultra-leftist government?

WHY has Gus Hall, head of the U.S. Communist Party praised almost every one of your policies and announced that the party will endorse and support your re-election in 1964?

WHY have you banned the showing at U.S. military bases of the film "Operation Abolition"—the movie by the House Committee on Un-American Activities exposing Communism in America?

WHY have you ordered or permitted your brother Bobby, the Attorney General, to go soft on Communists, fellow-travelers, and ultra-leftists in America, while permitting him to persecute loyal Americans who criticize you, your administration, and your leadership?

WHY are you in favor of the U.S. continuing to give economic aid to Argentina, in spite of that fact that Argentina has just seized almost 400 Million Dollars of American private property?

WHY has the Foreign Policy of the United States degenerated to the point that the C.I.A. is arranging coups and having staunch Anti-Communist Allies of the U.S. bloodily exterminated.

WHY have you scrapped the Monroe Doctrine in favor of the "Spirit of Moscow"?

MR. KENNEDY, as citizens of these United States of America, we DEMAND answers to these questions, and we want them NOW.

THE AMERICAN FACT-FINDING COMMITTEE

"An unaffiliated and non-partisan group of citizens who wish truth"

BERNARD WEISSMAN,
Chairman

P.O. Box 1792—Dallas 21, Texas

She continued to read and though she didn't know the meanings of the words "sophistry" and "pronouncements" she realized at once this was no welcome ad. This was a hateful ad. A cold chill ran through her as she continued reading and she pulled her robe into her body a little tighter.

The ad seemed to be about communists and the president's brother Bobby and Fidel Castro in Cuba. She had heard from the women she worked with at Wyatt's that Bobby was after the Mafia. She was happy about that, but sheltering Communists? That didn't make sense. How could he be trying to stop the Mafia but allowing Communists to go free. Weren't they pretty much the same? She didn't understand politics, didn't want to, and this ad was an example of why she didn't like political subjects. She had never heard of the CIA and coups. What was a coup? Who was being bloodily exterminated? And this horrible ad made it sound like all the people of Dallas agreed with the "American Fact-Finding Committee" a committee she had never heard of. The ad was signed "Bernard Weissman, Chairman" and gave his address, well, a post office box in Dallas. She threw the paper down and wondered what the president and his wife would think if they saw this trash. The whole city and its citizens were trying to make the city and themselves look wonderful for the president's visit and the paper runs an ad like this. *Well, I always said newspapers were just Jezebels for money*, she sighed to herself. *They'll print anything to make a dime*. She picked the paper back up and threw it in the trash.

* * * * *

Sitting behind the over-sized desk in his office at the Dal-Tex Building, Abraham Zapruder was reading the same ad in horror. What is it with some of these Texan Americans? If they had come from his country, they would know how very lucky they were to live in a country as great as the United States. Now, here was some crazy club had put an ad in the *Dallas Morning News* degrading our president. The ad matched the weather: gloomy and foreboding. It was 8:30 in the morning and the parade was due to begin in less than four hours. Would the city of Dallas cancel it? Knowing that one-time milkman mayor Earle Cabell, Abraham rather doubted it. Then again, maybe he would. It was well known among the Dallas politicos he met at parties that the honorable Mayor of Dallas and his Texas friends H.L. Hunt, D. Harold Byrd, George Bush and Henry Wade were not Kennedy supporters. In fact, they were just the opposite. He sometimes thought they were nutty, but to be a good business man, you had to be creative and diplomatic. And being creative usually meant you were a little nutty. He rose from his desk and walked to the window. He frowned and quickly looked up at the Texas School Book Depository. He noticed that there were men with trucks and dollies and ladders. *Well D. Harold's finally renovating that building,* Abraham thought to himself thinking of his friend D. Harold Byrd, who was now on an African Safari. *Smart of him to do it while out of the country, that way he doesn't have to deal with the headaches of renovation. I could have been on safari, but no, I don't hunt*, Abraham thought to himself. *A vacation would be great though. Maybe it would keep me from having these horrible nightmares*. Abraham, like Orville Nix, had been having nightmares for weeks. He would wake in the middle of the night in a cold sweat, sometimes with tears running down his face. He could never quite put it together though. His dreams were a fractal of horrible images and loud noises. His wife had said he was having them because he worked too much and was friends with the wrong people.

"I go to Mason meetings, I go to Dallas Council on World Affairs meetings, I go to parties, I do other things besides work," he told her, and my friends are what brings business to my company. And my dear, puts new dresses in your closet!"

She just clucked her tongue and walked away saying, "All these years Abe, and you still don't listen to me."

Just then, his secretary Lillian walked into his office with a cup of coffee. As if reading his mind Lillian said, "I'm sure the rain will stop before the parade

Mr. Z., not to worry. Besides, you could watch it all from right here from your window."

He looked up at her and smiled. He marveled at how women always did their best to make life easier for the men they cared about.

* * * * *

Across town, Forrest Sorrels was talking to his new friend Winston Lawson, a Secret Service agent from Washington D.C. assigned to the presidential detail, and tying up loose ends before picking up the other DC agents, Kinney and Hickey at the Sheraton Hotel on their way to Love Field. Lawson was in charge of numbering the cars in the motorcade and had been Forrest's daily companion since November 12th.

"You know, Win, I'm still catching hell about this motorcade route, but with all the bickering between Connally and Moyers, damn, this route was the best I could come up with. Connally was determined to go to the Trade Mart and threatened to not even be in the parade if the motorcade ended at the Women's Building in Fair Park. I told Gerald Behn if we took special precautions, the Trade Mart would work." Sorrel's friend Win Lawson nodded his head in agreement.[38]

*****

WINOS LIKED TO HANG OUT THERE WHILE PAN-HANDLING FOR THEIR NEXT DRINK. INDUSTRIAL BLVD. HAD POT HOLES AND BROKEN PAVEMENT UP AND DOWN THE BLOCKS FROM DRUNKEN ACCIDENTS, BAD WEATHER AND NEGLECT. THIS WOULD NOT HAVE BEEN A PLACE FOR FAMILIES TO TAKE THEIR CHILDREN TO SEE THE PARADE.

"Forrest, my men and I went over the Trade Mart with a fine-toothed comb," Win replied. "I don't relish having my SS boys in Washington look down their noses if they think we missed anything. Besides, you know as well as I that we can only do what we can do. The motorcade route looks good to me and since Lumpkin decided going down Main St. to Industrial meant going through the 'undesirable' part of town, what else could you do?" Winston empathized.[39] "Besides, the Democratic Party chairman Jack Puterbaugh and even Art Bales of the Army Signal Corps thought it looked fine to them.[40] Don't worry! I'm the one who will take the heat for it if there's anything wrong anyway!"

Lumpkin was the Assistant Police Chief of Dallas: George Lumpkin. Industrial Blvd was the 'wet' part of tee-totaling Dallas where liquor stores and dive clubs lined the streets. People had to drive from the suburbs to purchase liquor or wine, so the mix of people there was a potpourri. Winos liked to hang out there while pan-handling for their next drink. Industrial Blvd. had pot holes and broken pavement up and down the blocks from drunken accidents, bad weather and neglect. This would not have been a place for families to take their children to see the parade.

"That's just it Win, I don't want *any* of us to take any heat just because Connally and Yarbrough are bickering. Main-Houston-Elm seemed the best to me because of the size and cumbersomeness of the President's motorcade. Add to that the presence of that damned raised divider separating the Main Street lane from the Elm Street lane at the foot of the ramp up to the expressway, the whole damned motorcade would have to make a reverse S-turn in order to cross over the divider," Sorrels lamented.

"Well, Forrest," Win joked, "that's why you have the title Special Agent in Charge. You make the big bucks, you have to make the big decisions," he said laughingly.

"Yeah, big bucks," Forrest smiled. "Thank God all our suits are dark-colored so we can change out jackets with trousers when they get dirty." They laughed as they arrived at the Sheraton. It was 8:30 am, precisely the time Forrest had told Hickey he'd be there. Forrest was a stickler about timing.

"Hey, Win," Forrest said, "Let's not forget to ask Chief Curry if anything has changed. His walkie-talkie should be on. I don't want to ask in front of the other D.C. guys. We may talk slowly in Texas but we don't think slowly."

Kinney and Hickey were coming out the double doors of the Sheraton. The men got into the black car waiting for them on the curb. Little did they know this was the beginning of a day they would never forget; a day that would haunt them the rest of their lives.

This was America in the midst of a 'cold war'. Many Americans were still elegiac about World War II, the Nazi concentration camps, the communist witch hunts and the threat of nuclear destruction. Some of the soldiers from the war were now the wealthy and powerful men in charge of America. The administration did not want to present the American people with a level of discord throughout the world in regards to the land of the free, wealthy and brave. It was better to use rhetoric of security and patriotism and wealth rather than one of pragmatism. Americans wanted to feel good and the government wanted to ensure they did. The reigning administration desperately needed their votes. The easiest way to do this was not to tell the world of things that might worry them, but to put on grand gestures of transparency, teamwork, and hidden tyranny.

Minutes later, Forrest Sorrels and Win Lawson were on their way to Love Field Airport along with Samuel Kinney and George Hickey. In a flurry of shots, mishaps, and timing, these men would understand hours before the rest of the world how important this rhetoric had become. Timing would be the most important part of today's equation. Ignorance would come in a close second. The government factions working that day depended on ignorance for success. The American people understood ignorance.

Forrest understood ignorance as well; and he had always known how important timing was.

CHAPTER FOUR

OF PARADES AND PARODY AND PARALLELS

"Things do not happen. Things are made to happen."

John F. Kennedy[41]

At 8:30 the morning of November 22, 1963, Orville checked his camera for the third time to ensure the film was loaded. He couldn't remember if he had used indoor or outdoor film, but with a camera like this, he didn't think it would matter. Kodak film was one of his biggest expenses, and now that he had a color camera, he took movies of anything that caught his eye. He had rolls of film of the grandkids, of Cedar Crest, and of Riverlakes, but mostly of jet airplanes overhead. He was mesmerized by jets and in another lifetime, he may have been a pilot. But in this lifetime he was happy to take endless movies of jets flying through the Texas skies with all the power and grace of every hope he ever had for himself and his family. When he saw the film was loaded, he checked the lens to make sure the lens cap was off. He had forgotten to take it off one time after a day of filming golf games and when the Dynacolor guys developed it, they had laughed at him. That wouldn't happen again.

"Ella, I'm leaving," he shouted to her from the small living room. "Elaine and Gayle should be here soon. Don't forget, I'll meet you at the corner of Houston and Main."

"Okay, Orville," Ella shouted in return. "But if we get lost and can't get to you, meet us at Walgreens, okay?"

"Will do, Ella. You be careful and remember, this is a day for fun," he replied.

As he walked out the back door of 2527 Denley Drive, he locked the door behind him. He wanted his wife safe. He wanted her to enjoy herself. She worried far too much about things she had no control over. He wished he could give her a life she deserved, a life of leisure and unending prosperity. But knowing Ella the way he did, she would never be content to sit at home... except maybe when her 'stories' were on for a few hours each day. He smiled at the thought of her getting so involved in the lives of the characters of her favorite soap operas. It was as if they were her friends, and she actually cried when one would die or disappear from the show. She had told him once that she was glad she didn't have lives like theirs.

"No one leads a life like that in real life, Ella," he chided her one time. "Why would you think they do?"

"Well, of course people lead lives like theirs, Orville. The differences between people like them and people like us are they have power and money. We play golf and cards and with our grandchildren. They play with other's lives. We watch our money. They spend theirs and anyone else's they can get. They live dangerously, we live safely. They have to worry about people killing them or trying to steal their power or trying to steal their money. I wouldn't trade our lives for theirs ever."

As he turned the windshield wipers on to remove the stray raindrops on the windshield, Orville pondered on those thoughts as he lit a Lucky Strike. *Ella was right,* he thought on the fifteen minute drive to downtown Dallas. *Rich and famous people have much more to worry about then we do. All I'm worried about right now is where to park*, he chuckled to himself as he took a drag of his cigarette, *but having a lot of extra money wouldn't be such a bad thing.*

He decided he would park at the Terminal Annex Building where he had been transferred recently, and then walk across from the parking lot to the plaza area. There was a strip of grass between Main and Elm Street in the park named Dealey Plaza. If he stood there, he could see the presidential motorcade coming down Main as it turned onto Houston before turning again onto Elm.[42] Forrest was right. That would be the perfect place for taking a movie. If the streets were too crowded at Main and Houston, he could always move closer to Elm before the parade ended at the ramp to go to Stemmons Freeway and besides, his camera had a Zoom feature if he couldn't get close enough to the motorcade. He stopped for a moment and remembered seeing the map in the *Dallas Morning News* a few hours ago. It had shown a map of the parade going down Main, but his friend told him the parade would go down Elm. He believed his friend Forrest Sorrels.

Using the Keystone K-810 made Orville feel like a professional photographer, even though he was still learning how to use it. He was so excited because it had just been introduced in May, so even after six months it was still one of the newest model cameras. It used a wind up mechanism for the timing, something Orville really hadn't understood until he wound his last camera too tightly and broken it. The zoom lens on this new camera had a 9mm to 27mm focal length and made self-adjustments to light sensitivity. There was a small window to view how much film he had left and his favorite thing about it was the grip on the handle. All he had to do was clinch it in one hand and take pictures.[43] He thought that would come in handy if he had to hold one of his grandkid's hands… like Gayle's today at the parade.

As he parked the car in the parking lot behind the plaza, he waved at some of his friends who were taking a smoke break. They motioned him to come over, but he yelled, "I can't boys, gotta find a good place to take pictures."

*****

HE COULD NEVER UNDERSTAND WHY PEOPLE GRIPED ABOUT POWER AND TAXES AND 'TOO MUCH GOVERNMENT.'

HOW COULD THERE EVER BE TOO MUCH GOVERNMENT?

WITHOUT GOVERNMENT, HE WOULDN'T HAVE A JOB.

The 'boys' were wearing their khaki-colored GSA uniforms. That was another thing he loved about his job. He knew exactly what he had to do and wear; this made dressing up all the more special. He loved working for the GSA, heck, he loved the government. He could never understand why people griped about power and taxes and 'too much government.' How could there ever be too much government? Without government, he wouldn't have a job. There would be no military to protect us from our enemies… there would be no law of the land. He did agree about the taxes though. He hated paying them but knew they were a necessary evil to have the great country we had. What did too much government mean anyway? Even his son had said, "There's too much government" during their last discussion. *Yessiree*, he thought, *that boy of mine is thinking like those peace-niks. All that peace talk does nothing but make our soldiers think their efforts are for nothing. Where did he learn to think that way? Money, money, money is all he thinks about!*

His friends at the Terminal Annex smiled and nodded their heads as if reading his mind as he walked across the street to Dealey Plaza. There were people everywhere. God, they must have been twenty or thirty deep, but not on the Plaza. The parade wasn't supposed to begin for another couple of hours, but it seems that everyone had had the same idea he had: get there early. He noticed that many of the people at the plaza were moving towards Main Street, he guessed so the skyscrapers and taller buildings could block the cool breeze and sun. Funny thing, most of them must have arrived around the same time he did because he noticed there were no umbrellas or raincoats. What he did see were people young and old. Most of them were dressed as if they had just left church; the men were wearing their best suits and the women had on silk scarves and brightly-colored dresses. He thought the throng looked like a field of human flowers and almost got his camera out to film them then thought better of it. He wanted to save his film for the parade and to take pictures of Gayle. As he looked around the city plaza, he saw parents with their small children. He saw groups of women and men who seemed to be friends. A few of them held "Welcome Mr. President" signs[44] and he immediately thought of that ad in the damned newspaper this morning. He hoped the president hadn't had time to see that awful paper.

Orville milled around the plaza, admiring the stark white colonnades that formed Dealey Plaza Park. It was beautifully green on this sun-drenched November day. Orville had stood on the Triple Overpass (the railroad bridge that spanned Commerce, Main, and Elm Streets) in the early 40s and remembered that he thought the Plaza looked like the back portion of an arrow. Main Street served as the straight part of the arrow with Main and Commerce Streets curving towards it. The curved portions of Elm and Commerce Streets were adorned with white concrete pergolas on their slopes that descended toward what would come to be known as the Triple Underpass. The plaza was built as one of President Franklin D. Roosevelt's Works Progress Administration projects in 1940[45] on land donated by one of Dallas's business leader and philanthropist, Sarah Horton Cockrell. The WPA project, later named Dealey Plaza after another famous Dallasite, George B. Dealey, was replete with the planting of native Texas Oaks and the beautiful Art Deco styled structures. Orville often sat under the shaded structure on the Commerce side of the Plaza. It was a respite from the Texas sun and a perfect place to eat lunch or spend a contemplative moment away from work. On the Elm St. or northern side of the Plaza, there was a wooden picket fence that hid the parking lot of the Union Terminal train yards. Later this day, that area would be named the grassy knoll by award-winning United Press International journalist Merriman Smith who reported the events of the assassination by telephone.[46]

*****

That morning, across the street at 501 Elm in the Dal-Tex building, Abraham Zapruder was taking care of a stack of orders from Neiman Marcus. He had arrived punctually, as he did every day at 8 A.M. By the time he was finished with overseeing income, the rain had finally stopped. He decided to watch the parade, but of all days, he had forgotten his Bell & Howell camera.[47] He frowned as he related his forgetfulness to his secretary Lillian. Lillian and the girls in the office were again talking and wondering what the First Lady would be wearing.

She said, "Mr. Z., you've got plenty of time. Run home and get it. You'll be back in time before the parade gets to our part of the route, besides we're at the end of it all."

He looked at his watch and agreed. It was only 10 A.M. He should have plenty of time to get home and get back before the motorcade made it to the Dal-Tex building.

"Marilyn," he said, "would you come down with me to the Plaza to watch the parade?"

Marilyn Sitzman was his receptionist. She wasn't beautiful, but she wasn't ugly. Abraham would have labeled her 'interesting' or better yet, 'strong Texas stock.' She had dark wavy hair and was taller than Abraham and definitely taller than most women; about five foot eleven and she never failed to wear red lipstick, no matter what color clothing she was wearing.

"Of course, Mr. Z., I'll go with you. I think Beatrice and her husband Charles are going as well. What do you think Jackie will be wearing? The girls and I have made a pool. Whoever wins gets $20.00 and I feel lucky today."

Abraham Zapruder smiled as he left the office and returned home to get his camera. Zapruder made a fourteen-mile round trip drive home to pick up his camera. By the time he returned, crowds were already gathering to watch the motorcade.[48]

* * * * *

President John F. Kennedy and his wife Jacqueline landed at Love Field Airport in Dallas at 11:40 A.M. after a rousing breakfast speech at the Crystal Ballroom in the Hotel Texas. The president had donned a dark blue suit and the First Lady was wearing a bright pink Chanel suit with a matching pillbox hat. She was like a collectible porcelain doll. She never rode in motorcades with her husband: this was one of the first times and she wanted to look her best. She knew how important Texas was to her husband's reelection plans. Though the day had started with a fine mist and ominous clouds, the sun had shot them away and taken charge making sure November 22, 1963 was a clear, crisp day in Dallas. The bright colors of their wardrobe matched the beautiful day.

As they exited the airplane, hundreds of Dallasites had been present for the arrival of Air Force One at Love Field. There seemed to be even more excited Texans in Dallas than there were in Fort Worth. Governor Connally and his wife Nellie beamed proudly at the crowds that had gathered to get a glimpse of the couple. The throngs of excited onlookers made the Governor and his wife proud. Though they were on a tight schedule, Mrs. Kennedy, who was carrying a bouquet of red roses given to her on her arrival, was enthralled. The atmosphere of love was evident in the cacophony of cheers and plethora of welcome signs that greeted them. Mrs. Kennedy was so touched, she had gone out of her way to shake hands and greet the crowd. President Kennedy followed her lead. Fifteen minutes later, at approximately 11:55 A.M., the President and First Lady were ensconced in the motorcade on the way to Dallas. The 35th president was to give a speech at the Dallas Trade Mart and enjoy a steak luncheon. Religious, political, business, and civic leaders were invited to hear the speech and welcome the young couple. Neiman Marcus had even sent a pair of custom Texas saddles as gifts for the first couple to take home to Caroline and John-John. This was truly the best Texas would offer.

President Kennedy had wanted to come to Texas for three distinct reasons: to start his quest for re-election in 1964, to garner more contributions for the Democratic Party presidential campaign fund, and because the Kennedy/Johnson ticket had almost lost Texas in 1960 to Nixon. Yes, he wanted to make a good showing in Dallas. Dallas was one of the few Texas cities he hadn't won in 1960 and winning the oil rich vote in Dallas was imperative to the future of the Democratic Party and to his reelection. There were many political fences to mend in Texas. There was infighting in the party. Congressman Jim Wright, Senator Ralph Yarbrough, Governor Connally and Vice-President Lyndon B. Johnson all had bones to pick with each other or their cronies. It didn't help that some of their supporters including H.L Hunt, Ted Dealey, Clint Murchison, Syd Richardson, Mike Davis, George Brown, and D. Harold Byrd were dangling their bloated bank accounts in front of each politician like carrots to a herd of jackasses.

Then there was that mental military case in Dallas, General Edwin Walker, the John Birch Society Member and rumored Nazi who Kennedy had admonished publically. The man had even run against John Connally for Texas Governor the year before and after leading riots at the University of Mississippi later that year, JFK's brother Bobby had ordered Walker to be committed to an insane asylum. Yes, this was definitely nut country

He also *had* to do something about that bastard LBJ. His Vice-President from Texas had damned near ruined his presidency and if he didn't do something to fix it, he wouldn't be elected to a second term. There were rumors in Texas that Johnson had paid people to buy the elections in Texas, Chicago and West Virginia. There were rumors that LBJ had gotten kickbacks for ensuring General Dynamics got the military fighter jet contract in Ft. Worth. Then there were the Billie Sol Estes and Bobby Baker scandals.[49] On top of that, even at his age, LBJ had as many 'lady friends' as Kennedy had. There always seemed to be an 'incident' lurking in the shadows whenever Lyndon Baines Johnson was near.

Knowing this, President Kennedy had brought his best defenses to Texas. He donned his Peace Corps mantel, charismatic lasso, and beautiful wife and brought them to Texas to fight the war of votes and help alleviate the dissension. If he could divert a Cuban missile crisis, by God he could tame these Texas mavericks and that out-of-control LBJ.

*****

SECRET SERVICE AGENT SAM KINNEY WAS TOLD TO REMOVE IT. HE WAS HESITANT, BUT HE DID WHAT THE D.C. BRASS TOLD HIM AND HAD THE PROTECTIVE BUBBLE-TOP REMOVED.

There were several motorcycle officers and four of the motorcycle officers from the Dallas Police Department flanked the presidential limousine. In the lead car, Forrest and Win were riding with Dallas Police Chief Jesse Curry and Dallas County Sheriff Bill Decker. Win had mentioned to Forrest this was unheard of. Normally, the lead car was all Secret Service agents. Forrest had suggested that because of the Adlai Stevenson incident in Dallas a few months earlier, the Dallas Police and Sheriff Departments wanted the public to know they meant business and this was a united front. In an unmarked white Ford were the commanders of the Dallas crime fighters along with Winston Lawson and Forrest Sorrels of the Secret Service. Behind them in the second car, the President and Mrs. Kennedy sat in the backseat of a dark blue Lincoln Continental limousine. President Kennedy, noting the beautiful day, had requested that the protective bubble-top be removed while they were at Love Field[50] so he could better interact with the crowd.

Secret Service agent Sam Kinney was told to remove it. He was hesitant, but he did what the D.C. brass told him and had the protective bubble-top removed. Kennedy and his First Lady would be sitting at the back of the car, and the First Lady's Secret Service Agent Clint Hill would be behind the car along with Secret Service agents Hickey and Kinney. In the middle of the huge blue Lincoln stretch limo, in jump seats a little lower than the front and back seats, Texas Governor John Connally and his wife Nellie would be sitting. The driver of the presidential car was Secret Service Agent William Greer, accompanied by Secret Service Agent Roy Kellerman.

The four motorcycle officers from the Dallas Police Department flanked the presidential limousine. Several dignitary cars followed whose passengers were also in convertibles: Vice-President Lyndon B. Johnson and his wife Ladybird; Senator Ralph Yarbrough; Democratic Representative Ray Roberts; and Dallas City Mayor Earl Cabell, who was the brother of the former CIA Deputy Director, Charles Cabell. Charles Cabell had recently been fired by John F. Kennedy. Kennedy had flatly turned down Cabell's request to employ fighter planes during the Bay of Pigs Invasion in Cuba and after its failure, Kennedy asked for Cabell's resignation.[51]

There were three Secret Service cars interspersed between the dignitary cars then several photographer cars; including two buses. Forrest had had Chief Curry set up a police unit on the overpass looking down on the parade. He tried not to worry about how open the whole motorcade would be. *It's a short parade* he tried to reassure himself. *It'll all be over in less than thirty minutes.*

The motorcade was huge and daunting to Forrest, though the amalgam of powerful interests in Dallas that day was bigger: some were even riding in open cars of the motorcade; others were conspicuously out of town. The eyes of Texas were upon them all.

A few had brought cameras with them, including Orville Nix, who didn't realize he was about to take a home movie that would be speculated about and hidden more than any home movie he had ever taken, and would become a piece of a puzzle he would have never tried to work. To many, the film he was about to take would become a modern day Holy Grail.

CHAPTER FIVE

12:30 PM CST -11/22/1963

"If anyone is crazy enough to want to kill
a President of the United States, he can do it.
All he must be prepared to do is give his life for the President's.

John F. Kennedy[52]

A dark past is inherently built into everything. It navigates, it determines, it concludes. It is evil, it is pure, and it is objective. One never leaves the past; it burrows into the psyche of its witnesses and remains trapped there forever. It spreads like a virus to those who look for truth and infects those with a conscience. Only those free of morals and intellect are immune… or crazy.

On November 22, 1963, the past came down upon Dallas. Some would say this day was the fruition of the sins of the fathers. There were so many fathers in Dallas that day. Some were at the parade with their wives and children. Some were in the motorcade. Some were there with their mistresses. Others were there in spirit, but not in body… those had sent their stand-ins. Others had sent patsies. Some were aware of what was about to transpire, but the majority of Dallas was not.

The citizens of Dallas were so delighted to see the president and First Lady that between 150,000 to 200,000 people lined the streets… almost a quarter of the population of Dallas in 1963. They were dressed in their work clothes, or Baptist Sunday best to see the first Catholic president and his wife. Many schoolchildren skipped school to come to the parade. Others had used valuable days off to see the president. It was a worldwide event being hosted in Dallas. Sadly, for many Dallasites, this would be the last day they would tell a stranger they were from the glistening city.

* * * * *

Orville Nix, father and grandfather, looked down at his watch and realized it was 12:05 P.M. His wife Ella, daughter-in-law Elaine, and eldest granddaughter Gayle were not there yet. Dressed in his newest suit, he moved to the edge of the Kelly-green grass strip that separated Main from Elm and looked over the crowds and crowds of people. Orville was 6’6, so it was easy for him to stand on his toes and see. There was no sign of his family. But how could there be? The onlookers were as thick as the molasses Orville had mixed with butter and slathered on his breakfast toast this morning. There would be no way he could find Ella, Elaine, and Gayle if he walked down Main. He decided to stay where he was and let them find him.

At 12:11 P.M., Ella, Elaine, and five-year-old Gayle were braving the crowds to make their way to Main and Houston. People were smiling. Bright confetti rained down upon them. Red, white and blue bunting festooned between the buildings. People were cheering and with each shout Gayle would scream, “He’s here Mama, He’s here Granny! He’s here!”

Ella looked every time she shouted and every time she said, ‘No Gayle, not yet, but he’s on his way. Just like Santa Claus.”

Elaine, who was holding her eldest daughter’s hand, was wearing her new button-down turquoise dress with a smart, self-tying belt in the front. Gayle would grab the belt from time to time, untying it and Elaine would have to stop among the crowd to tie it back again. One time as she was tying it again for the eighth time, a man came up behind her and said, “Let me do that for you, honey.” Elaine smirked at him and grabbed Gayle’s hand. *What is wrong with people today?* she thought to herself. She looked up and realized they were near a place she would never go to: the Carousel Club.[53] Elaine stood in front of the window so her daughter wouldn’t ask questions when she saw the horse and half-

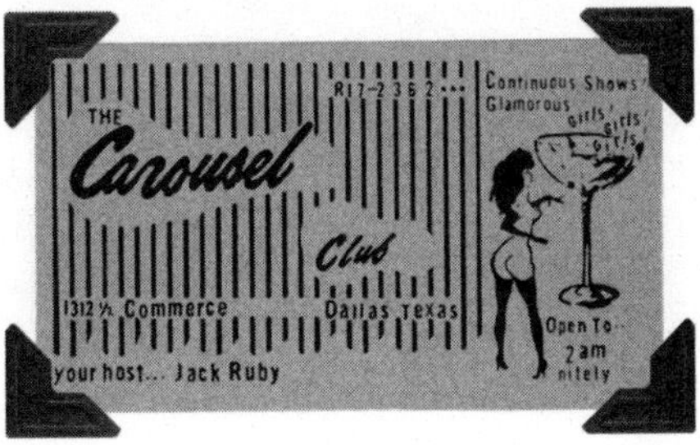

dressed woman that adorned the door to the place. Thankfully, at that moment, Gayle announced she had 'to go to the bathroom.'

As they neared the Adolphus Hotel, Elaine realized there was no way they would make it several more blocks and the only place close with a restroom was the Walgreen's store[54] across from the elegant Hotel.

"Granny!" Elaine said loudly. Ella couldn't hear her over the din of the crowd. "GRANNY!" she yelled again. This time Ella turned around at the sound of her name and smiled. Elaine said, "Gayle has to go to the restroom, is it okay if we stop at Walgreens?"

"Well of course, that's where I wanted to go after the parade so she could play the jukebox, but we can do it now."

Elaine didn't think playing the jukebox during the president's visit was a very good idea, but she wasn't one to argue with her mother-in-law.

"Gotta go, Mama, I gotta go!" Gayle wriggled and cried.

The threesome hurried across Main to Walgreens. Just as they were entering the store, a group of men in dark suits and sunglasses were leaving a booth that faced the window. One of them handed a leaflet to Elaine as he pushed past her. She looked down at the writing. In bold letters were the words, "WANTED FOR TREASON"[55] with mug shot looking photos of the president. Elaine wadded it up and threw it into the busboy's dirty dishes bin. The busboy made a face at her. She looked over her shoulder to see if she could still catch one of the men who gave it to her. They were gone. She would have liked to give him a piece of her mind. *How revolting,* she thought to herself. *Whoever printed these should be ashamed! What a horrible way to make people in Dallas look; uneducated, rude and hateful.*

CONFIDENTIAL

WANTED

FOR

TREASON

THIS MAN is wanted for treasonous activities against the United States:

1. Betraying the Constitution (which he swore to uphold):
He is turning the sovereignty of the U.S. over to the communist controlled United Nations.
He is betraying our friends (Cuba, Katanga, Portugal) and befriending our enemies (Russia, Yugoslavia, Poland).
2. He has been WRONG on innumerable issues affecting the security of the U.S. (United Nations-Berlin wall-Missle removal-Cuba-Wheat deals-Test Ban Treaty, etc.)
3. He has been lax in enforcing Communist Registration laws.
4. He has given support and encouragement to the Communist inspired racial riots.
5. He has illegally invaded a sovereign State with federal troops.
6. He has consistantly appointed Anti-Christians to Federal office: Upholds the Supreme Court in its Anti-Christian rulings. Aliens and known Communists abound in Federal offices.
7. He has been caught in fantastic LIES to the American people (including personal ones like his previous marraige and divorce).

CONFIDENTIAL

Commission Exhibit 770

"Mama," Gayle cried, "I have to go *now*!"

"I'll take her, Elaine," Ella offered. "You just save our booth."

Elaine wriggled into the booth and gazed out the window. People were everywhere, inside and out. Elaine looked down at the watch she had gotten from her parents when she graduated from South Oak Cliff High School a little over a year ago. It was 12:19 P.M. She could see the crowds looking towards their left. The president must be coming and there would be no way they could see him from inside. She sighed in disappointment. She wanted her daughter to see the president as badly as she wanted to.

* * * * *

A few blocks down, Abraham Zapruder had rushed back from home to the Dal-Tex Building and was searching for a good place to film the Presidential Parade in Dealey Plaza. His receptionist, Marilyn Sitzman was with him, along with his bookkeeper Beatrice and her husband Charles Hester. He took pictures of all of them with his movie camera to check out the lighting before the parade began. Though Abraham was an amateur photographer, he wanted to make sure he got a wonderful film for his grandchildren and wife. They began their search for the perfect place to film at the far east side of the Plaza.

"Oh my, Mr. Z., this is the perfect place for pictures," Marilyn cried. "Make sure you get one of Jackie, I just know she'll be wearing something elegant."

* * * * *

Zapruder chuckled and looked at his watch. It was 12:20 P.M. He wasn't happy with any of the places they stopped at while walking through the plaza. He walked to the furthest point of Dealey Plaza, the part closest to the underpass, and saw a raised pergola and a few ledges. The first one he tried was too narrow and since he had vertigo,[56] he had a hard time balancing himself. He then moved to another raised ledge, but there were too many branches and shrubbery obscuring his view. He finally found the place to take what would become the most historic home movie in history - a pergola about four feet high.

"Hold onto me, Marilyn, I don't want to fall," he said to his receptionist as he raised his Bell & Howell camera up to his face. About that time, motorcycles leading the parade turned onto Elm Street and he began filming. He heard Beatrice and Charles Hester cheering and clapping behind him.[57]

Across the street from Abraham Zapruder, Orville Nix had a tornado of thoughts racing through his mind, the most important one being, "Were Ella, Elaine, and Gayle okay?"

Just then, he heard a siren on Houston Street. *Had someone been run over?* As he turned around, he saw a man having an epileptic seizure[58] across the street from the reflecting pond in the plaza. He was lying on the corner of Houston Street and Main, and the old red courthouse behind him seemed to be watching the man seize, with its ornate windows and blood-red brick. For a moment he froze, thinking of his experience with Edward as a child. The man was seizing violently and he could hear the chatter of men and women around him. They all just stood there watching the man as if they were watching a *Punch and Judy Show* playing out in front of them. He thought to run towards the man, and then decided against it. He couldn't help the man, he could just empathize. The words of his daddy immediately rang in his ears, "*You can only do what you can do, Orville.*" He looked up at the skies thinking of Edward and noticed the Texas School Book Depository and the buildings across the street from it: the Dal-Tex Building and the County Court House. For a moment he wished he had worked in one of those buildings because the upper floors would have been a great place to watch the parade. Some of the windows seemed open, so he supposed that people had the same idea he had: watch the president from a comfortable place and enjoy the cool day. At the Dal-Tex building, he saw three women leaning outside the window. He still couldn't shake the thoughts of Edward, so he turned again to look back where the man was. It was over. The ambulance was closing the back doors. The small crowd of onlookers had dispersed. He remembered that his sister Grace had said that sometimes excitement led to seizures with Edward. Maybe that man was excited about the parade. Then he thought about what his daddy had said years ago: "Hug your brother and thank him for making your life easier today." He wondered if someone's life had been made easier in downtown Dallas today. Maybe it was a distraction. *But a distraction for what? To make people go home?*

About that time, he heard the thousands of people cheering more loudly and heard the roar of the motorcycle escort engines. "Oh my God," he thought, "I'm going to miss the whole parade." He aimed his Keystone camera toward Houston Street where he had been waiting for his family. He looked towards the area where the epileptic man was earlier, again thinking of his brother Edward. He put his new camera to his eyes and took a few frames, but he didn't get a close up of the president. All he had gotten was a shot of the president and his wife talking to each other and smiling happily and then Senator Ralph Yarbrough 's car moved into his viewfinder. That wouldn't do. He would rather not have a movie of Ralph Yarbrough since he couldn't stand that lying no-good. He walked faster down Main as the motorcade was moving very slowly it seemed to him the cars were moving less than five miles per hour. He wondered which car his friend Forrest was in as his eyes scanned the motorcade. The day was so beautiful and the sun so bright, it was as if everything from the people to the sidewalks glittered like gemstones.

He looked up at the Texas School Book Depository. The Hertz sign on top of the building blinked 12:30 P.M. in glittery red neon.

> *****
>
> **HE SQUEEZED THE CAMERA GRIP AS HE RAN TOWARDS THE SLOW-MOVING MOTORCADE.**
>
> **WHAT WAS HAPPENING?**

Suddenly a shot rang out. Orville knew that sound. It was gunfire. Time stopped and Orville would later wonder how strange it was he had just looked at the huge clock atop the Texas School Book Depository Building. The cheering he had heard moments earlier had turned into screams. It was cacophonous. People were dive-bombing onto the ground in front of him as if terrorized missiles were dropping from the buildings and trees. He squeezed the camera grip as he ran towards the slow-moving motorcade. *What was happening?* Bang! Bang! Why were the cars moving as if in slow motion? Two more shots rang out in quick succession. This time he looked up towards the stockade fence. He was sure that's where the shots came from. But he didn't smell smoke. He didn't see muzzle flashes. By this time Orville was acting on primal impulse. He saw people covering their children. He saw people running in all directions. *Would he be shot? Should he find a place to hide?*

There was no place in the plaza to take cover. He again looked towards the presidential limousine and in that horrific moment saw the president's head explode into brilliant shards of red confetti: glittery, red confetti. *What was happening?* The two motorcycle policemen were stopping and looking to their right.

The First Lady, wearing a pink suit and pink hat seemed to be trying to get out of the car. A man in a dark suit had jumped onto the back of the president's car, *was it Forrest?* trying to push her back into the slow moving, midnight blue limousine. She seemed to be reaching for something. He heard another shot, *or was it a backfire? My God, there are guns everywhere. Glints of shiny somethings were everywhere. Flashbulbs? Fireworks? Gunfire?* He watched the limousine finally speed up and head towards the Triple Underpass. He stopped to catch his breath. He looked down at his hands and they were white knuckling the grip of his camera. *Had he been taking pictures?* Again, he looked up towards the stockade fence on the Elm Street side of the Plaza and policemen and people were running towards it. He began running and filming this time, since he couldn't remember if he had been filming before, and filmed the hordes of people running up the plaza to the stockade fence and train yards.[59] He thought that the shots had come from there. As he skillfully made his way through the crowds, he felt as if he were in a minefield. He looked to his right; another group of people were hurrying towards the Texas School Book Depository. Behind him, people were scampering towards Main Street. To his left people were moving quickly toward the policeman standing atop the Triple Underpass. He stopped filming. He had to find his family. But he also had to know what he had just witnessed. People were screaming. Some were still lying on the grass. *Were they hit?* He walked up to a few of them to check if they were okay. They were sobbing and scared. He saw a young couple across the street shielding their two young children. By this time, photographers were everywhere. So were policemen. *Where the hell had they been before? Why was this happening?*

He overheard a couple standing behind him absolving, "He deserved it, and I hope he's dead, that damned communist."

He wanted to hit these people! He wanted to make sense of this madness. He wanted answers. How could someone have fired four shots or more without anyone catching them? What had just happened? He needed a cigarette. His hands were shaking. He stared up at the stockade fence. He was convinced at least one of the shots had come from that area. He fumbled into his suit jacket and reached for a cigarette.

My God, the President has been shot in my hometown, he thought with a tear in his eye. He realized at that moment that the nightmare he had been having for weeks had come to life and he suddenly became light-headed. This is what his dreams had meant. The thirty-fifth President of the United States had been shot in Dallas and he had witnessed the entire horrible event.

CHAPTER SIX

OF SECRETS, NEGOTIATIONS AND FIRSTS

"Let us never negotiate out of fear.
But let us never fear to negotiate."

John F. Kennedy[60]

Orville was still shaking as the crowds began to disperse. He lit another cigarette. Newsmen and police were swarming the area. People were standing with their mouths open. Some people were running. Others were crying. All Orville could think to do was to find his family. He began sprinting down Main Street hoping he would find his wife, daughter-in-law, and granddaughter. He passed the old red courthouse and a few boutiques looking in the windows as he walked. The quiet was almost as deafening as the cheers were minutes ago. The whole city was stunned. It was as if a grimy, shameful pall had put its hands over the mouth of the shiny city.

The men and women who had lined the streets in droves were now huddled around radios and televisions. No one really knew what happened. Orville overheard a couple of women walking in front of him wailing, "They killed him." He quickly walked past them and overheard a group of men describing the shots.

"I swear to God," a small chunky man was saying, "I thought some yahoo was throwing firecrackers."

"Ah, Virgil, who the hell would have firecrackers at a parade?" another man in the group said. Another one of the group, this one wearing a brown hunting hat said, "No boys, them were rifle shots. It's hunting season you know, and some nut job just decided to shoot the president. He must have taken four or five shots. Wonder which building he was in?" he said while looking up at the tall buildings.

Virgil said, "I think he could have been in any of those buildings. Ever one of them has five or six stories. Hell, it would be like hiding in a deer blind." The other men nodded their heads in agreement.

The last man in the group spoke slowly and somberly. He had a tear in his eye and seemed much older than the other four.

"All I know is that there hasn't been a president killed in office since Garfield. And now here - in *our* city - the president has been shot. I think we may need to move further west, hell, even past Fort Worth. This city will never be the same. I hope our president makes it. I pray that he lives."

The other four nodded their heads in agreement. Orville silently agreed with them as he walked towards Walgreens. He peered inside and saw Ella, Elaine, and his white-headed granddaughter seated in a booth. He breathed a loud sigh of relief, realizing he had been holding his breath most of the last hour. Gayle looked out the window and shouted, "Paw-Paw!" He could hear her through the thick window glass. He smiled as he entered the store, and surveyed the people inside. No one was talking. Everyone seemed to be whispering. He realized that Walgreens, like all the stores on Main St., had become individual wakes, all memorializing the fallen president.

Ella jumped up from the booth and hugged him. "Good Lord, Orville, I was scared for you. You're alright! We kept hearing people talk about gunfire and war zones and the president being shot. Is it true?"

Orville nodded his head in affirmation. Ella could tell he had been crying. She kissed his cheek gently and pulled him into the booth.

"Paw-Paw," Gayle exclaimed in her little girl voice, "I only saw the president drive by real fast. Did you seem him better? What did he look like? Did he wave at you? I wanted him to wave at me but there were too many people standing in the way" she said with a pout.

"Yes Darlin', I saw him, and I waved at him for you," Orville replied as she jumped into his lap.

As he patted her back he didn't know if he could ever tell her about the glittery confetti that was once the President's head. Or the blood all over the First Lady's painfully beautiful pink dress. Or the sight of the governor screaming in pain while his wife cradled him. Or the parents fearing for their children's lives, shielding them with their bodies. He put his palms to his face and tried to shake the memory. Gayle hugged him and looking over his shoulder saw the table jukeboxes. "It's okay, Paw-Paw. Music will make you feel better. Can I play an Elvis record, Mama? Can I, Granny? Mama loves Elvis and Paw-Paw is sad," Gayle begged.

"No, Gayle, this isn't the time," Elaine said sternly.

"Here's a dime, Gayle, play whatever you want," the over-indulgent Ella said without making eye contact with her daughter-in-law. "Life goes on Elaine. She's too young to understand."

The coin clicked, the tabletop jukebox crackled and the only sounds within the store were those of Elvis singing, "Bossa Nova, Baby" and Gayle's voice singing along with him.[61]

* * * * *

Abraham Zapruder was shaken. He could feel the sweat inside his hat's headband and under the arms of his suit. He was sweating on the 22nd of November, one of the few cool months Texas has. The temperature was 73 degrees. *Am I having a heart attack*? he thought to himself, *or is it just from standing on the four foot pergola? This wasn't just the vertigo, no, it wasn't the vertigo. There were gunshots coming from behind him. Was it from his building? Was it D. Harold Byrd's building?* There were people screaming. Everyone was running. He stopped for a moment and took inventory, something he was prone to do during times of crisis. "Always look for the silver lining," his father had told him. He looked in front of him to Elm St. then began to walk towards his office. He had just watched his beloved president's brains blown all over Elm Street. Poor Jackie no longer had a husband. Poor Caroline and John-John no longer had a father. Poor America no longer had a young, exciting president. Poor the World. He broke down in tears. Marilyn Sitzman came running up from behind him, pulling at his arm screaming, "Mr. Z., they killed him. He's dead!"

*****

THERE WERE PEOPLE SCREAMING.

EVERYONE WAS RUNNING.

HE STOPPED FOR A MOMENT AND TOOK INVENTORY, SOMETHING HE WAS PRONE TO DO DURING TIMES OF CRISIS.

Policemen, motorcycle cops he thought, were swarming the area he walked through. One bumped his shoulder. He grimaced and looked behind him at Elm Street. The motorcade had sped away moments ago.

At that moment he stopped and all the fears and sympathy he had for the First Family dissipated into business. A *Dallas Morning News* reporter, Harry McCormick approached him on his way back to the Dal-Tex building.[62]

"Hey Mister, you have a movie camera there, did you get the president being shot on film?" McCormick asked. "If you did, you've hit the jackpot," he continued, "and my company would pay lots of money to see it." Abraham ignored him and kept walking, all the while thinking to himself, *"My God, I have it all on film. I have it all on film."* He walked faster towards the Dal-Tex building with a purpose, McCormick chattering behind him. *Maybe he had the killer on film. Maybe his film could be evidence. The money for this type of evidence would be priceless.* For Abraham Zapruder, this film would be worth more than his company *Jennifer Juniors* would ever make.

Realizing this, Abraham's first phone call was to his business partner and lawyer, Erwin Schwartz. At the same time, he told Lillian to call the Dallas Police Department.[63] Minutes later, Abraham Zapruder's office on the fourth floor was bombarded by all sorts of people. Two Dallas Police officers arrived, after receiving the call Zapruder asked his secretary Lillian Rogers to make, and demanded the film.

"Give us the film, it is evidence," one announced to Zapruder.

Abraham refused to give it to them on advice from his attorney. The policemen ensconced themselves in his office. Five minutes later, Darwin Payne, a writer from the *Dallas Times Herald* arrived and tried to purchase the film.[64]

"It's not for sale," Zapruder tells him, "I don't even know what it shows, and how did you know I had it?" he asked Payne.

"With all this going on today? I just happened to ask some of the bystanders questions at the Texas School Book Depository and some were your employees. They told me you had taken a movie." Payne replied. "Will you grant an interview for the *Dallas Times Herald?*"[65] Abraham was beside himself at this point. All he could think about was the horrific murder of his beloved president, then the money he could make from the film he just took, and *where the hell is Erwin?* Any other day he felt like this, he would have left the building and gone to sit on the bench outside his office building. If it was a really bad day like today, he would have walked to Dealey Plaza, planted his face into his hands and wept until the bad thoughts were out of his system. He didn't have that luxury today. At that moment, the phone rang. It was Erwin Schwartz.

"Hurry Erwin, I need you here," Abraham pleaded as he explained what was happening in his office.

"Tell Marilyn to put the film into the safe until I get there," Schwartz told Zapruder, "Let no one touch it." He hung up the telephone with a loud click.

Though his film would later prove to be the most compelling evidence, it wasn't treated as such immediately after the assassination.

Around 1:15 P.M., Harry McCormick arrived with Orville Nix's friend Forrest Sorrels of the Secret Service. McCormick had told Sorrels about Zapruder's film and Sorrel's interest was keen.[66]

"I can get you a copy sir," Zapruder told Sorrels, "but on the advice of my attorney, I must retain the original."

When Darwin Payne realized his competitor's reporter was so heavily involved in Zapruder's decision making, he protested loudly.

"Hey, Mr. Zapruder, what's with this? I thought I was going to get the exclusive interview and purchase of the film!"

"I met him first, Payne," McCormick replied. "The *Dallas Morning News* gets the story," and smiled at his journalistic victory.

At that moment, Erwin Schwartz entered the offices overhearing the verbal scuttle between the competing newspaper reporters. Always the negotiator, he said, "Yes, Mr. Payne is it? Yes, Mr. McCormick here spoke with my partner and client first. As is the democratic way, we will work with him. Now, Mr. McCormick has suggested we take the film to the WFAA studios, which is co-owned by the *Dallas Morning News* and see if they can develop the film for Mr. Sorrels and the Secret Service."

In the offices of *Jennifer Juniors*, the employees were hunched around a small television set, as was most of America. At 1:39 P.M., the most trusted newsman in the world, Walter Cronkite, puts on his dark-framed glasses and delivers the lines that are as iconic as they are anguished:

> *"From Dallas, Texas, the flash apparently official, President Kennedy died at 1:00 P.M. Central Standard Time. Two o'clock Eastern Standard Time, some thirty-eight minutes ago." As his voice cracks with sorrow, he continues:*
>
> *"Vice-President Lyndon Johnson has left the hospital in Dallas, but we do not know to where he has proceeded. Presumably he will be taking the oath of office shortly and become the thirty-sixth president of the United States."*[67]

As America heard this, a collective cry rose from each home, office, school, and city. Surely, this was the most heartbreaking day of this century.

Zapruder, Schwartz, McCormick, and Sorrels departed for the studio at about 1:45 P.M. in a car driven by police officers C.R. Osburn and Joe B. Jones.[68] Payne was left behind to inform his editor he didn't get the story.

The WFAA studios in Dallas were all aflutter. They were about to get the exclusive interview from a man who took a home movie of the assassination. The program director, Jay Watson, was making necessary phone calls and approval to break into regular programming for an on-air interview with Zapruder.[69] In the photographic department, the WFAA chief photographer and Assistant News director Bert Shipp was frantically searching for older 8mm equipment to process the Zapruder film.[70] The only equipment the studio had available was for 16mm film. In an effort to seal the deal for the exclusive interview, Shipp offered to call his friend Jack Harrison at Kodak about processing the film.

In the meantime, Zapruder was being readied for the interview. A man of large stature, Abraham Zapruder was visibly shaken, yet he enjoyed the attention he garnered so quickly. Dapper in his white shirt, dark suit and bowtie, he made an endearing, as well as believable witness. At one point during the interview, he explained to Jay Watson, who was doing double duty as a news anchor, that he heard shots coming from behind him.[71] In no official record would he speak these words again.

*****

AT ONE POINT DURING THE INTERVIEW, HE EXPLAINED TO JAY WATSON, WHO WAS DOING DOUBLE DUTY AS A NEWS ANCHOR, THAT HE HEARD SHOTS COMING FROM BEHIND HIM. IN NO OFFICIAL RECORD WOULD HE SPEAK THESE WORDS AGAIN.

The parent network, ABC, carried the interview live as well. CBS's Walter Cronkite may have broken the news of the president's death, but now thanks to ABC, the world knew there was photographic evidence of the JFK Assassination. Even more stunning, the filmmaker believed shots may have come from behind him. During the interview, Erwin Schwartz held the precious undeveloped film while standing nearby. He realized he was holding history, fame, and fortune.

While Zapruder was being interviewed, Forrest Sorrels told the two Dallas Police officers Osburn and Jones they would need to drive the trio to Kodak. Shipp had told Sorrels his friend Jack Harrison at Kodak would be able to develop the film.

Around 2:40 P.M., Zapruder, McCormick, Schwartz and Sorrels arrived at the Kodak Film Developing Plant near Love Field. Ironically, Air Force One was departing Love Field with the dead president's body and the newly sworn in president, Lyndon Baines Johnson at the same time. It was as if twin scenarios were being born at the same time: one on celluloid, the other in veiled secrecy.

The three men entered the large Kodak processing plant and were quickly met by Kodak manager Phil Chamberlain.[72] It was immediately developed, and as soon as it dried Chamberlain carefully ran the film through a viewer and the horrific murder was viewed for the first time by those in attendance. Chamberlain was aghast. Sorrels was dumbfounded. Zapruder broke into a sweat at the too-soon reliving of the president's murder. Erwin Schwartz was abnormally speechless. Forrest's walkie-talkie crackled and he excused himself from the viewing. He has been called back to the Dallas Police Department due to the arrest of Lee Harvey Oswald.[73]

Chamberlain, still shaken by what he has seen but realizing the importance of the six feet of film celluloid, refused to run it through the viewer again for fear of destruction. He regretfully told them that his plant had no facilities to make copies. He suggested Zapruder and Schwartz take it to another film processing lab, Jamieson Film Labs of Dallas.[74]

By this time, Zapruder was beyond flustered. The day had been like the Roller-Coaster at the Texas State Fair: up, down, and rickety. He had run the gamut of emotions from terror to thrill and desperately wanted copies of his film. Erwin agreed that this had to be done that day, so they drove to the Jamieson plant to have copies made. It was 4:30 P.M. but the normal tangle of traffic one would see on a Friday drive home was absent.

* * * * *

Due to the horrible events of the day, the Dallas Independent School District canceled all Friday night football games. Most of the larger companies in their glistening skyscrapers sent their employees home. Those same shiny skyscrapers held secrets from their employees and from the city; secrets that would not be revealed for decades. Some of the buildings housed secrets more sinister than the others including the men who met at the Mercantile Bank[75] as well as the Republic Bank Tower.[76] The whole of Dallas seemed to have shut down with news of the assassination. Flags all over the city had already been lowered to half-mast. For five sets of eyes in one office building, solemn looks were shot to one another like a ritual in a fraternal pledge ceremony. The look conveyed the promise of silence in a noise that will last for over fifty years. One of the set of eyes looked up at a portrait of Lyndon Baines Johnson holding court in the boardroom. He seemed to be participating in the ritual as well.

* * * * *

Across town, the two shrewd business partners left the Jamieson Film Labs where copies of the valuable film were made and developed. They then returned to the Kodak Lab where print enlargements of specific frames were made. Zapruder and Erwin left the Kodak plant about 9:45 P.M. with three copies of the film and the original. They then drove to Sorrel's office in downtown Dallas. There they gave him two copies: One was immediately dispatched to the FBI investigators in Washington D.C., the other kept by Sorrels.[77] Abraham realized he hadn't eaten at all that day and his stamina was depleted.

"I have to go home Erwin. I haven't spoken with my wife at all today," he told his friend.

"Be prepared, my friend, and prepare your family," Erwin told Abraham. "This will be the first of many hectic days. You have history in your hands and the world will want a piece of it. Make no promises until you've spoken with me."

Abraham nodded his head affirmatively and drove home.

The next day he sold the rights to his film to Richard Stolley of *Life* magazine for $150,000.00 plus royalties (or $979,500.00 plus royalties applying today's Consumer Price Index).[78] This was a considerable amount of money for twenty-six seconds of film, though the public was told it was only $25,000.00. It was only later that the secret sum of cash Zapruder was paid became known. Erwin Schwartz did his job well.

CHAPTER SEVEN

A TIME TO FABRICATE AND DESTROY

"I do not want it said - I do not want it said of our generation of Americans what T. S. Eliot said in his poem, 'The Rock,' of another group of people: 'And the wind shall say these were a decent people, their only monument the asphalt road and a thousand lost golf balls'. We can do better than that."

John F. Kennedy[79]

Orville Nix and family left Walgreens and silently drove home. Gayle was napping in the backseat of Orville's 1957 red and white Plymouth Fury[80] on her mother's lap. Ella rode in the front with her shaken husband.

"What did you see Orville? Did you see him get shot?" she asked him.

"I saw the nightmares I've been having come to life Ella. Come to life! At one moment I was taking a film of him smiling to his wife and the next moment I saw him shot." Ella saw his eyes filling with tears.

"Did you get his…well…did you get…?"

"Are you asking if I got the president's death on film? I don't know Ella, I just don't know. People were screaming and crying and I was scared. All I could think about was whether or not you and Elaine and Gayle were okay and then when I saw people covering their children and racing all around the Plaza, I just… I just… I just don't know if I took anything or not," he said despondently.

Ella reached across the red vinyl car seat and patted her husband's shoulder. She couldn't think of a time she had ever seen him this way.

As they reached their home on the corner of Denley Drive and Elmore St., Orville helped Ella, then Elaine out of the car. Gayle was still sleeping, and he carried her to Elaine's car. He gently opened the car door and placed his granddaughter inside. He looked at his young daughter-in-law and thought of the First Lady again. How terrible to be so young and lose the father of your children. He hugged Elaine and told her to have his son call him when he got home from work.

"I will Paw-Paw, try to get some sleep, it's been a hard day for you," Elaine replied. She pushed the reverse button and backed the small white Valiant out of the driveway and headed home to 1203 Savoy near Kiest Park in Oak Cliff.[81]

Ella was sitting at the table with her head in her hands as Orville entered the small home. She had already turned the black and white television on and the news on every channel was all about the death of John F. Kennedy.

"What is the television saying?" Orville asked his wife.

"They're saying that the president was shot and died at Parkland Hospital," Ella replied.

Orville had taken out his Keystone camera and was checking the footage indicator window. The number was now at twenty-three. That morning, he had loaded his new roll of Kodacolor Type A film through the aperture and pressure plates and replaced the camera cover. Then following the instruction booklet, he ran the film through it until the number twenty-five appeared in the center of the footage indicator. This meant he had twenty-five feet of film to use. That it now measured only twenty-three meant that he probably didn't film the president being shot.[82] I must have been filming the ground while I was clinching the camera grip, he thought to himself. The memory of everything he saw was still so vivid in his mind. The shots—at least four, maybe even five. The people-running to the stockade fence, the Texas School Book Depository, the Triple Overpass. The president—his head exploding into glittery pieces before Orville's eyes. He decided to go use more of the film the next morning to try to recreate his ineffable memories.

As he looked up at the television again, there was a man being interviewed by WFAA. He recognized the balding man wearing the bowtie, though he didn't know where he had seen him. He got up from his vinyl recliner and turned up the volume. [83]

WATSON: *A gentleman just walked in our studio that I am meeting for the first time, as well as you- this is WFAA-TV in Dallas, Texas. May I have your name please, sir?*

ZAPRUDER: *My name is Abraham Zapruder.*

WATSON: *Mr. Zapruda?*

ZAPRUDER: *Zapruder, yes sir.*

WATSON: *Zapruda. And would you tell us your story please, sir?*

ZAPRUDER: *I got out in, uh, about a half-hour earlier to get a good spot to shoot some pictures. And I found a spot, one of these concrete blocks they have down near that park, near the underpass. And I got on top there, there was another girl from my office, she was right behind me. And as I was shooting, as the president was coming down from Houston Street making his turn, it was about a half-way down there, I heard a shot, and he slumped to the side, like this. Then I heard another shot or two, I couldn't say it was one or two, and I saw his head practically open up, all blood and everything, and I kept on shooting. That's about all, I'm just sick, I can't…*

WATSON: *I think that pretty well expresses the entire feelings of the whole world.*

ZAPRUDER: *Terrible, terrible.*

WATSON: *You have the film in your camera, we'll try to get…*

ZAPRUDER: *Yes, I brought it to the studio, now.*

WATSON: *We'll try to get that processed and have it as soon as possible.*

WFAA then shows a video tape of the hearse with Kennedy's body leaving the Parkland Hospital driveway. Watson next shows a photograph of the Texas School Book Depository and points to the sixth floor window.

WATSON: *There is a picture of the window where the gun was allegedly fired from that killed President Kennedy-*

ZAPRUDER: *I must have been in the line of fire.*

WATSON: *... today. Excuse me, go ahead sir.*

ZAPRUDER: *I say I must have been in the line of fire where I seen that picture where it was. I was right on that, uh, concrete block, as I said. And as I explained before, is a sickening scene. At first I thought perhaps it's a, uh, it sounded like, uh, somebody make a joke, you hear a, a shot and somebody grabs their stomach."*[84]

Orville watched the Zapruder interview stunned at the immediate fraternity he felt with this man. He looked down at the camera he still had in his hand and for a split-second thought of taking it to the television station. Even if he had taken a film, it would only be second best after this Zapruder fella had shown his. He then thought of what the newsman said, about the alleged gunmen at the Texas School Book Depository.

"Ella," Orville called, "Ella, I don't think the shots came from the Texas School Book Depository. I don't remember looking that way. That's the building with the big Hertz clock on it."[85]

Ella walked into the small beige living room and sat on the brown herringbone print couch she had bought from Montgomery Wards.

"Well, where do you think they came from?" she asked her husband.

"I remember looking towards that part of the park that doesn't match the rest, the part that has a fence. Do you know where I mean?" he replied. Ella nodded her head in agreement. "And I remember thinking that's where the shots were coming from. There's some trees up there, and during that time of day it's shadowy but there was so much going on...so many people screaming and running and..." his voice faltered as he put his head into his hands and began to cry again. Ella had been married to Orville for over twenty-five years and had seen him cry twice: when Edward died and when his son was born. In the course of twenty-four hours she had now seen him cry two more times. She was worried for him.

Ella jumped up from the couch and hurried over to console her husband. She ran her palm in a circular motion on his back. In the background, the television was now reporting on the arrest of Lee Harvey Oswald. They were calling him a Russian defector and pro-Cuban protester.

"Oh Ella, I was so worried that something may have happened to you or Elaine or Gayle. I should have run up to the park area to see if someone was behind that fence. I feel so helpless. I feel like I could have done more. Why did this have to happen in our city?" he said tearfully.

The ringing of the telephone broke the solemn moment. Orville jumped up to answer it as he always did. He hated it to ring more than twice without it being answered.

"Hello," Orville answered as he picked up the black telephone. "Dad, are you okay?" It was his son Orville, Jr. on the line. "Elaine says you were pretty shook up about what you saw today. Can you believe .it? Those idiot Democrats, I'll lay a dollar to a donut that they killed each other off. That, or Bobby made the Mafia pretty mad. Think it could've been a Mafia hit?" Orville hadn't even thought of someone else killing Kennedy, he just knew that Oswald wasn't behind the stockade fence.

"Well Jr., the TV says it's some scrawny little Communist guy named Lee Harvey Oswald. They say he killed a policeman too."

"Yeah, we were watching that too. You know what? He lived in that boarding house that Elaine's Uncle Eual's patient, Gladys Johnson owned in Oak Cliff at 1026 Beckley St.[86] Doctor Eual Dipprey, the Chiropractor. His office is on Zangs St., not too far from there. Small world isn't it? Eual called us just a few minutes ago and also told us that Gary, his son, was in the same class with Allan, the son of the officer they say Lee Harvey Oswald killed, J.D. Tippit.[87] And did you hear Oswald screaming, 'I'm just a patsy?' Think he was set up? I told Gary and Eual that you may have taken a movie of the assassination but you didn't know. Eual wants a copy if you did. Do you think you did, Dad?" Orville Jr. peppered his dad with questions.

"No son, I don't think I did. The film indicator shows I didn't take much of anything, probably just the ground while I was running. I'm going back down there in the morning and try to retrace my steps. Want to go with me?"

"I can't Dad, I'm off tomorrow and I promised the kids it would be junk food breakfast Saturday so Elaine can get some sleep."

"Junk food breakfast? What the heck is that?" Orville asked his son.

"You won't approve of it Dad, but I take them to the 7-Eleven and let them get cupcakes, candy, and cokes for breakfast. It's just a treat I do for them every now and then," Orville told his dad sheepishly.

"If Elaine needs some sleep, why don't you just bring the kids here? You know how much your mom loves to have them over for the weekend," Orville admonished his son.

"Mom needs her rest too, Dad. She works hard like you. Besides, Elaine and I don't want to take advantage. The kids are with you and Mom all the time."

"We love having them here, son. I was happy to see Gayle today. I was missing Cindy and David, but after what happened, I'm glad they weren't with us at the parade. I think of little John-John and Caroline. I'm still upset about it all. What do you think is going to happen to the country? Do you think we'll be invaded by Russia or Cuba?" he asked his son. Orville knew his son knew much more about political events than he did. Orville hardly ever read the paper.

"Nawww, I don't think so Dad. I think there may be more to this though. They caught Oswald awfully fast. When have you ever known the Dallas Police Department to work that fast? And you know what else? If anything, I would think they would have had Oswald in the "Decker Hold" by now.[88] Wonder why he isn't? The people who didn't like Kennedy are *really* not going to like having that snake LBJ as president. It embarrasses me that he's from Texas. Welp, he's the president now though and didn't even have to get Billie Sol Estes to buy him votes to get there. And yes, I'm sure there will be a war of some kind, but not with the Russians or Cuba. LBJ will make sure the military production stays in Texas. I tell you, Dad, you need to vote for Barry Goldwater in '64." [89]

"I've never been a Republican, and I'm not a 'changing now. I gotta go, son, talk to you later." With that, he hung up the phone. As he did, he noticed a shadowy figure outside near the front porch. It was late afternoon and the sun was going down. He walked to the front door and opened it. The figure he had seen a moment ago was no longer there. As he stepped out the screen door, the smell from the Fleming and Sons Paper Company made his nostrils flare in protest. He took a few steps out and looked all around the porch and yard. He noticed the chrysanthemums were starting to bloom yellow and gold in the deep blue planters Ella had bought during their summer trip to New Mexico. One of them looked like it had been moved; a stem was broken. Had someone been there?

CHAPTER EIGHT

OF CAPITALISM AND SECRECY: THE AMERICAN WAY

"The very word 'secrecy' is repugnant in a free and open society; and we are as a people inherently and historically opposed to secret societies, to secret oaths, and to secret proceedings."

John F. Kennedy[90]

Orville endured a sleepless night replaying what he saw on November 22, 1963 over and over. People, shots, blood. People, shots, blood. Like a bad opera, the scenes in his head were horrific and accompanied by a musical score of high sopranos shrieking instead of screaming… screaming instead of singing.

Before bed, Orville and Ella had spent the evening in front of the television watching all the different stations and listening to the story of Lee Harvey Oswald come to light. This scrawny assassin wasn't any older than his own son, Orville Jr., and he too was a family man with two small daughters and a wife. Why would a man kill the president, then a police officer and then go see a movie at the Texas Theater? Why didn't he get as far as he could out of the city? Why didn't he run? Why was he acting so calm at the Dallas Police

Station? Orville supposed he didn't think like a criminal which is why he couldn't understand the whole Oswald scenario. The thought made him feel better. He remembered the phone call with his son the day before, and for a split second wondered if Oswald worked for the new president LBJ or whoever had bought the 'Welcome Mr. Kennedy' advertisement in the *Dallas Morning News* yesterday. *What the heck was the John Birch Society anyway?* It sounded like some bird watching group to him.[91] As if reading his thoughts, he heard the paperboy's delivery *thump* of the day's newspaper at the front screen door. He looked at the clock next to his bed; it was 4:45 A.M.

He got up quietly so as not to wake Ella and made some coffee. As the coffee percolated, he opened the door to get the paper. He never locked the door as he couldn't remember a time when there had been any crime in his neighborhood, save for kids playing pranks at Halloween.

Then he remembered the strange figure he had seen yesterday. Aw, it had to be the excitement of the day. Why would anyone be looking into our window? We're not rich, and this is a rented house. He pushed any thought of larceny out of his mind and sat down at the small, aluminum dining table to read the day's paper. Orville had a hard time reading, and many times he became frustrated with the words reporters used. He had no problems today though and, as he unfolded the paper, the headlines screamed, "KENNEDY SLAIN ON DALLAS STREET."[92] There beneath the headlines were pictures of LBJ and President Kennedy. President Kennedy's picture was larger than LBJ's picture, something Orville reckoned the new president wouldn't like too much. All Texans knew Lyndon Baines Johnson liked being in the spotlight. In between the pictures was the article Orville read that morning. It was entitled, "Pro-Communist Charged with Act." Well, that puts an end to my thoughts about LBJ hiring him. Oswald was just a Communist mad at the president, Orville thought as he read along.

Orville took a sip of coffee, heavy on cream and sugar and lit a Lucky Strike. He read that the Communist Oswald had used a Mauser 7.65 mm rifle.[93] "*Well, he was either a really good shot or it was a lucky strike. How would he have gotten four or five rounds off in that short of time?*" he wondered out loud.

"Lucky Strike?" said Ella yawningly as she shuffled into the kitchen. "Can you not find your cigarettes?" she asked as she kissed Orville's forehead.

"No, my cigarettes are right here. Did I wake you Ella? I'm so sorry. I was just reading the paper out loud. It says here that this commie pinko Oswald shot the president with a Mauser rifle. The boy must have been a really good marksman because Ella, I heard at least four or five shots down there at Dealey Park, maybe more."

"I'm sure we'll hear more about it today. He's in jail now, so the police will find out. And they're so spittin' mad about him killing one of their own, I'd be surprised if they didn't get a confession quick," she said.

Orville drank the last of his coffee and passed the paper to his wife.

"I'm going to go back down there this morning and try to remember what I saw. I'm going to take my camera," Orville said.

"Well dress warm, Orville, its cold this morning. Do you want me to make you some breakfast?"

"No, when I get back, we'll go out to eat. How does that sound?" he winked at her and left to get dressed.

Ella smiled as she read the paper then said, "No, Orville, wait for me, I didn't get to see where you were yesterday, I'm going with you. I want to see what you saw."

Thirty minutes later they were in the red Plymouth on their way back to downtown Dallas. As they neared Dealey Plaza the whole of it seemed as faded as wilted roses.

Orville parked behind the Terminal Annex building like he had the day before. The air was thick with low lying clouds and as he and Ella walked, their breaths intermingled with the fog. It was as if the clouds were trying to cover the horror that had occurred in this exact place less than twenty-four hours earlier. But instead of cleaning the air filthy with murder and secrecy, the clouds seemed to enrobe them into invisibility. Metaphorically, the clouds would linger for years.

Orville and Ella walked to the corner of Main and Houston where Orville had waited for the motorcade and his family. He pointed to the place where the epileptic man had had a seizure, then mysteriously vanished.

Many years later, researchers found this man to be a part-time employee in the *Dallas Morning News* mailroom. He was taken to Parkland Hospital, but there is no record of his discharge as he walked out without being questioned. Why? Many believe that because President Kennedy was brought into the hospital several minutes later, no one was paying attention to him. Is this story one more coincidence of many that day or was he in Dealey Plaza for a diversion?

"It was like watching Edward, wasn't it?" Ella empathized. Orville nodded his head in affirmation.

"Ella," Orville sadly said, "I wish I could have done more for Edward because he always did so much for me. He never cried about his illness. He hated that we all had to take care of him. He found happiness in our happiness, never thinking of himself. He taught me more than my own daddy did. All I could think of was, I can't help him, I can't help him. Then the president is shot, the first lady is a widow and again, I couldn't do anything to help, Ella." Tears welled in his eyes.

"He was watching over you yesterday, Orville… he was! You didn't get shot did you? With all the bullets flying around it's a wonder only two men were shot. You were meant to be alive, Orville. God isn't finished with you yet." Orville kissed his empathetic wife and silently thanked God. She was right.

Orville wiped his face and began filming as he walked with Ella.

"Here's where I walked after I realized I wanted to see the president a bit closer. I looked up at the Hertz sign and then back to the president's dark blue limousine. Right then the shooting began and I heard at least four or five shots. Bam… Bam then real fast Bam-Bam. They seemed to be coming from the stockade fence. You know, Ella, my daddy always said you never hear the first shot, just the ones afterwards, I know I heard at least four."

The Dallas Morning News

Johnson Takes Nation's Helm, Pages 4 and 5

John F. Kennedy Life History, Pages 16 and 17

KENNEDY SLAIN ON DALLAS STREET

JOHNSON BECOMES PRESIDENT

Receives Oath on Aircraft

Lyndon B. Johnson

Gov. Connally Resting Well

Impact Shattering To World Capitals

Pro-Communist Charged With Act

Four Hours in Surgery

Friendly Crowd Cheered Kennedy

FUNERAL FOR PRESIDENT WILL BE HELD ON MONDAY

John F. Kennedy

GRAY CLOUDS WENT AWAY

Day Began as Auspiciously As Any in Kennedy's Career

Orville panned his camera towards the area of which he spoke. Ella's eyes followed the direction of his camera. She saw the bright white pergola and its crescent moon shape to the front of them. She marveled at the cutwork design of the pergola that she thought would be a lovely place to plant vines. To the left of it, she saw the stockade fence of which her husband spoke; dark tan against the bright white of the Plaza shelter.[94] The sun empathized with her feelings as well as those of her husband's. She was staring at the Elm St. part of the Triple Underpass bridge as a single ray of sunlight shone through brilliantly forming a cross of shadows. She felt goosebumps at the sight. It was as if God was mourning the loss of the young president as well.

Orville's voice shook her back to reality.

"Mrs. Kennedy was trying to get out of the car, she was crawling across the trunk and then some man jumped on the back of the car. I guess he was a Secret Service man and pushed her back in as the car sped away towards the Triple Underpass. It all happened so fast but seemed to last for hours," Orville lamented as he looked up towards the Texas School Book Depository. The Hertz sign blinked 7:30 A.M.; nineteen hours later than the time Orville had looked up at it before. The president hadn't been dead twenty-four hours, yet the world was already a different place.

* * * * *

Across the street at the Dal-Tex building, Abraham Zapruder was meeting with Richard Stolley from *Life* Magazine along with Forrest Sorrels and some other Secret Service men.[95] They all screened the film and were disturbed by the graphic presidential murder the film portrayed. This was at least the fifth time Abraham had watched the horror movie he had taken.

"I don't want Mrs. Kennedy or her children to see this, Stolley. I don't want this film exploited by turning it into a Hollywood movie or trading cards. *Time/Life* can have the film, but only if the more graphic frames aren't shown," Zapruder said tearfully.[96] Stolley eagerly agreed to the shaken business owner's stipulations.

On November 29th, 1963, exactly one week after the assassination, *Life Magazine* published thirty-one frames from the Zapruder film, omitting the graphic frames numbered from 312-315 under Zapruder's direction.[97] Later, it was discovered that critical frames were transposed to depict a more forward motion of Kennedy's head rather than a rearward motion. It was explained thusly many years later:

> *"James Wagenvoord, the editorial business manager and assistant to Life Magazine's executive editor, Dick Pollard, realized that a mistake had been made: "I asked about it when the stills were first printed, (they didn't read right) and then duped for distribution to the European and British papers/magazines. The only response I got was an icy stare from Dick Pollard, Life's Director of Photography. So being an ambitious employee, I had them distributed. In 1965 FBI director J. Edgar Hoover explained this reversing of the Zapruder frames as a 'printing error'.*[98]

This "error" would be the second of many errors with regards to the Zapruder and Nix films, but by this time, Zapruder's evidentiary film could no longer be considered such as it had been altered by *Life* magazine under Zapruder's direction. For a quarter, any person could purchase the only known photographic evidence of the charismatic president's murder. This evidence was on coffee tables, libraries, offices, and subways around the world. The horror movie that was the Zapruder film was enough to shock any reader viewing the magazine and any future juror, and this issue of the magazine did not even reveal the most horrific frames. Of course, by the time this *Life* issue was released, Lee Harvey Oswald had already been publicly declared the lone assassin and Jack Ruby had ceremoniously executed him for the Kennedy family and America. Scholarly JFK researchers and those not so scholarly would say this "printing error" was the first indication that there was more to the assassination than the public would ever know. If there wasn't a conspiracy to kill the president, there was a definite conspiracy to withhold the truth from the American people and the world. Why? Were we not able to handle the truth? Were we too naïve? Were we too stupid? Abraham Zapruder wasn't, but Orville Nix may have been.

In one week's time, Zapruder's personal name had become more famous than his company name. Moreover, Zapruder's personal wealth multiplied substantially. Not only would he receive $150,000 paid in $25,000 increments, he would receive half of any royalties *Life* procured from its usage in films, television, and print. Orville Nix would receive $5,000 total in his lifetime. In retrospect, the filming positions of both Zapruder and Orville Nix matched the dissimilar way their films and their lives were treated. Though their journeys into this event paralleled, they diverged soon after. Some would say their experiences were just another example of the American way in action: capitalism, secrecy, and the inequality between rich and poor that still rears its ugly head today.

CHAPTER NINE

FORTY-SEVEN HOURS AND WHITE RESISTOL HATS

"Before my term has ended, we shall have to test anew whether a nation organized and governed such as ours can endure. The outcome is by no means certain."

John F. Kennedy[99]

Orville and Ella left Dealey Plaza on Saturday, November 23, 1963 to return to Oak Cliff. They decided to eat a late breakfast at Austin's Barbecue, a small diner at the intersection of Illinois and Hampton Streets in Oak Cliff.[100] Orville went to Austin's often; sometimes in the morning for breakfast after working the night shift, other times after a particularly hot day at golf. The large plastic cups the owner Austin Cook allowed his customers to take home held enough tea to quench a hot golfer's thirst.[101] The diner was crowded as usual, but even more so today. Every red vinyl booth seemed to be talking about the assassination. Orville and Ella heard snippets of conversations through the scrannel of tunes from the miniature jukes boxes at each table as they waited to be seated.

"Did you see that little commie they picked up?" A burly man asked his friend between Hank Williams yodels.

"Yeah, he has a black eye. If I had gotten hold of him, he would've had worst," the other wearing dusty jeans and boots said.

In another booth, two young women wearing an excessive amount of black eyeliner and overly-bleached, teased blonde hair were hunched over yet talking loudly.

"Tippit worked here you know, as the security guard on Saturday nights usually. I always thought he kinda looked like Kennedy. He had that dreamy, wavy hair. Kenny got mad at me one night because I kept smiling at him," the blonde with the pink scarf knotted at her neck said. "He usually stood right by the door." Their miniature jukebox was playing Bobby Vinton's *Blue Velvet.*

"Kenny gets mad at any guy you smile at, Betty. I don't know why you're still going out with him. Besides, he should feel badly now knowing that Officer Tippit won't be around for you to smile at anymore anyway. It's so tragic isn't it? He had a wife and kids. I just can't believe all this is happening," the blonde with the yellow scarf tied in her hair said as she took a sip of her over-sized drink.

At that moment a short woman adorned in a sheen of perspiration, black hairnet, and red stained apron told Orville their table was ready. They walked to the back of the diner and took their seats, taking care not to tear their clothes on the rips in the red vinyl chairs.

* * * * *

At the same time, Richard Stolley was returning to *Life* Magazine with the Zapruder film in hand. In downtown Dallas, Lee Harvey Oswald had been arraigned for the murder of President John F. Kennedy and was again being questioned by a myriad of investigators at the Dallas Police Department. The infamous Katzenbach memo from J. Edgar Hoover perfectly summed up the nicely gift-wrapped package that was presented to America and the Kennedy family in the form of Lee Harvey Oswald: "The thing I am most concerned about, and so is Mr. Katzenbach, is having something issued so that we can convince the public that Oswald is the real assassin."[102] Nicholas Katzenbach was not only the Assistant Attorney General, he was the Kennedy emissary to the South in all things legal and had now been anointed the American public's exorcist to lay to rest all rumors of conspiracy and subterfuge. He conceived the idea of the Warren Commission and later served as Attorney General after Robert F. Kennedy resigned. In the midst of southern race riots, the Bay of Pigs Invasion, and the Cold War, Katzenbach was part of an administration and governmental mindset that believed the people of America were too fragile to handle much more tragedy than they had already seen in the three short years of Kennedy's tenure.[103] In many ways, it was a noble intention: protect the public from knowledge that could hurt. Unfortunately, every good has a bad, and this same worldview would be molested to deny the truth of what really happened on November 22, 1963.

The Dallas Police and Sheriff's Departments had their own agenda that, luckily for Hoover and Katzenbach, paralleled theirs. The boys in the white open road brim hats[104] that were the elite Homicide detectives at the Dallas Police Department were well aware that they had just become front-page news and they were ready to show the world how Texas justice worked. One of the ways they did that was by interviewing Oswald for twelve hours over a three day period. Unfortunately, no official stenographic or tape recordings of these interviews were kept.[105] Instead, memoranda notes from a myriad of investigators, including a postal inspector, paint a picture of a man who was calm, stoic, and quiet about his participation in the death of the president and a police officer. The notes also contained inconsistencies that are still being questioned today.[106]

*****

Orville and Ella ate a quiet lunch that Saturday afternoon and went back home to watch news coverage about Lee Harvey Oswald along with people all over the world. Orville would later learn that he and Ella were not the only people glued to their television sets. From Nov. 22 through 25, 1963, 96% of TV-owning households tuned in for an average of more than 31 hours apiece. On Saturday, November 24, 1963 more facts about Lee Harvey Oswald were being reported about the man who would be labeled the lone assassin. Captain Fritz of the Dallas Police Department said they had found three shell casings on the sixth floor of the Texas School Book Depository and a rifle had been hidden under some boxes by a stairway nearby. Of course, Fritz failed to tell the people of Dallas that he had taken one of those shells and put it in his pocket, only later to give to the FBI. The first reports were that the rifle was a Mauser. It had now been determined it was an older rifle, an Italian made Mannlicher-Carcano.[107] Even later still, word would come that Abraham Zapruder's friends, Jeanne and George de Mohrenschildt were close friends of Lee Harvey Oswald and his wife Marina.

A young local CBS reporter, Dan Rather, appeared on television near the place where Orville had filmed President Kennedy smiling at the First Lady. Like Orville and Ella, Rather seemed mesmerized by the crowds of people who had shown up at the Plaza that afternoon. Orville listened to him talk about school children cheering at a school as if happy the president had been assassinated.[108] *That couldn't be*, Orville thought, and at that moment, he swore to never watch Dan Rather on TV again. *Why was this upstart news reporter trying to make the whole city look like a bunch of murderers, even the children? Wasn't it enough that the president had been shot in Dallas?* Orville changed the channel and turned back to watch the television. The news report showed a wreath being placed near the point the president was shot and Orville got a tear in his eye at the sight. His emotions turned again though, as he and Ella watched the thin, well-spoken Oswald being questioned by reporters. Oswald had a black eye and it was hard to hear the reporter's questions because there were so many people in the Dallas Police Department, all of them talking at the same time. Just the sight of this man made Orville's stomach turn.

"Good Lord Orville, that man doesn't look strong enough to fire a rifle once, let alone four or five times," Ella commented.

Orville shook his head in agreement. "What I don't understand, Ella, is why I heard shots from the fence. They're saying this man was in the School Book Depository Building. Do you think there could have been another shooter?" he questioned.

"Well, Lord no, Orville! If there had been another shooter, don't you think they would have mentioned it by now?" Ella replied.

"Are you saying I'm losing my mind woman? I heard shots come from the damned fence!"

Orville got up to light a cigarette and then opened the front door and went outside. He was becoming tired of this round the clock television talk about the death of the president. He wanted things to be like they were before.

He looked up at the sky, wondering if he should get his camera to take pictures of the beautiful Texas sunset. As colorful as it was, the blood red streaks emanating from the Midas-like sun, tinged with hot pink reminded him of blood all over the golden President and First Lady. He took a long drag from his cigarette and closed his eyes, the smoke filling his lungs, the memory of the shots coming back to him. *I remember running towards Elm Street. I remember people falling all around him, trying to shield themselves from omnipresent shots. I remember looking toward the stockade fence. The shots definitely came from there.* If his own wife didn't believe him, would anyone else? He opened his eyes and again looked toward the skies. The same God who made such beauty had put him into a position to see such evil. Orville wondered if he would ever use his camera again.

But the evil wasn't over. During the night, the police reportedly received threats on Oswald's life through the switchboard.[109] Again, no record was kept of them. Henry Wade, the Dallas District Attorney, was not about to risk losing the chance to convict the president's killer. He made plans to safely transfer the president's murderer to the Dallas County Jail. Wade had already lost the ability to keep the President's body in Dallas to the boys of the Federal Departments. That wouldn't happen with Oswald… at least that's what he told the public.[110] Plans are made to transfer Oswald to the Dallas County Jail, directly across from the Texas School Book Depository, at 10 A.M. the next morning. An armored car would be the decoy while Oswald is transported in an unmarked squad car.[111] Postal Inspector Harry Holmes requested to interview Oswald, delaying the transfer by almost an hour and a half.[112] Oswald was finally seen being brought down to the basement by elevator surrounded by investigators in white Resistol San Antonio model hats.[113] As they escort Oswald in front of news cameras through hallways lined with police, reporters and investigators from dozens of law enforcement agencies, Oswald was seen wearing a white t-shirt and dark sweater.[114]

Ella watched the television as she dressed to go to work at Wyatt's Cafeteria. Orville paced around the living room; he had felt anxious since last night. They have never watched television like this their whole lives.

"He's wearing different clothes, Orville," Ella mentions, "Do you think his wife brought him a change of clothes because he was cold?"

Orville noted the dark sweater Oswald was now wearing, rolled up at the sleeves. The V-neck white t-shirt he wore under it provided a sharp contrast on the black and white television.

"Maybe," he replied.

They continued to watch the news as several men in white and light colored cowboy hats entered the basement with Oswald in tow.[115] Men in suits were everywhere; some holding cameras, some holding paper, some just walking around. Oswald was obviously handcuffed and there was a large man holding his arm on the right, leading him along. The world would later learn that man was James Leavelle.[116] L.C. Graves, in a dark suit and fedora was on his left. Orville knew many of the FBI and Secret Service agents from work, but he recognized none of these men. The group of three slowly moved through the Dallas Police Department basement, as if in a wedding march. There were flashbulbs and shouts from reporters. *It's like an Elvis concert*, Orville thought to himself. Just then, a short, stocky man wearing a dark gangster-like hat jumped out from the right side of the television screen. A gunshot rang out. Oswald cringed in pain. The news announcer shouted in an anxious voice, "There's a scuffle. Oswald has been shot. Oswald has been shot."

Orville was shaking. The sound of the gunshot echoed throughout the televised basement, loud and clear. He jumped at the sound.

"Not again!" he yelled. "Not again!" Orville, Ella and millions of people had just witnessed the first televised murder in the history of media.

An ambulance seemed to appear out of nowhere. *How did it get there that fast?* There is pandemonium. The white Resistol hats were wrestling the short, dark Fedora to the ground. The fedora-man is later identified as Jack Ruby, the owner of a burlesque joint called the Carousel Club and passionate Kennedy supporter.[117]

Again, the country was horrified, though some found yet another reason to smile in less than two days. The man who killed the beloved president was dead. He has been executed in the same way he executed the president. What goes around comes around.

Or does it? Again, five sets of eyes wink at each other knowingly. The plan was working out better than they had hoped. The country would endure and LBJ's troubles were lessening by the minute. The industries that had made them rich, had given them power and kept them there was now secure until the next political threat came along. They weren't at the Lamar Hotel in Suite 8F,[118] in Houston but they were close enough. Many of these men were also members of the Dallas Citizen's Council, including the wounded governor, John Connally and Abraham Zapruder.

There would be no trial for Henry Wade to preside over now. Almost forty-seven hours after President John F. Kennedy was killed, Lee Harvey Oswald had died a similar death.

CHAPTER TEN

OF FUNERALS, FILMS AND FOOTBALL

"As we express our gratitude, we must never forget that the highest appreciation is not to utter words, but to live by them."

John F. Kennedy[119]

November 25th, 1963 was the culmination of the four saddest days of November. It was the day of President John F. Kennedy's funeral. Orville had to work that day, but he and his co-workers spent many a moment in the break room watching the funeral. The boss didn't mind, the whole country was mourning.

When the funeral procession began, Orville was amazed at the regalia and respect that had been planned in only three days. But, as he thought, there were many new developments in the three short years during which John F. Kennedy was the most powerful man in the free world. Kennedy had begun the Peace Corps. Kennedy had pushed for NASA and the space program. Kennedy had started the Navy Seals. Kennedy had taken the country to the brink of World War III and brought it back during the Cuban Missile Crisis. The man had done so much in such a short time. Orville wondered how much more he could have done had he lived.

As he looked around the breakroom at his coworkers, he noticed that some of them were smirking, others were somber and others ignored the funeral processional all together.

"Say Orville," one of the younger GSA employees said, "weren't you down there when the President got shot?" Orville nodded his head in affirmation.

"Did you see it all? Did you see that lunatic Oswald?" his young friend asked.

"Well, I didn't rightly look up at the Depository I thought the shots came from the fence," Orville replied.

Another man interjected, "Hey, that's where I thought they came from too. I was on the roof of the building here and I didn't see any shots come from where they caught that commie pinko. You know, Orville, our boss Mr. Price was up there too with binoculars I think."

Shortly after, Orville saw his friend Forrest Sorrels walking through the building. He seemed to be in a hurry.

"I'll be back in a minute, fellas, hold my spot," Orville said as he hurried after his friend from the Secret Service.

"Say, Forrest, hey!" he yelled. Forrest turned around and smiled as he recognized his friend.

"Orville, how are you buddy? What do you think of all this craziness? My God, the president shot in Dallas, what is the damned world coming to?" he said to Orville.

"I keep dreaming of it, Forrest. I keep seeing his head blow up."

"Wait, Orville, did you take a film of it? Pictures?" Forrest asked.

"Naw, I don't think so. I know I got a shot of him as the motorcade turned onto Elm, but after that, I just don't know. Where do you think the shots came from, Forrest?"

"I think they came from that little hill area up by the railroad yard,"[120] Forrest replied. "I thought I saw something."

"I thought they came from that area too, but hell, this Oswald kid wasn't anywhere near there, and now he's dead too. Oswald must have been the shooter or why would he have been shot by that strip club guy?" Orville asked his friend then stopped.

"What do you think you saw, Forrest?" Orville tentatively asked his friend. He knew Forrest didn't like to talk about work.

"Maybe nothing, you never know, Orville, you never know. There was so much happening that day but I'll check it out. I gotta go. Washington is calling at all hours still and there's way too much paperwork to do. Come see me next week after everything is calmed down and we'll have lunch," Forrest said as he slapped Orville's back and left.

Orville made his way back to the break room. An older guy, one Orville didn't think highly of, grabbed him by the arm, pulling him to a complete stop.

"Hey, Orville, have you heard the latest joke about the assassination?" the guy asked.

Orville grimaced and said nothing, waiting for the guy to tell his joke.

"What was LBJ doing right before the shots?" he said, obviously waiting for Orville to say 'What?'

Orville shook his head, still not saying a word.

"He was ducking!" the man guffawed as he slapped Orville's back. The idiot was laughing so hard he fell into a coughing attack.

Orville walked away thinking he wished the guy would choke, the sounds of coughs and laughter filling the silent hallway.

* * * * *

The week was another short one. Thanksgiving Day fell three days after JFK's funeral, and Ella and Orville spent it alone. His son, Orville Jr., went to his mother-in-law's house for Thanksgiving; they would spend Christmas at Orville and Ella's house. It was the saddest Thanksgiving Orville could remember, and when it came time to give Grace for the Thanksgiving meal he had a hard time finding the words to say. Out of nowhere, he remembered a bit of a prayer he had heard at John F. Kennedy's funeral, and used some of the words in his Thanksgiving prayer:

"Dear Lord, keep our hearts strong and our minds pure. Save us from the evil that seems to be all around us. Thank you for the blessings you have given our family and our country. Please help the Kennedy family in their time of grief and allow their children to grow up with love instead of hate. *We ask your blessing and your help, knowing here on Earth, God's work must truly be our own.* In Jesus' name, Amen."[121]

*****

DEAR LORD, KEEP OUR HEARTS STRONG AND OUR MINDS PURE. SAVE US FROM THE EVIL THAT SEEMS TO BE ALL AROUND US. THANK YOU FOR THE BLESSINGS YOU HAVE GIVEN OUR FAMILY AND OUR COUNTRY. PLEASE HELP THE KENNEDY FAMILY IN THEIR TIME OF GRIEF AND ALLOW THEIR CHILDREN TO GROW UP WITH LOVE INSTEAD OF HATE.

Ella looked across the table at her husband and smiled. She recognized the words from the Kennedy speech she and Orville had spoken of often. Orville was a good man.

Two days later, Orville Jr. called and asked his dad if he would go to the South Oak Cliff High School game and take pictures of Elaine's brother's girlfriend. She was a majorette.

"Junior, you know I watch midget wrestling on Saturday night," Orville admonished.[122]

"It'll only take a minute, Dad, and you said you still had film you had to use. Please? I promised my brother-in-law at Thanksgiving I would do it, but I can't take the three kids. Well, just this one time, Dad?"

"Which brother-in-law? It can't be Tommy, he's too young. You mean the curly-headed brother?" Orville didn't know Elaine's brothers well.

"No Dad, not Tommy, Sonny, Elaine's older younger brother. Wait, does that make sense?" his son asked.

"Okay, son, I'll take pictures, but I'm leaving after halftime to get home to my wrestling."

He hung up the phone and grabbed his hat and camera. He looked down at the camera's film counter. There was still fifteen feet left to use, even after filming on the Saturday before Oswald was killed.

"Ella, I'm going to the football field, I'll be back in a couple of hours. Junior wants me to take some film of that girl Elaine's brother is dating. Lock the door."[123]

He didn't give Ella time to say a word; he knew she'd be mad. He started the shiny, red Plymouth Fury and drove the short drive to South Oak Cliff High School, the school from which his son and daughter-in-law had graduated. The sound of the marching band put energy in his step and he realized he hadn't felt that way in over a week. He sat down in the stands and filmed the halftime entertainment. As it ended, he looked down at the camera counter and it was at zero.

Good, he thought to himself. *I'll just take it to Dynacolor while I'm out and maybe I'll have it back by Tuesday*. He drove to the lab and dropped off his film then made his way back home.[124]

As he turned the corner onto Denley, he thought he saw a figure standing near the side of his house. It was becoming foggy, like most late November evenings, and he put his bright lights on. The lights glared back into his eyes and the dark figure he saw was no longer there. *You must be seeing things, Orville,* he said to himself. He turned the car off and went into the house looking at his watch. It was a little after 10 P.M. He hadn't missed midget wrestling.

Orville fell asleep watching his favorite show; it wasn't even funny tonight, or possibly it was just his mood.

He woke with a start to the ringing of the telephone. He quickly answered it, worried that something had happened to Junior or one of the grandkids.

"Hello Mr. Nix? This is Dynacolor film lab. You need to get down here right away. We've developed your film and you must see it before we turn it over to the FBI."

Orville rubbed his eyes trying to shake the sleep away.

"What? Why the FBI?" he asked.

"Well Mr. Nix, you have the assassination on your film and the FBI has sent a message out to all film labs that any assassination footage must be immediately turned over to the FBI. We thought we might have overlooked your film with all the developing we have done the last week, but it looks like you just dropped this off earlier in the evening. It seems everyone thinks they have film of the assassination and we're way behind. Can you come down now?" the technician asked.

They overlooked my film? What? He was still waking up from the phone call and didn't understand what they meant. He looked down at the watch he was still wearing. It was now after 2 A.M.

He rubbed his eyes again. "Yes, I'll be down there. Which way do I come in?" he asked.

"Just knock on the front door where you drop off film. We'll be waiting." The technician hung up. Orville dialed his son's number. The phone rang three or four times before Junior answered.

"Hello?"

"Junior?" Orville said, "I need you to get dressed and go down to Dynacolor with me. You may have to miss church tomorrow. They say I have film of the assassination."

"What?" His son asked incredulously. "Okay Dad, let me get dressed. Don't ring the doorbell, I'll wait for you on the porch so the kids don't wake up. See you in a few minutes." Orville Junior lived at 1203 Savoy near Kiest Park, about five or ten minutes from Orville's house on Denley Drive in Oak Cliff. Orville checked on Ella and found her sleeping. He silently dressed and left quietly so as not to wake her. She had to work the next day.

As he drove to his son's house his mind was filled with thoughts. He had read of Abraham Zapruder selling his film to *Life* magazine for a lot of money.

Could his film be better? Could it be worth as much? Would this be the break he had waited his whole life for? Would it show as much as the Zapruder film? Would he become famous? Could he tell Ella she could finally quit working? He wondered what he had actually taken. It couldn't be very long, unless he had misread his film counter. Wait. Could the processing lab be wrong? Surely they knew that the footage he had taken on the Saturday after the assassination wasn't real. Maybe they were talking about the filming he had done while standing at Main and Houston. Yes, that was probably it. They had developed the part of the film he had taken showing the president smiling at his wife.

As his mind settled on that thought, he had turned onto Savoy Street. His tall, lanky son was sitting on the porch steps waiting for him. He ran to the car blowing his hands. It was cold that night. As he opened the door, Orville's heart swelled. He loved his son and was very proud of him.

"Gosh Dad, so you *did* take assassination pictures! This is exciting! I wonder what it shows. I wonder if it's like the Zapruder film in the magazine? You think your film will be in a magazine? I can't wait to see it!" Orville Junior's words came out in a staccato pace.

*****

THEY FOLLOWED THE MAN INTO THE BACK OF THE BUILDING. THERE THEY ENTERED A LARGE ROOM THAT WAS VERY DARK, FILLED WITH TABLES, METAL CANISTERS OF FILM, AND ANOTHER MAN.

"I don't know, son, I was thinking on the way over here that it just may be the part I took when the motorcade was turning from Main onto Houston Street. Remember when I told you I had taken film of the president smiling just before the car turned onto Elm?" Orville said.

"Yeah, that's probably right. But still, you have history, Dad. History! How long will it take us to get there?"

Orville drove a little faster than normal to get to the Dynacolor Lab on Halifax Street. It was on the other side of downtown Dallas. As they pulled up, both quickly walked to the door and knocked. The door opened immediately.

"Mr. Nix?" the young technician asked.

"Yes, I'm Orville Nix, and this is my son Orville Junior," Orville replied. He didn't recognize these men and he had been to Dynacolor more times than he could remember.

"Come with me, sirs."

They followed the man into the back of the building. There they entered a large room that was very dark, filled with tables, metal canisters of film, and another man.

The other man spoke. "Mr. Nix? I apologize for bringing you down here in the middle of the night, but as I do want to follow governmental rules, I also want to keep our customers happy. In my opinion, this is *your* film even if the FBI does say give it to them.[125] I thought it only right for you to see it before we give it to them. We don't have a projection screen here, but I think this white wall will do."

With that, he loaded the 8mm film into the Keystone projector carefully by the sprockets and turned the projector on. Orville and his son still stood in the places they stopped as they entered the room, excited and anticipatory.

The film was a bit grainy, Orville thought he may have used the wrong filter as he watched it, and the first image was overexposed, as most films were during that time from the feeder film collecting more light when loaded. Still, Orville could see the President's limousine passing in front of the Dallas County Courthouse at the corner of Houston and Main where he had waited for his family to meet him.

The president seemed to be sharing a joke with the First Lady whose pink suit and hat were vibrantly attractive that sunny day. Orville remembered thinking her beautiful; the vibrant pink of her suit set off her black hair and alabaster skin perfectly and the president's teeth seemed whiter than the motorcycle helmet of the policeman riding on the left side of the limousine. The next few frames showed the Secret Service car and one of the occupants who was standing and wearing a dark suit; he seemed to be looking up at the buildings. The spectators he captured on film were all clapping and excited. He noticed a couple wearing black clothes: the woman in black sunglasses, scarf and coat, the man in a white shirt and black suit. Behind them was a Negro man who looked like a milkman or delivery man. He was wearing a light-colored uniform and a hat and his hands were filled with a coat or bags - Orville couldn't tell. The next few frames showed the car Senator Ralph Yarbrough was in and at one point, the Senator seemed to be waving towards him. After seeing the Senator, he realized he hadn't gotten to see the president that well, and started walking quickly towards Elm Street across the Main Street swath of grass. He had his zoom lens activated. He saw the motorcade pass under the Hertz sign and then pandemonium. Something happened! He heard a shot. The limousine seemed to slow down and the president's hands went to his neck as if loosening his tie. The film he was watching was at a strange angle. The limousine had definitely slowed down. The First Lady looked like she was putting her white gloved hands around his shoulders. It was at this time he thought he heard more shots 'bam-bam and then bam' and he looked towards the stockade fence area. The president's head exploded into what he remembered as a red glitter spray forward into the air and towards Governor and Mrs. Connally, whose heads were the only things Orville could see. The

First Lady reacted along with the bystanders lining the parade route as the president fell to his left into her arms. His film caught people running, falling down, scared. There was a man across the street shielding his children. There were people on the Elm Street side of the grass running. Some men were on the steps, two of them wearing reddish-colored shirts. One ran up the stairs into the shadows, probably in fear he would be shot. The beautiful First Lady was jumping over the car, seemingly trying to get out and a dark-suited man jumped on the back of the car, pulling her back in. Three of the four motorcycle cops seemed to be looking at the fence or grassy knoll area. Suddenly, the limousine started moving faster and sped away towards the Triple Underpass, leaving the other cars behind. He panned around the fence area again then the next frames showed the ground. He must have been running and quit squeezing the camera. A few frames later, a blue Chevrolet and a white one with men with cameras slowing down to take pictures were seen. Some of the motorcycle officers sped up and others stopped to run up to the Stockade fence area where Orville had heard the shots. It was surreal reality. Then it was over. The whole assassination sequence couldn't have lasted more than six or seven seconds, but it seemed like hours.[126] Orville looked down at the shiny linoleum floor of the film processing plant and shook his head. His son Orville put his arm around his father in empathy.

*****

IT WAS SURREAL REALITY.

THEN IT WAS OVER.

THE WHOLE ASSASSINATION SEQUENCE COULDN'T HAVE LASTED MORE THAN SIX OR SEVEN SECONDS, BUT IT SEEMED LIKE HOURS.

The next part of his film showed the frames he had taken the next morning when he went back down to show Ella what he had seen and where he had been. This time he took a couple of frames of the Texas School Book Depository, as that is where the Dallas Police Department said Lee Harvey Oswald shot the President. He captured a few frames of the sixth floor. He still felt the shots had come from the picket fence and spent more time taking pictures of that area. This morning's filming showed people in mourning at Dealey Plaza, revisiting, like he was, the scene of the crime.

The last part of his movie was the South Oak Cliff football game he had taken just hours before. He wasn't sure which girl he was supposed to be filming, so he filmed everything he saw. The film ended at that point.

The Dynacolor employees turned the lights on. The four men stood there in silence, until Orville spoke up.

"Do you mind if we watch it again?" Orville asked.

"If you'd like," the technician answered.

The four men watched the film twenty or thirty times that early morning. With each viewing, Orville noticed something he hadn't noticed before: white hosiery on a woman with a golden coat and wearing white nurse's shoes,[127] three men instead of two on the stairs leading up to the white building area,[128] the United States flag furling and unfurling on the presidential limousine, a man sitting on the curb watching the parade.[129]

Finally, one of the technicians suggested that Orville give the viewings a rest so as not to damage the frames from the heat of the projector's bulb. He wound the film onto a metal canister and gave it to Orville. No other copies were made. Orville promised to take the original film to the FBI the next day which for most workers would be in a few hours; Sunday, December 1, 1963.

He and his son drove home in silence. The lack of sleep and spectacle of what they had spent the last hour viewing was overwhelming.

As Orville pulled into his son's driveway, Orville Junior said, "I'll call you tomorrow, Dad, to see what the FBI says. Try to get some rest. I love you."

Orville drove home with only one thought. At least one of those shots had to have come from the stockade fence area. He didn't care what the Dallas Police Department said. He knew what he saw. He knew what he heard. He knew he was right.

The sun had begun to rise and a new day was dawning.

CHAPTER ELEVEN

NEW YORK, NEW YORK

"Every American ought to have the right to be treated as he would wish to be treated, as he would wish to have his children treated."

John F. Kennedy[130]

Orville was up early on Sunday, December 1st, 1963 to fulfill his promise of taking his film to the FBI. Since he had to work, he left earlier than usual to make the stop at the Santa Fe Building at 1114 Commerce before going to work at the Terminal Annex.[131] He had called Forrest before he left and his friend had told him to go to the twelfth floor and drop it off at J. Gordon Shanklin's office.[132] But first, Forrest had accosted him with a flurry of questions.

"Orville, what does it show, your film I mean?" he asked.

"Well Forrest, it doesn't show much, its only 8 or 9 seconds long I think and since I took it while I was running, the film is at a funny angle, kinda like Elm St. is on a hill."

"Well it does slope a little Orville, don't be so hard on yourself, I know you take movies all the time. Does it show the assassination?" he asked slowly.

Orville replied, "It does, Forrest, it does. It's not up close, because I was standing on Main, but you can see enough to give you nightmares. I tell ya Forrest, from the snap of his head and from the sounds I heard, I just know there were shots from the fence area. I don't understand why no one is checking into it. Don't you agree?"

"I do Orville. I thought they came from there too, but Chief Curry says Oswald was the man, and I don't dare start a war between the Secret Service and the Dallas Police. There are good men there. We all have to work together. Meet the FBI guys downtown, tell them I told you to come. Take your film and we'll talk next week. Thanks for calling me, my friend," and with that, he hung up.

Orville put down the phone feeling better that his friend had the same thoughts he had had - there were shots from more than one place. He slapped some aftershave on, grabbed his hat and opened then back door. He stopped. He had an idea. He grabbed the paper and looked through it. *Was it Life magazine or Look that paid Zapruder all that money, he couldn't remember.* He found the paper again and saw it was *Life* magazine. He picked up the phone again and dialed the operator. He asked to be connected to *Life*.

A young lady answered the phone. "*Life* magazine, how may I direct your call?"

He explained in his long, Texas drawl that he had taken a film of the assassination. He was immediately transferred to a man named Jackson.

"Before you waste both our time, let me preface this with a warning that we are tired of false alarms regarding the assassination. It seems everyone has a film of the assassination. Give me your name, tell me what you have, let me verify it and I'll get back with you this afternoon."

Orville obeyed and gave him his name, Dynacolor's phone number and the number for the FBI. He also told him he had shared this information with Forrest Sorrels of the Secret Service.

"Fine, fine Mr. Nix. It sounds as if your report is legitimate. I'll be in touch with you later after it's verified," and he slammed the phone down.

Those damned Yankees are the rudest people to walk the earth. They act like the world revolves around them, Orville thought to himself. He grabbed his keys and hat and left.

* * * * *

Orville did as Forrest advised and met with FBI agent Joe Abernathy.[133] He promised to have the film back to Orville by the next day. Orville didn't get it for three days and after calling the FBI offices four and five times a day, they returned it to him. He needed it back because *Life* magazine had indeed returned his call and were now interested in talking to him about buying his film. UPI's Burt Reinhardt had gotten wind of his film while it was at the FBI and contacted Orville as well. Orville explained to Reinhardt that he had already been contacted by *Life* and that maybe they could both bid on his film. His dreams of becoming rich and famous and retiring to a leisurely life of golf and poker returned quickly. He didn't think about the assassination of a president he had filmed, except in the mornings when he awoke from the nightmares.

The call from *Life* magazine was one of the high points of Orville Nix's life. Orville had never been further east than Mississippi and honestly didn't care much for people from New York. He had seen his fair share of Northerners talking in accents he didn't understand around the GSA building on their visits from Washington and New York and he had found the ones he had met brusque and rude. *Life* offered to fly him to their offices in New York and pay for his hotel. They also offered to pay for Ella's trip. Ella would have nothing to do with it as she was scared of air travel, so Orville asked Junior to go along with him.[134]

"Besides," Ella scolded, "someone has to stay and make a living. Not all of us can go gallivantin' around the country like we're important people."

"I'll only be taking Friday off, Ella, and if they paid the other man $25,000, surely they'll pay me at least half of that," he said to his wife.[135] "That's worth a day's loss of pay! And just think, honey, you could quit working. We could take more vacations. This could be the best thing that ever happened to us," he told her with dreams of financial security, fawning women, and new fedoras dancing in his mind.

Orville Junior was excited as well. He had always wanted to visit New York, and at the tender age of twenty-four was about to. He had bought a new suit at

Turner Brothers just for the occasion - his mom had helped pay for it. He wished that his wife Elaine could go along, but it would be nice flying with his dad. He knew how much his dad loved airplanes.

On the morning of December 6th, exactly two weeks after the assassination, Orvilles Sr. and Jr. boarded a 7:00 A.M. American Airlines Electra flight to LaGuardia Airport. (Twenty-two days later, the other airport of that city, New York International Airport at Anderson Field, would be renamed JFK airport in honor of the newly-fallen president.[136])

Orville and his namesake left Love Field Airport on a prop airplane with excitement and anticipation. Twenty-four hours later, they would be home frustrated and disgusted.

After the layover in Washington DC, the two Orvilles landed at LaGuardia. The skies were grey and gloomy, matching the skyscrapers that looked down upon them as the driver of the car *Life* sent to retrieve them drove more recklessly than any driver they had ever seen in Dallas, save for the drunk ones on Industrial Blvd. The driver stopped at the New York Hilton in Midtown and opened the trunk.

"Youse gentlemen don't have long to get it together. Run up and drop off your bags and change your clothes. I'll be waiting here for youse. Your appointment at the *Time/Life* building is in an hour, and its right down the street hee-yah, at 1271 Avenue of the Americas," he admonished in his thick New York accent.

The two men gathered their small suitcases and pushed their way through the revolving door of the Hilton. Orville Jr., noticing a lady behind going into the hotel, stepped aside and said courteously, "Ladies first, Ma'am."

She looked at him disdainfully and exclaimed, "Go to hell!"

Orville Jr. was stunned and stood blocking the revolving door. Other people were trying to get in and were shouting, "Move it, buddy" and "Get out of the way." Was she being rude because she detected his Texas accent? Or was this how women in New York acted.

"Dad, did you hear what that lady said to me?" he asked.

"I heard her, Junior, just ignore it. I told you Yankees were rude. Don't talk to anyone else until we get to the meeting."

Though it had been one hundred years since the Civil War, the long unspoken distaste for Southerners and Northerners alike still reared its ugly head from time to time. With the murder of JFK, all those feelings seemed to find their way back into the public psyche, and Dallas had been labeled the "City of Hate" by the rest of the country.[137] This incident was only one of many being played out across the country when a Texan, Dallasite or not, went to another state.

This was not the Dallas of "America's Team." The Dallas Cowboys Football team could barely win a game, much less become the darlings of the NFL. A few years later, Lamar Hunt, son of H.L. Hunt, would coin the term 'Super Bowl' in Dallas.[138] But it wasn't during this time. This was the Dallas before the Texas Rangers Baseball team. They wouldn't appear for nine more years, again, thanks to the Hunts. In fact, the Hunt family and its progeny did all they could after the assassination to dispel the hate rumors. Was it penance they were paying or was it a love for the city? JR Ewing of the show *Dallas*, a caricature of big Texas Oil (some would say the Hunts), came fifteen years later.[139] Finally, people began questioning, 'Who shot JR?' instead of JFK for a time. It seemed that the only bright sign in Dallas was the flying red neon Pegasus Horse of Magnolia Oil (later Mobil Oil) atop the Magnolia Hotel.[140]

Orville and his son didn't open their mouths again except to say "thank you" until the driver deposited them at the *Time/Life* Building. Located in Rockefeller Center, it was one of the fanciest buildings Orville and his son had ever seen. They noted the serpentine patterned sidewalk design that led from the sidewalk all the way into the lobby.[141] Once inside, there were huge murals lining the walls, much like the ones in Dallas at Fair Park. The building was forty-eight stories tall, and *Time/Life* publishing occupied twenty-one of those levels. The glass in the building was all green, making it look like a modern day abode for the Wizard of Oz. In fact, to Orville Sr. the editors could very well be his Wizards of finance as he and his son walked to the elevator.

Two men, wearing dark suits and thin dark ties, approached them and asked, "Are you Orville Nix?"

Orville Sr. replied, "I am. And who might you be?"

"I was sure you would recognize my voice. My name is Burt Reinhardt, we talked briefly in Dallas, and this is my associate Maurice Schonfeld. We're from UPI and would like to purchase your film," the man replied.

Orville Jr. spoke up. "Well sirs, we're here on *Life's* dime and we have an appointment with them to purchase the film."

"We understand, we'll be waiting down here when you're done," the man named Schonfeld replied.[142]

Father and son looked at each other, obviously amazed at the men's confidence that they would be talking again. They made their way to the elevator, and were met by James Wagenvoord, a kind assistant editor who took them to the 34th floor where they met Edward K. Thompson, then editor for *Life* magazine and later, the founder of *The Smithsonian* magazine.[143] Other men in the room included Art Keylor, General Manager and Chapin Carpenter, the *Time/Life* financial director.

"I hope you had a grand trip, we're happy to have you here," the young Wagenvoord welcomed them. "Now let's view this film." Several other people were in the room, but Orville wasn't introduced to them, and he guessed they were employees or reporters. The room full of men sat in the large boardroom, in the iconic Eames chairs that were made specifically for *Time/Life*.[144] Orville had never sat in a chair so comfortable and so moveable. A woman came in and gave them both cups of strong coffee. Orville asked for cream and sugar. The lights dimmed and the film played. And played. And played. Orville Jr. looked at his dad and whispered, "How many times do they want to see it?"

Orville Sr. shook his head and glared at his son in a silent "shut up."

After over fifteen viewings of the film, Mr. Thompson spoke with the other men in the room in low tones that Orville couldn't hear. The lights came back on and Keylor said, "Mr. Nix, we find this film to have nuisance value only. Still and all, we'd like to offer you three thousand dollars for it."[145] What Orville didn't know was that none of these men were film technicians: they were all executives.

Orville Jr. looked at his dad in disbelief. *What a slap in the face*, he thought. His father stood slowly, the veins in his neck swelling, his face turning an oxblood red. His son knew he should say something as he was worried that his father was either going to have a stroke, or berate these rude men at any moment. Mr. Wagenvoord was appalled and embarrassed. He quickly looked down at the tall Texan's huge hands and realized they were tightly clinched. He wondered if he should call security while at the same time hoping the kind visitor would punch one of his pompous bosses in John Wayne style.

"Well sir, thank you for your offer, but we'll be leaving now," Orville Jr. said and with that, they took their film and walked quickly to the elevator. The men in the room shook their hands and Orville Jr. wondered if his dad was going to break their arms when he saw how hard he squeezed their hands.

They rode the elevator silently down the thirty-four flights, until Orville Jr. looked at his father and said, "It's not over, Dad, maybe the guys from UPI are still waiting."

"Maybe," Orville replied with a resigned sigh.

As the elevator doors open, Orville looked out into the lobby and the two men from UPI were still waiting. His face reverted to its normal color.

"Did you sell it?" Reinhardt asked.

"We weren't happy with their offer," Orville Jr. spoke for his dad. "We were expecting more than three thousand dollars," he explained.

"Well, let's go to our offices and talk," Mr. Reinhardt replied.

"Nossir, not now," Orville Sr. replied, "We haven't eaten all day and I need a smoke. Give us the address and we'll meet you after we eat."

Reinhardt gave him a business card and the men agreed to meet after dinner. Orville and his son exited the *Time/Life* Building in disgust.

As they walked the long blocks through Midtown Manhattan, Orville said to his son, "Why the hell did we come here? These men want to offer me money for nuisance value? My film is a nuisance? What the hell does that mean, son? I know I'm not an educated man, but by God, this film is history. Any loony tune could see that. Nuisance value?"

"Dad, I'm sure it's just the Yankee way of doing business. Let's get something to eat and talk to the UPI guys. Maybe they'll offer you more." Orville Jr. was worried about his father. He watched all the dreams he had dreamed of for a few days slip away into cynicism. When they finally found what looked like would be an affordable restaurant, they walked in and sat down. Orville Jr. pulled two menus from the counter, passed one to his dad and began looking at the fare. The diner smelled of old grease and older coffee.

"They want a $1.65 for a hamburger? Without any French fries?" Orville Sr. exclaimed. "Good Lord, what are the burgers made with? Beef from Rockefeller's private reserve?"

His son chuckled. "Heck, $1.65 would buy my whole family burgers at Griff's in Dallas.[146] Maybe the burgers are made of steak."

They ate their expensive hamburgers with no fries and 75 cent coffee then hailed a cab. This trip was costing far more than it was making for Orville. He could practically hear Ella's disapproval in his head.

At UPI, Reinhardt and Schonfeld watched the movie several times. By now, Orville was no longer excited about his fantasy retirement; he was more excited to get back home to his wife. After an hour or so, Reinhardt said, "Quite frankly Mr. Nix, we don't think we should offer you more than the three thousand dollars *Time/Life* offered, but since you've traveled all the way here, we'd like to offer you a bit more. The film is grainy. It doesn't look as if you've used an expensive brand of film. Would $5,000.00 and a new hat seal the deal?"[147]

Orville again felt patronized. *Why did these men think they could insult him and offer him money in the same breath?* He looked at his son and nodded his head in agreement. He just wanted to get out of this hell-forsaken city.

Orville Jr. said, "That will be fine. But we want a copy of the film and you're not to reveal my dad's name as the maker of the film. My mother doesn't want a lot of phone calls." They shook hands and Orville Sr. signed the contract written on notepaper. He would receive a copy of the film and a cashier's check for five thousand dollars within the next five days. He also would receive a new fedora. As they were shaking hands to leave, Orville said, "Can we have the film back after the copyright term is over?"

"That will be 25 years or more," Mr. Reinhardt said, "but yes, you certainly may."[148] They shook hands and the Nixes left.

Orville was downtrodden. He had been treated rudely. He had been insulted. His dreams of retirement had evaporated at the fancy *Time/Life* Building. Now he just wanted to get home to Texas. The two men took a cab back to the Hilton and retrieved their bags. Though their tickets weren't for departure until the next day, they went straight to LaGuardia to catch the earliest flight from New York they could board. *I would have been treated better if I had been a business man, or had a degree*, Orville chided himself silently. Next to him, his son was also berating himself. *Maybe I should have asked for more; maybe I should have been a better negotiator. I won't let this happen again, never.* Neither of them put voice to their thoughts; they both napped on the three hour flight home.

The next day, December 7th, 1963, Fox Movietone ran a newsreel in movie theaters about the assassination.[149] UPI news subscribers also received several frames of the film. All of them mentioned Nix's name, in direct violation of the newly- signed and verbal contracts.

This would be the beginning of the many lies Orville Nix would be told until he died.

* * * * *

The American people were also being lied to in regards to the assassination. As of December 1963, questions were already being asked about the assassination. Nothing seemed right. Nothing seemed fair. So many logical questions weren't answered. Fifty years later those feelings still exist and questions linger. Through five government funded commissions to find the truth as to what happened that day, classified files still exist.

In 2013 President Barack Obama approved the CIA's measure of keeping classified the over 1,100 files relating to E. Howard Hunt (CIA agent and Watergate burglar), William Harvey (when the CIA wanted to create an organization capable of carrying out assassinations in 1960, they gave it the code name of ZR-RIFLE and put Harvey in charge), David Sanchez Morales (David Morales was a career CIA officer who served as the chief of operations at the CIA's Miami station in 1963 where he worked with David Phillips and Howard Hunt), George Joannides (declassified CIA records show that Joannides obstructed two official JFK investigations by not disclosing what he knew), and David Atlee Phillips (who oversaw CIA anti-Castro psychological warfare operations in 1963) until at least 2017.[150]

Aren't fifty years filled with lies and waiting and spending taxpayers' dollars on committees enough? Releasing all documentation and demanding transparency from our government in regards to the JFK assassination is long overdue. If Oswald acted alone, what on earth could be in those files that could hurt our National Security?

In Orville Nix's case, why would *Life* magazine consider his film a 'nuisance?' In hindsight, it's a good thing *Life* magazine didn't want the Nix film. If UPI hadn't bought it, researcher Jones Harris would have never gotten a chance to see it, and without Jones Harris, the Nix film's importance may never have been known.

CHAPTER TWELVE

OF CONSPIRACIES AND MADNESS

"The great enemy of the truth is very often not the lie, deliberate, contrived and dishonest, but the myth, persistent, persuasive, and unrealistic."

John F. Kennedy[151]

The first time Orville heard the words "conspiracy theory" was from a man named Penn Jones who lived in Midlothian, a southern suburb twenty-five miles from Dallas.[152] To Orville, Midlothian was 'out in the country', so how could a man from the country know anything about what happened in Dallas that day? Orville soon found out that he knew a lot. While *Life Magazine* was protecting the Zapruder film and by contract not showing the more horrific frames of the film and never in movie form, Orville's film, now called "The Nix Film", was being shown in movie theaters. UPI did not protect the Nix film like *Time/Life* protected the Zapruder film. Why?

Because UPI had negated their contract within 24 hours of signing it, specifically ignoring Orville's request to not use his name, Orville and Ella had begun to receive phone calls; long lost family members, friends, some nut cases, and strangers like Penn Jones. At first, the phone calls were mainly friendly ones, but Ella was skeptical. She was not one for public drama, though she didn't mind a bit of personal drama from time to time - it kept her family on their feet. So when Penn Jones called, she was concerned. Orville had told her of his dismay over the way he had been treated by those Yankee newspapermen on his trip, and she wasn't about to allow a reporter from Texas to do the same.

"I think the whole country is going mad," she told her husband after speaking with another stranger who had told her Jackie Kennedy was the one who was supposed to be shot, not her husband.

* * * * *

Penn Jones was an amiable fellow, though sometimes frightening. His tenacious quest to find answers to assassination questions was at once noble and irritating… he never let go of an issue until he was convinced the person was being truthful. He grew up in the same era as Orville and Ella, and like them, never forgot his roots. In his first phone call to Orville, he explained his background and Orville was instantly endeared to him. Mr. Jones had bought a newspaper in 1945, *The Midlothian Mirror,* and as his biography states, he "quickly established a reputation as an outspoken advocate for transparent, responsible, and honest local government as safeguards for democracy."[153] With the Kennedy Assassination, Jones would become an outspoken advocate for transparent National Government as well. In 1962, his outspoken and controversial opinions led to the firebombing of his newspaper.[154] Penn Jones was no stranger to hostility. He called Orville on December 8th, 1963, a day after UPI had screened the Nix Film in select movie theaters.

"Mr. Nix, this is Penn Jones of the *Midlothian Mirror*. Do you have a moment to speak with me?" he asked after Orville answered the telephone.

"Sure do, Mr. Jones, how can I help you?"

"I've just become aware that you took a film of the JFK assassination. I understand your film shows the pavilion and little hill by the picket fences. I think you have the most important film of the assassination as I think your film will show there was another shooter besides Lee Harvey Oswald. I was wondering if we could meet this week and discuss this. Do you have time?" Jones asked.

"Well, I work nights, but I could get up early, say Wednesday, and we could meet for lunch somewhere or you could come here."

"I'd like to come there if it's alright by you, Mr. Nix, say Wednesday at 1 P.M.? Is that too early?"

"No, that would be fine. My address is 2527 Denley Drive and I'm on the corner of Elmore and Denley, across the street from the Cedarcrest Shopping Center. I'll see you then."

* * * * *

That short conversation would be the first of many conversations Orville would have the next few years with reporters and researchers alike.

Penn Jones wasn't the first to question the logistics of the assassination. On December 19th, 1963, Mark Lane wrote an article for the *National Guardian* entitled "A Defense Brief for Oswald".[155] This piece wasn't viewed by a large audience. On December 21, 1963, another article, this one entitled, "Seeds of Doubt: Some Questions about the Assassination," by Jack Minnis and Staughton Lynd was published in the New Guardian.[156] In it, the authors question several areas of contention that exist still today: the wounds, the rifle, the Parkland doctors' interviews, the target and the bullets. Conspiracy thoughts were already being proposed by cutting-edge independent journalists across the country.

*****

THE BOOK WAS A STINGING AND NAME-DROPPING BOMB OF A BOOK THAT WOULD BE CONSIDERED SLANDEROUS BY MANY AMERICANS.

THE ELUSIVE 'HEPBURN' NAMED EVERYONE A SUSPECT FROM THE FBI TO THE SECRET SERVICE TO TEXAS OILMEN.

Later, in the spring of 1964, six months after the assassination, Thomas Buchanan's book, "Who Killed Kennedy?" was the first of many books to be published suggesting there was a conspiracy to kill the thirty-fifth president.[157] In his book, Buchanan asserted that "the assassination had been the work of Texas oil interests who felt that Vice President Lyndon B. Johnson, once elevated to the presidency, would protect their favorable percentage depletion tax treatment more vigorously than the Kennedy administration." [158] Was this more hatred directed toward the City of Dallas and Texas? Or could Buchanan have been on to something as early as 1964? Another book, of mysterious authorship and not published in America was Hepburn's *Farewell, America.*[159] The book was a stinging and name-dropping bomb of a book that would be considered slanderous by many Americans. The elusive 'Hepburn' named everyone a suspect from the FBI to the Secret Service to Texas Oilmen.

Everyone who had lived in Texas for more than two years, especially the Dallas and surrounding areas, knew about the Big Oil boys. This group of men consisted of D.H. Byrd (owner of the Texas School Book Depository), Clint Murchison (owner of the Dallas Cowboys), H.L. Hunt (owner of Hunt Oil as well as most of the East Texas Oilfields), Sid Richardson (Murchison's partner), and the malleable LBJ state politician from the Dallas area Sam Rayburn. Many in this group were members of Suite 8F.[160]

In the early months following the assassination, sides were again being taken: either Lee Harvey Oswald was a lone nut or there was a conspiracy to kill the President. Why was it so hard for Americans to believe there could have been a conspiracy (even if not against the murder of a president), but a conspiracy against the world to hide the truth? Was it hard because we would have to admit that our country lied to us? Because it would be one more foundational truth of Life, Liberty, and Justice found to be a lie? Were we all really in need of an emotional escape and believing that Lee Harvey Oswald did it alone could keep our small, little minds at ease? Or was it because we were losing God to the likes of atheist activist Madeline Murray O'Hair who was desperately trying to assassinate all vestiges of Him by taking prayer out of the classroom? Or was it just madness caused by the Hippie movement and the use of mind-altering drugs?

Contrary to history books, newer books explain the LSD phenomenon as one not just for 'rock and rollers' and 'beatniks', but the mind-altering drug of spiritual seekers and the intelligentsia. Timothy Leary, Abbie Hoffman, JP Morgan's Vice-President Gordon Wasson, and Henry and Clare Luce all were acid-eaters of one type or another.[161]Why would this matter in a JFK Assassination book? This push to change accepted behavior and beliefs were another example of how strong the media/government relationship was becoming. In November of 1963, *Life* magazine was arguably the most important general news source in the United States. The top management of *Time/Life Inc.* was closely allied with America's intelligence agencies and was used often by the Kennedy Justice Department as a conduit to the public.[162]

If socialites like the Luce's could imbibe in the usage of illegal drugs, then it set a precedent for those that weren't leaders of society and gave an okay to those who were. Henry Luce and his wife Clare, the publisher and editor-in-chief of *Time/Life* were using LSD during the mid-sixties and that bled over into their publications during the period. Their magazines ran several articles during Luce's navigational tenure of the magazines' content and author Stephen Siff credits *Time* and *Life* coverage, with "raising public awareness that a drug with the unique effects of LSD existed and was possibly desirable."[163]

Ironic isn't it? *Life* magazine was withholding exhibition of the extant Zapruder film for fear of public shock, but was touting the benefits of LSD, now known to remain in your brain for the remainder of your life. This was truly history making madness.

Philosophically, in the mid-sixties, the great intellectuals Jacques Derrida and Michael Foucault were wrestling with the concept of madness and history. It seemed fitting as one of the most popular modern leaders, JFK, had just been assassinated. In the *Ideology of Tyranny: The Use of Neo-Gnostic Myth in American Politics*, author Guido Giacamo Preparata discusses madness and history. In Chapter Seven he states:

> *According to Derrida, Foucault's imprecision (in regards to his take on the relation of the history of madness and Descartes) was to have cast maladroitly the conflict opposing sense to nonsense as a historical theme: as if the chasm between the clear rays of reason and the 'dark light' of madness could only be grasped as a significant development of our times. Derrida contended that there existed, in fact, a "virgin soil"- some sort of primordial grounds- upon which, "obscurely" the battle had ever unfolded. The madman himself does think: the "ancient madness" is the ultimate wisdom, but the difference is that the madman cannot articulate ("speak") such madness. His is the "garrulous silence of a mind that cannot think its words." There wasn't madness before modernity, and reason thereafter. Rather there exists a plane, for Derrida, where the two appetites lie inextricably, though antagonistically twined to each other, and the alternate convulsions of the one and the other are what we designate as the signs of reason or unreason. Bataille's project was thereby vigorously reaffirmed; Derrida referred to it as the "hyperbolic project," which was to enable "the violent release of the word"—a word shedding its "alien" light on the inexpressible realm of the impossible, of nothingness. So, there was something deeper and prior to madness, and in the vision of Derrida, this was a pseudo-divine principle of "difference": that is, a life—and meaning-giving essence by which the play of opposites—like reason and unreason—punctuates a trace, a scribble, a text.*[164]

In regards to the JFK assassination, this play of opposites can be seen in every online forum, every review of a book on the assassination and in every heated debate overheard at a conference. Are we allowing madness to become articulate; letting it 'speak for itself' as Foucault suggested or are we giving the many government subsidized official reports on the JFK assassination that are filled with madness a 'tongue of logic' as Derrida opined?

Orville Nix asked himself that question each time he answered the telephone or was stopped by a stranger.

CHAPTER THIRTEEN

OF CHARACTER AND CABALISTS

"We'll know our disinformation campaign is complete, when absolutely everything the American people believe is false."

William Casey, Director of the CIA [165]

The Kennedy family was like most families, a mix of dysfunction and success. The paternal head of the family, Joseph Kennedy, made his millions by bootlegging Scotch during prohibition and having astute investment acumen in the stock market. He married well: Rose Fitzgerald was the daughter of the famous politician 'Honey' Fitzgerald and their union produced a family of nine children. Though his business sense was impeccable, his paternal instincts weren't as much: he had his eldest daughter Rosemary lobotomized.[166]

No self-made man put greater pressure on his children than did the elder Kennedy. When first son Joseph Jr. was killed during World War II, Jack became the designated heir. Himself a Navy veteran and survivor of a collision with a Japanese destroyer, he would write to his friend Paul Fay that, once the war was over, "I'll be back here with Dad trying to parlay a lost PT boat and a bad back into a political advantage."[167]

Joseph Senior was important to his son and groomed him to become the politician he had wanted his namesake to be. There was no doubt: Joseph piloted all nine of his children's lives.

"From the time Jack first ran for Congress, his father had taught him everything from wearing a suit and the best way to cut his hair, how to appear youthful and wise and serious at the same time," says David Nasaw, whose biography of Joseph P. Kennedy was published in 2012.[168] Joseph not only advised his children, he shared with them the tricks for becoming aristocratic. Joseph had learned these talents from his days of being looked down upon for his profession and because he was an Irish-Catholic. He had endured the stereotypes, biases, and ignorance that comes from narrow-mindedness and was not about to let them get in the way with his desire to ensure his children important futures in society: he had taken care of their economic needs through his career decisions. He sensed the upcoming stock market crash and quickly removed his funds.[169] Like all financially successful people, Joseph Kennedy had astute business acuity and was a seasoned political adviser for his sons.

He made sure his son Jack was a public figure years before he ran for office. "Why England Slept" released in 1940,[170] was a book-length edition of a thesis Jack wrote at Harvard about the British in the years before World War II. Most theses don't get published by a big publishing company, but then again, most people don't have Joseph Kennedy for a father. An introduction was provided by one of the country's foremost image makers, *Time* magazine publisher Henry R. Luce. "You would be surprised how a book that really makes the grade with high-class people stands you in good stead for years to come," Joseph Kennedy had advised his son.[171] Again, the *Time/Life* influence intertwined with John F. Kennedy long before the acid-eating days and purchase of the Zapruder film that would follow.

Even with all the revealed skeletons in the Kennedy's closet and rumors of infidelity, the short JFK administration got more things done in his 1,036 days in office than presidents who have served eight year terms have since. John F. Kennedy's personal talents included charisma and hope. "He had a gift for rallying the country to its best, most humane and idealistic impulses," says Pulitzer Prize-winning historian Robert Caro[172] It also helped that he had a beautiful and elegant wife, Jacqueline Bouvier Kennedy

But the 35th president of the United States also had a gift for making enemies of one-time friends. As such, many of these factions and people were forced to practice self-preservation, at any expense. His father had not taught him how to deal with this type of issue.

John F. Kennedy and Robert F. Kennedy were trying to eliminate the Mafia (a group rumored to have helped him win the 1960 election), the CIA (the embarrassment over the revelation of the Bay of Pigs debacle forced the Mayor of Dallas, Earl Cabell's brother Charles to lose his job as Deputy Director of the CIA), dump LBJ from the ticket in 1964 (a fate Johnson's ego could not live through), prevent Israel from getting nuclear weapons (note FDR was not fully behind the creation of Israel or European powers that profited from British colonization), and attacking the international drug trade in Vietnam.[173] Kennedy had also made himself an enemy to General Edwin Walker of Dallas and the John Birch Society.

Another party acting on self-preservation was J. Edgar Hoover who the Kennedys hated and who hated the Kennedys with equal fervor.[174] For all these reasons, the Kennedys had created many enemies; some with whom he shared the White House and his Administration.

So could any of these people or groups have had enough power and persuasion to assassinate John F. Kennedy?

There are always those people behind the scenes who are keepers of powerful people's secrets. These people are usually personal assistants, right-hand men, or personal secretaries. Though they don't always know it, they too hold great power and could also be considered threats to their boss's enemies.

> *****
>
> **THERE ARE ALWAYS THOSE PEOPLE BEHIND THE SCENES WHO ARE KEEPERS OF POWERFUL PEOPLE'S SECRETS.**
>
> **THESE PEOPLE ARE USUALLY PERSONAL ASSISTANTS, RIGHT-HAND MEN, OR PERSONAL SECRETARIES.**
>
> **THOUGH THEY DON'T ALWAYS KNOW IT, THEY TOO HOLD GREAT POWER AND COULD ALSO BE CONSIDERED THREATS TO THEIR BOSS'S ENEMIES.**

Evelyn Lincoln, Kennedy's personal secretary for twelve years, was privy to things even the First Lady did not know. Lincoln shared much of her knowledge of these secrets and enemies in her book, "Kennedy and Johnson." She had intimate knowledge of the power plays in Washington during her tenure as President Kennedy's secretary and could exhibit evidence of the dislike of the Kennedys by Hoover and his alliance with Lyndon Baines Johnson.[175] Evelyn Lincoln knew that LBJ would not be on the 1964 ticket and worried about JFK's visit to Dallas. LBJ's presidency, once established, gave J. Edgar Hoover a job for life; and Hoover had plenty of power and information on the highest ranking officials in the world. Other facilitators were the men of Suite 8F who were worried JFK would take away their tax shelters. The men of Suite 8F were part of the LBJ corruption network in Texas and with their oil-rich bank accounts they could provide funding for the operation of killing a president.[176] And of course, the Military Industrial Complex (a faction former President Eisenhower warned about) had their dislike of the Kennedys. Later, it was discovered that Robert Surrey was General Edwin Walker's right hand man and that he was the one responsible for having the ugsome 'Wanted for Treason' pamphlets printed the day JFK was assassinated.

But the most subversive hatred came from that ghostly branch of government President Harry S. Truman had begun in 1946 to fill a void for the "lack of coordinated intelligence in Washington; the Central Intelligence Group."[177] Twenty months after its genesis, the decision was made to 'pull the plug' on both the Central Intelligence Group and the National Intelligence Authority operations and convert them into one entity. Finally by 1947, the CIA and the National Security Council were both generated under the National Security Act of 1947, allowing the CIA to "be responsible for discovering intelligence, securing its validity, and deciding the level of national security."[178] Truman had created a Shelleyesque monster not unlike Frankenstein in its part CIA, part NSC and part OSS body.

By the time John F. Kennedy had become President, the CIA was a powerful governmental force. Former President Eisenhower had allocated millions of tax dollars to build the CIA headquarters in the deep-forested area of Langley, Virginia in 1959.[179] It didn't take long for this new defender of national security to begin to resemble a Mafia crime syndicate. As author and University of Georgia Professor of Law Donald E. Wilkes, Jr. describes the agency in 1975:

> *"Lavishly but secretly funded, unrestrained by public opinion, cloaked in secrecy, conducting whatever foreign or domestic clandestine operations it wished without regard to laws or morals, and specializing in deception, falsification, and mystification, the CIA was riddled at all levels with ruthless, cynical officials and employees who believed that they were above the law, that any means were justified to accomplish the goals they set for themselves, and that insofar as their surreptitious activities were concerned it was justifiable to lie with impunity to anyone, even presidents and legislators. Many of these individuals, thinking he was soft on communism, that he would reduce the size of the military industrial complex, and that he was to blame for the Bay of Pigs disaster (the failed CIA-sponsored invasion of Cuba in 1961), hated and despised Kennedy. The CIA routinely circumvented and defied attempts by the executive and legislative branches to monitor its activities. It was involved in innumerable unlawful or outrageous activities. It illegally opened the mail of Americans. It interfered with free elections in foreign countries and arranged to destabilize or overthrow the governments of other countries. It plotted the murder of various*

foreign leaders. It arranged to hire the Mafia to help with some of these proposed murder plots."[180]

One month after John F. Kennedy was murdered; former President Harry Truman warned the world of the monster he created:

> *I think it has become necessary to take another look at the purpose and operations of our Central Intelligence Agency—CIA... for some time I have been disturbed by the way the CIA has been diverted from its original assignment. It has become an operational and at times a policy-making arm of the Government. This has led to trouble and may have compounded our difficulties in several explosive areas. We have grown up as a nation, respected for our free institutions and for our ability to maintain a free and open society. There is something about how the CIA has been functioning that is casting a shadow over our historical position and I feel that we need to correct it.*[181]

By 1963, there had been several CIA assisted coups including Guatemala and Iran, as well as "shadow government assassinations and assassination attempts on/of José Figueres, "Papa Doc" Duvalier, Fidel and Raul Castro."[182] The CIA became a force with which to be reckoned, and the transformation paralleled the elegance of Camelot. The term 'spying' was replaced by the politically correct phrase 'intelligence gathering' and covert operations included wire-tapping, propaganda, and counter-insurgences.[183] Ironically, in 2013, fifty years after this, the National Security Administration has admitted to doing the very same things.[184]

The CIA covert actions and problems with Cuba though, along with Vice-President LBJ's scandals, caused the most embarrassment, as well as failure for the counter-intelligence portion of JFK's presidency. This may have led to mixed feelings for the president as he was obsessed with covert operations and secrecy. He loved reading Ian Fleming's *James Bond* books and had even recommended them to CIA Director Allen Dulles.[185] The CIA had tried to appease the president in as many ways as they could while still maintaining their objectives. It was no secret to the CIA that both JFK and RFK wanted Castro out of the way, so the CIA set out to find ways to do that. The Church Committee, (yet another governmental committee appointed to investigate assassination conspiracies) convened and found no less than eight separate plots against Castro during JFK's presidency. These ranged from an attempt to give him a poisoned wet suit for scuba diving to poisoned cigars to "a more determined effort, through agents recruited by the Mafia, to poison his food."[186] So when the Bay of Pigs failed, the Kennedys were crushed; both personally and politically.

For his part as president, JFK took responsibility for the failed attempt to overthrow Castro. But privately, he blamed the CIA, forcing Allen Dulles, who ironically (or maybe not so ironically) would become a member of the

Warren Commission on JFK's assassination, into resignation.[187] Kennedy then implemented National Security Action Memorandum Number 55, transferring control of paramilitary operations to the Defense Department. There is no doubt that JFK's faith in the CIA was severely undermined by the Bay of Pigs debacle.[188] Could all these things have led to a CIA involvement in the JFK assassination? Several incriminating coincidences give credence to the theory including:

- Lee Harvey Oswald's friend in Dallas, oil man and rumored CIA operative George de Morhenschildt was also married to Abraham Zapruder's former business partner, Jeanne LeGon.[189]
- In the summer of 1963, pro-Castro Oswald publicly scuffled with the nation's most well-known anti-Castro group – the DRE – and their arrests and resulting debates were covered on radio, TV and in the newspapers. The DRE was financed and directed by the CIA's Miami propaganda and counter-intelligence bureau.[190]
- Author Jefferson Morley's discovery that the CIA liaison officer to the House Select Committee on Assassinations, George Joannides, was from 1962-64 the case officer for DRE, the very same Cuban exile group with which Oswald had had multiple interactions in the summer of 1963. See above.[191]
- CIA money paid to an "Oswald Project."[192]
- FBI director J. Edgar Hoover told LBJ the day after the assassination that someone had impersonated Oswald in Mexico City in September 1963 according to CIA wiretaps and photos. That part of Johnson's presidential tapes – fourteen minutes – was erased and considered lost until this was found.[193]
- A typewritten letter from Oswald was sent to the Soviet Embassy in Washington DC two weeks prior to the assassination saying Oswald had met with Comrade Kostin in Mexico City. It showed up two days prior to the assassination because the FBI had stopped and searched it, as it did with all mail going to the Soviet embassy. Following the assassination, the Soviets considered the letter proof of a U.S.-based conspiracy and gave it (back) to the FBI. This *document* actually did show up in the *Warren Commission Report.*[194]
- The Warren Commission, which concluded in 1964 that Oswald acted alone and was not part of a conspiracy, was never told about the CIA's possibly relevant anti-Castro activities, despite the fact that former CIA director Allen Dulles was a Warren Commission member.[195]

- Withheld 'classified' documents numbering over 1,100 from the CIA concerning the assassination of JFK.[196]
- The following quote from a *Life* journalist, Andrew St. George, interviewed by Gaeton Fonzi:

> *Sometime in the early Fifties... assassination became an instrument of U.S. national policy. It also became an important branch of our invisible government, a sizable business, and a separate technology involving weapons and devices the ordinary taxpayer paid billions for but was never permitted to see, except perhaps in the Technicolor fantasies of James Bond flicks."*[197]

But was there a secret war between President Kennedy and the CIA with FBI aid? Public evidence does not support it. What it *does* support is that the JFK administration was no different from the administrations before and those after in using covert operations. Conflicting quotes from President Kennedy cause doubt for CIA support but his actions speak differently. A little over six months after the Bay of Pigs, Kennedy approved Operation Mongoose, a secret plan to overthrow Castro involving four hundred American employees, two thousand Cuban agents, a small Navy and Air Force and more than fifty business fronts.[198] Their activities included intelligence gathering, minor sabotage, and propaganda.[199] Later CIA covert activities spread to the Far East, Africa, and Latin America. The CIA was becoming far too powerful, even in 1963. In an article written in The *New York Times*, by JFK's close friend Arthur Krock, the writer quotes a high-ranking official in the government as saying:

> *"The CIA's growth was likened to a malignancy which this 'very high official' was not even sure the White House could control ... any longer. If the United States ever experiences [an attempt at a coup to overthrow the government] it will come from the CIA and not the Pentagon. The agency represents a tremendous power and total unaccountability to anyone."*[200]

Every president since JFK has used the CIA to hide the darkest secrets our government possesses. This secrecy handling has, in modern times been shared by the FBI, Homeland Security, the Drug Enforcement Agency, and the National Security Agency. Should Americans have the right to know about them all? Who determines what the American public can and cannot know? What does keeping secrets say about character?

In 1963, Orville Nix had never questioned these things. He counted on his government to protect him from evil. He never thought of how they protected him, just that he was protected from communists, nuclear warheads, and terror. As for keeping secrets, he was firmly against it and raised his son to think the same way.

"If you don't have your word, you have nothing," he told his son, "and keeping secrets is like telling lies… lies that always come back to bite you in the butt."

The phone began to ring again for the twentieth time that day. Before the second ring, Orville answered it.

"Hello?" he said.

A muffled male voice, like spoken through a blanket of fog, came through the black telephone receiver. "You need to keep your mouth shut or someone will shut it for you," he said with no detectable accent. Orville could hear clicking in the background.

"Who is this?" Orville responded.

"Keep your mouth shut or you'll find out," the voice said. The next sound Orville heard was the dial tone.

Orville hung up the phone and stood there looking at it. He then walked across the room, locked his front door then went back across the kitchen to lock the back door. In the twenty years he had lived there he had only locked all the doors one time, when he, Ella and Junior had taken a week-long vacation. He would find himself locking the doors nightly from that day on. He wouldn't tell Ella or his family about this phone call until several months later after receiving several more.

CHAPTER FOURTEEN

UPI, RUMORS AND THE CIA

"The very word 'secrecy' is repugnant in a free and open society; and we are as a people inherently and historically opposed to secret societies, to secret oaths and to secret proceedings."

John F. Kennedy[201]

The doorbell at 2527 Denley rang promptly at 1 P.M. on Wednesday, December 11, 1963. Orville answered it to see a diminutive man with a kind face smiling at him. It was Penn Jones.[202] This would be the first of several meetings between the two men.

"Mr. Nix? Mr. Orville Nix?" Penn asked as Orville opened the screen door emblazoned with an iron work flamingo.

"You must be Mr. Jones," Orville replied as he held out his right hand to shake in greeting. "Come in, come in. Would you like some coffee or a glass of iced tea?"

"Coffee would be great, Mr. Nix, just black." After he showed Jones into the living room, Orville noticed the man reaching to open his briefcase as Orville walked into the kitchen to make the coffee. Jones took some papers out.

"Mr. Nix," Jones said while Orville was in the kitchen, "I hope you will be patient with me. You see, I think there's something funny going on. I don't know your political leanings, but I think that 'ole hound dog faced' LBJ has had his men in the military kill our President."

Orville came back in with two cups of coffee; one black, one with sugar and cream.

"My son feels the same way, Mr. Jones."

"Call me Penn, call me Penn," he interjected. "Your son, huh? Is he a college student?"

"Naw, he works for the Appraisal District and Monkey-Wards on the weekends doing accounting. He's a Republican."

Penn smiled and said, "Well, kids will do what kids will do."

Orville smiled at this funny, but intelligent man. He took an instant liking to him.

"Let me get right to the reason for my visit. You see, Mr. Nix, I've looked at those Zapruder frames in *Life* magazine. I think the shot that killed the president came from the front. Your film might show it."

"Well, I don't own it anymore Penn, UPI does, but I have a copy of it if you'd like to watch."

"Oh please, may I?"

"Sure thing, let me get it," Orville replied.

Orville excused himself and went to the bedroom to get his projector and screen. He had the copy of his film hidden under the mattress. He set the equipment up and turned off the lights. They both watched it several times. With each viewing, Penn would move closer and closer to the screen. After about twenty minutes of watching the film, Penn rose and stood right in front of the center of the screen. The footage played against his beige shirt and hat like a fabric cartoon.

"I'm no photo expert Orville, but I see things. Like there, right there."[203] He pointed to a dark shadow in the center of the pergola. "You see that?" Penn asked excitedly. "It looks like a man holding a rifle." Orville couldn't make out what it was Penn thought he saw. Each time the film played, Penn pointed to the same place. It wasn't the place Orville thought the shots came from, but he didn't want to embarrass himself or his new friend by saying so.

"Do you mind if I call some friends about seeing your film?" Penn asked him.

"Well Penn, I'd rather you not use my name. You see, I have a government job and I don't want them to get wind of my film and then find some reason to let me go. It happens you know."

Penn nodded his head in agreement.

"I don't blame you, Orville, you can never be too careful. In fact, I don't think you should tell many people you took this. I think you would be safer if you didn't. Well, I'll get back to you. Thank you for letting me come by and for letting me see the film. I do believe you have something of great importance here."

*****

"I DON'T BLAME YOU, ORVILLE, YOU CAN NEVER BE TOO CAREFUL.

IN FACT, I DON'T THINK YOU SHOULD TELL MANY PEOPLE YOU TOOK THIS.

I THINK YOU WOULD BE SAFER IF YOU DIDN'T.

WELL, I'LL GET BACK TO YOU. THANK YOU FOR LETTING ME COME BY AND FOR LETTING ME SEE THE FILM. I DO BELIEVE YOU HAVE SOMETHING OF GREAT IMPORTANCE HERE."

With that, they shook hands again and Penn Jones left with a tornado of thoughts in his head.

Great importance? Orville thought. *Those jackasses at Time/Life called it a nuisance.* He scowled at the thought of his trip to New York. Orville grabbed his new fedora, the one the UPI men had sent him along with the five thousand dollar money order and copy of his film. There wasn't even a thank you letter with it.

"I need to play golf," Orville said to himself out loud and grabbed his golf clubs. After the excitement and disappointment of the last month, he needed to hit some balls.

* * * * *

Later that afternoon, 3000 miles away in New York, the men from UPI were anxiously reviewing the Nix film again, but not from an investigative standpoint; no, this time for money. Whether it was because they came in second to scoring the publishing coup of modern times, the Zapruder film, or that they just wanted to stay atop of breaking news stories, they were well aware that the public had developed a huge appetite for all things JFK and huge appetites meant huge profits.

During those frantic four days in November, UPI had first reported the assassination, AP was the first to report Oswald's arrest and *Time/Life* got the Zapruder film. Each of the three top media magnates claimed a first place ribbon in the race to get the news out to the world. In January of 1964, less than a month after purchasing the film from Orville Nix, UPI published a book of the Nix and Marie Muchmore frames entitled, "Four Days".[204] Marie

Muchmore had also taken a home movie, but hers was much shorter than the Nix film. The UPI book contained 143 pages from the Nix and Muchmore films, news stories, personal accounts, speeches, and letters, and sold for $2.95. UPI made the money they paid for the films the first day of publishing. By the next month, they had made a healthy profit. *Time/Life*, on the other hand, was protecting the Zapruder film. No one was allowed to see it. Though *Life* had paid 3000% more for the Zapruder film than UPI had for the Nix film, they were in no big rush to recoup their investment. Why? Was *Life* magazine protecting the American public from something the CIA did not want seen?

Rumors abounded in the 1950s and 1960s that many of the top news agencies, magazines and newspapers were CIA fronts. It wasn't until many years later when findings from the Church Committee were released that the American people were told these rumors were indeed facts. In many instances, CIA documents proved that journalists had been engaged to perform tasks for the CIA with the consent of the managements of America's leading news organizations. These news organizations included William Paley of the *Columbia Broadcasting System*(CBS), Henry Luce of *Time/Life Inc.*, Arthur Hays Sulzberger of the *New York Times,* Barry Bingham Sr. of the *Louisville Courier-Journal*, and James Copley of the *Copley News Services.*[205] Other organizations which cooperated with the CIA include the *American Broadcasting Company* (ABC), the *National Broadcasting Company* (NBC), the *Associated Press* (AP), *United Press International (*UPI), *Reuters, Hearst Newspapers*, *Scripps-Howard, Newsweek* magazine, the *Mutual Broadcasting System*, the *Miami Herald,* and the old *Saturday Evening Post* and *New York Herald-Tribune.*[206]

By far the most valuable of these associations, according to CIA officials, have been with the *New York Times*, CBS, and *Time/Life Inc.* In fact, if it weren't for the JFK assassination, *Life* magazine had plans to ruin Lyndon B. Johnson's political career.[207] Former editorial business manager for *Life* magazine, James Wagenvoord said in an email to John Simkin:

> *"Beginning in later summer 1963 the magazine, based upon information fed from Bobby Kennedy and the Justice Department, had been developing a major news break piece concerning Johnson and Bobby Baker. On publication Johnson would have been finished and off the 1964 ticket (reason the material was fed to us) and would probably have been facing prison time. At the time LIFE magazine was arguably the most important general news source in the US. The top management of Time Inc. was closely allied with the USA's various intelligence agencies and we were used after by the Kennedy Justice Department as a conduit to the public…*
>
> *The LBJ/Baker piece was in the final editing stages and was scheduled to break in the issue of the magazine due out the week of November 24th (the magazine*

would have made it to the newsstands on November 26th or 27th). It had been prepared in relative secrecy by a small special editorial team. On Kennedy's death research files and all numbered copies of the nearly print-ready draft were gathered up by my boss (he had been the top editor on the team) and shredded. The issue that was to expose LBJ instead featured the Zapruder film".[208]

* * * * *

In 1967, CBS would ensure Orville Nix never gave another interview.[209] And for their part, *Time*, who owned *Life* magazine, had control over the Zapruder film and would not give it up until 1975 when they sold it back to the family for one dollar. This was confirmed by Richard Stolley, the man who first saw the Zapruder film and later became editor of *Life* magazine: "the order to acquire the film and withhold it from public viewing came from *Life's* publisher, C.D. Jackson via Henry Luce.[210] For many years, Luce's personal emissary to the CIA was C.D. Jackson, a *Time Inc.* vice-president who was publisher of *Life* magazine from 1960 until his death in 1964.

The CIA's practice of controlling the media had ensured that any secrets the Nix and Zapruder films would later reveal would not be found out now. The CIA didn't know the Church Committee, convened in 1973 would spill many secrets of how they used the aforementioned newsgroups to propagandize, disseminate disinformation, and smear the lives of innocent people. Orville Nix was one of the CIA's practice victims...UPI just took advantage of him. Latter day reporters who worked for the CIA included Richard Billings and Hugh Aynesworth. Both also worked on the Jim Garrison staff during the famous Clay Shaw trial.

At first, UPI's interest in Orville Nix and his film was more for greed than for sharing information. This was proven with Orville's own experience and Marie Muchmore's experience with UPI.[211]

The UPI tag team of Reinhardt and Schonfeld had licensed the Marie Muchmore film for a song; one thousand dollars. In later years, Maurice Schonfeld would write about it in the *Columbia Journalism Review,* bragging about how he and Reinhardt procured the film:

"I've got a lady here who says she has a movie of the assassination. What do I do with her?" asked the deskman. "Lock the door," said Reinhardt.

Reinhardt hurried to the office and set about shaking Miss Muchmore's confidence in the value of her film by asking if she was positive that she was filming at the very moment of the assassination, if the film was in focus, if the exposure was right. UPI would be pleased to develop the film and see if it was any good and then make an offer, Reinhardt said, or, if Miss Muchmore preferred to play it safe, UPI would make a blind cash offer. Miss Muchmore chose to play it safe and accepted a check for $1,000. Reinhardt took the film to *the Eastman Kodak lab in Dallas. At first it seemed that Miss Muchmore had gotten the better of the deal. All we had was a grainy, jerky glimpse of the last seconds of the assassination and the confused aftermath; but back in New York we slowed the picture down, blew it up, zoomed in and stop-framed and turned it into two minutes of respectable TV news. By the time we released the edited sequence, however, Jack Ruby had killed Oswald, the president's funeral had just occurred, and showing the film seemed in such poor taste that most UPI client stations chose not to show it."*[212]

How unfortunate for UPI.

* * * * *

UPI, under the direction of Burt Reinhardt, developed several projects with the Nix and Muchmore films. They produced the above-mentioned book, "Four Days," including several color frames from the movies. They made a composite movie in 35mm from the original 8mm movies by David Wolper. The composite used the technique of repeating a frame several times to give the appearance of slow motion or stop action during key sections of the films; a technique that wasn't truthful, but was widely used at the time. Reinhardt, Schonfeld, and Mr. Fox, a UPI writer, made the composite movie available to researchers at their projection studio in New York in 1964 and 1965.[213] Researchers who viewed this "technique" film at the time included Mark Lane, Sylvia Meagher, and many others.[214]

That UPI offered the film to researchers was a transparent gesture, unlike the secrecy with which *Life* magazine surrounded the Zapruder film. The grandest gesture made by UPI though, was due to the insistence of one man in New York who vehemently believed he too had seen an image, though different from the image Penn Jones had seen. This man was named Jones Harris.

Jones Harris, the colorful son of actress Ruth Gordon, is a man of many influences and connections.[215] With his refined vocabulary, charming demeanor, and unique style, he has always been a force with which to be reckoned. He believed from the day the thirty-fifth president was murdered that there was a conspiracy within a conspiracy. He began making phone calls and interviewing witnesses as early as December of 1963. Then, after the Warren Commission was convened due to the overwhelming public questioning of Lee Harvey Oswald's guilt, a twenty-six volume set was published listing their findings and photo, audio, and witness exhibits. Few people could afford such a complicated set of findings, but Jones Harris, a man of independent means, could. He was appalled and mystified as he pored over the laborious tome day and night. He knew several people within the JFK administration, several of them lovely women. He had been advised by one of them, Pamela Turnure, the petite and beautiful press secretary for First Lady Jacqueline Kennedy, that even some of the Secret Service men felt there was a conspiracy to kill JFK.[216] "She said that they thought there was gunfire from more than one place," he related to the author. "That's when I went to Dallas to interview witnesses myself."[217]

Early in 1964, not long after Penn Jones visited him, Orville Nix got a phone call from a man asking if he knew Jones Harris. Orville, thinking this was the friend of which Penn Jones spoke, said, "Not that I recollect, though I do know a Penn Jones."

The caller hung up and Orville long wondered why the phone call was made. Later in the year he would find out why.

Burt Reinhardt and Reese Schonfeld were contacted by Mr. Harris in order to view frames from the Nix film. Harris was, and still is, convinced that in the Nix film, the viewer could see a man dressed in a police uniform, aiming a long-barreled revolver at the President. Behind this image is the automobile that Forrest Sorrels questioned Jack Ruby about, Honest Joe's Gun and Pawn Shop Edsel. Honest Joe's Gun and Pawn Shop unique car was parked by the Dallas Police Department basement doors the day Jack Ruby shot Lee Harvey Oswald.[218] Coincidental? Harris thinks not. In a telephonic interview on November 9th, 2013, with me, the author, Harris told me:

> *Dearest Gayle, have you read the full Warren Commission testimony of Forrest Sorrels? I know he was friends with your grandfather, but do you realize what a bad day he too was having on November 22, 1963?*

Think about it…he was sitting in the same seat as JFK was except in the car in front of him. He was looking out the right window. He saw things that he only told a few people. I think that must have been one of the saddest days of his life, not only because the President died, but because he saw the person that did it. I'm convinced because he is the only one who mentions Honest Joe's car not once, but twice in his testimony. And no one ever questioned him.

I was well aware of the Mafia connection to the assassination, even as early as 1963, but what kept me researching the case was the government involvement---and your grandfather's film proves it. You see, in the river of time, Forrest Sorrels was 7 to 8 seconds ahead of President Kennedy. He would have been looking the same direction Kennedy was looking and I believe he saw something on the knoll. Why else would he be the only one to mention the Honest Joe's car? The Zapruder film doesn't show that area, but the Nix film does. It is the most important film of the assassination. [219]

Jones Harris contacted Reese Schonfeld of UPI. Schonfeld relates the UPI experience with Jones Harris:

"In some of the pictures published in the Warren Report, Harris found something new. First off, he saw a station wagon with a machine gun mounted on the roof. Such a station wagon did exist in Dallas—it was used to advertise a Dallas gun shop—and it was Harris's theory that the station wagon and the shop were involved in some way in the Kennedy assassination. Then he found a curious shape on the grassy knoll, a shape that could be read as a man aiming a gun at John F. Kennedy. We gave Harris some of the key stills made from the Nix film. They showed the knoll and, atop the knoll, "the pergola"—a concrete structure consisting of two octagonal towers connected by a wall thirty-eight inches high and 100 feet long. In the process of enlarging these stills, two things happened: the station wagon went away and the head, shoulders, arms, and gun of the rifleman was standing behind this car, leaning on it, as he took aim."[220]

In 2013, during an interview conducted by the Sixth Floor Museum with the late Eddie Rubinstein, Honest Joe's son, he too would relate the sightings of his dad's car that day. He recounted the Secret Service coming to the business and later the FBI asking questions because someone had "reported that a young guy got out of Honest Joe's car and was carrying a long package wrapped in newspapers and ran up to the knoll."[221] The Secret Service had asked if it was him to which he adamantly responded "no." Rubinstein later relates during the same interview that he and his friend had gone to Austin the weekend the president was assassinated. As they were having breakfast at Nighthawks diner, they saw a picture of his dad's advertising vehicle on television. For a scared moment, Eddie Goldstein thought his dad may have been involved in the death of Lee Harvey Oswald because his mother (Eddie's grandmother) was a huge Kennedy supporter. This love for Kennedy would also be the reason Jack Ruby gave for killing Lee Harvey Oswald.

This station wagon, some would call a van or truck, was also seen the day Lee Harvey Oswald was shot by Jack Ruby. The Dallas Gun Shop was actually a Pawn Shop named Honest Joe's and indeed had a non-working machine gun attached on the back.[222] Honest Joe's had two advertising vehicles: a jeepster and an Edsel.[223] Harris's contention of seeing a gunman was later dismissed by a study conducted by a firm UPI had hired- ITEK, a CIA run film analysis plant. What the public didn't know, nor did the unquestioning Schonfeld, was that the ITEK study did indeed state there could have been another gunman there: just not the one Harris claimed to see. Little did Schonfeld and Reinhardt know, Jones Harris had teamed up with renowned photo analyst and photographer Bernard Hoffman who had devised a way of enhancing film using a microscope called photo-micrography. Hoffman was a famous photographer and inventor and became fast friends with Jones Harris who, unlike Schonfeld, respected Hoffman's work. Nevertheless, Schonfeld and Reinhardt had found another money-making opportunity from the Nix film:

> *Harris wanted Hoffman to analyze the key frames of our original film, hoping to be able to firmly establish the existence of the rifleman. If the UPI-owned Nix film bore out Harris's theories, it would obviously be worth a lot of money. Reinhardt and I cooperated. We produced the original so that Bernie Hoffman could make the best possible reproductions. As the custodian of the original, I worked through the winter of 1965-66 with Hoffman and Harris in Hoffman's photo lab, searching with them for the frame that would prove, once and for all, that there was a man with a gun on the grassy knoll, where no man was supposed to be, as well as a car parked where no car was meant to be parked.*[224]

The urge to make money superseded the urge to find the truth. Schonfeld continues:

> *At this point, the question was how to proceed. Jones Harris wanted the publicity which only a national magazine could provide, but he seemed reluctant to carry his research any further.*
>
> *Additional research in to the film would be extremely costly. UPI was unwilling to pay for it, since there would be no immediate financial return (UPI does not sell exclusive stories and it is impossible to assign a dollar value to a wire service scoop). Also, there was always the chance that further analysis would reveal that the shape which seemed to be a man was nothing but a mass of shadows, so that a great deal of money would be spent for what would finally be an epic nonstory—about a frame from a film no one had heard of which proved only that there was nothing remarkable to be seen. But if this sort of nonstory could*

> *hardly succeed as a wire-service piece, it could very well go over big on the cover of a national magazine: a blown-up frame of the knoll, a white circle drawn around the shadowy shape, and a bold title reading "WAS THERE AN ASSASSIN ON THE KNOLL? See page 6." So, though as a journalist I hated giving up control of the story, as a businessman I realized that it made more sense to take it to a magazine than for UPI to go on with it.*[225]

Schonfeld shopped the Nix film and the Jones Harris discovery to Richard Billings, an assistant editor at *Life* magazine. Billings was unable to interest the CIA fronted *Time/Life* powers that be, because in doing so, the Warren Report findings would be questioned. This, of course was not the excuse they gave for being disinterested. Jones Harris spoke with Billings personally, aside from Schonfeld and showed him the enhanced frame Hoffman had made from the Nix film. The blood drained from Billings face as he stared at the frame. "Would you mind if I show this to the head of our photo lab?" he asked Harris. Harris agreed. They walked to the lab where Harris was introduced to a distinguished, white-haired man. Billings handed the enlarged frame over to the man, who Jones Harris later learned was George Karas. Karas looked down at the blowup slowly, inspecting the image with a technical eye. A few seconds later, he looked up at Billings and tears were gushing from his eyes as he shook his head in horror. Jones Harris realized Mr. Karas had seen the same image Jones had seen when he first saw the Nix film: an image of a sniper in front of a car. Without saying a word as his tears flowed freely, Karas handed the frame back to Billings who quickly escorted Harris from the lab. For the second time, *Life* magazine had a chance to break a story about the Nix film, but did not. Their excuse, Billings said was, "They felt that they had already given sufficient space to the Kennedy assassination."[226]

Schonfeld gave up on the Nix film for the time being. Jones Harris did not. In 1965, Jones Harris would ensure the Nix film would garner UPI's attention once more.

CHAPTER FIFTEEN

OF COMMISSIONS AND COMPLICITY

"And no official of my administration, whether his rank is high or low, civilian or military, should interpret my words here tonight as an excuse to censor the news, to stifle dissent, to cover up our mistakes, or to withhold from the press and the public the facts they deserve to know."

John F. Kennedy[227]

By November 25th, 1963, newly-sworn in president Lyndon Baines Johnson knew that there were questions about his predecessor's murder and the events in Dallas. President Johnson ordered the FBI and the Department of Justice (run at this time by Nick Katzenbach instead of JFK's distraught brother, Robert F. Kennedy) to investigate the assassination and the murder of Oswald.[228] A myriad of investigative committees were suggested. Politicians were eager to subdue the grief the American people were experiencing due to the death of the president: they also wanted to squelch the rising voice of conspiracy. That Katzenbach was well aware of the need to silence the questions surrounding JFK's assassination is evidenced in the now infamous Katzenbach memo he sent to JFK Presidential Adviser Bill Moyers:

> *"The public must be satisfied that Oswald was the assassin; that he had no confederates who are still at large; and that evidence was such that he would have been convicted at trial."*[229]

With LBJ's blessing, on November 26th, 1963, Waggoner Carr, the Texas State Attorney General, held a joint press conference in Washington with Herbert Miller, head of the Criminal Division of the U.S. Department of Justice calling for state and federal cooperation in making public all known facts surrounding the assassination of JFK. His announcement was met with vicious negativity. The world press, in town for President Kennedy's funeral, broke into an uproar. Many of the newsmen cursed and denounced Carr for "being a Texan and a Texas official."[230] Carr wasn't deterred. He assembled an organization to conduct the inquiry including two attorneys who had been members of the prosecution team at the Nuremberg war crimes trial: Robert G. Story and Leon Jaworski, (the Houston lawyer and later, special Watergate prosecutor.)

On November 27th, Senator Everett M. Dirksen proposed a Senate Judiciary Committee investigation, and Representative Charles E. Goodell proposed a joint Senate-House investigation.[231] Also, Waggoner Carr had announced that a state court of inquiry would be established. President Johnson was keen to this idea. The committee cited a statement by Leon Jaworski, who worked for the offices of both the Texas Attorney General and the U.S. Attorney General, indicating that LBJ told him on November 25th that he (LBJ) was encouraging Carr to proceed with the Texas Court of Inquiry.[232] A court of inquiry is a legal device to look into matters which are questionable. As Carr explained in an interview with James Kerr in 1974:

> *"The Texas 'court of inquiry' has subpoena powers, can take testimony under oath, and quite often results in evidence being developed to justify the filing of criminal charges or providing grand juries with enough facts to return indictments. My plan was to have everyone subpoenaed who knew anything about the assassination and related events."*[233]

Carr went about investigating all leads and a few days later found that LBJ had appointed Chief Justice Earl Warren to head the Warren Commission in investigating the death of John F. Kennedy; an appointment rumored to be declined by Warren but accepted after being presented with 'delicate' information provided by J. Edgar Hoover and disgust by Senator Richard Russell, the Head of the CIA Committee.[234] Russell suggested that Castro may have had a hand in the assassination and had no confidence in Earl Warren. Russell later made it public that he disagreed with the Warren Commission's 'single bullet theory' and wanted to dissent.[235] Warren obviously wasn't a friend of many.

Waggoner Carr tried his best to be civil to the man he had to work with politically for the country, but personally couldn't stand. Keeping his promise of sharing information with Warren's federal investigative committee, when Carr found evidence of an FBI connection with Lee Harvey Oswald, he lost no time in contacting Warren and an emergency joint-meeting was held. One of the key facts Carr found was that Oswald was an FBI informant being paid $200.00 as informant S179. Is this why the government claims it cannot find the tax returns for Oswald?

That was the last time the two investigative bodies met. According to Carr, from that time on, Warren blocked his requests and used intimidation tactics to close the Texas Court of Inquiry. Warren soon made himself inaccessible to Carr, forcing Carr to communicate through Katzenbach. Carr relates his experiences:

> *"Once I sat in Katzenbach's office for three days and most of three nights, just trying to get some word from him. I became outraged at what I considered rude, high-handed treatment and decided to bring matters to a head. I stood up, put on my hat and called out, 'I might not be a big shot like the Chief Justice, but as a state official I certainly had the authority to go back to Texas and open my public investigation in competition with Warren's secret inquiry.' This turned the trick. Warren immediately signed an agreement that from then on nothing would be withheld from the Texas investigators: a contract he soon violated".*[236]

In fact, the Warren Commission gave no credit or even mentioned the contributions of the Texas group of investigators save for a pat on the back at the end of his testimony regarding Dallas District Attorney Henry Wade. It was just one of the many gloss-overs readers, researchers and witnesses would find wrong in the twenty-six volume *Warren Commission Report*. The author has included a list of many more oversights at the end of the book.

When the Warren Commission was convened in 1964, many people living in Dallas, especially Orville Nix, thought all the questions people had been asking one another would be answered. He couldn't go a day without hearing one or several questions about JFK's assassination. Since he had been there, people looked to him to find answers. Sadly, he didn't have the answers.

People questioned how Lee Harvey Oswald had been arrested so quickly. Was there a connection between Oswald and the policeman he allegedly murdered, J.D. Tippit? Was there a connection between Oswald and Ruby? And yes, speaking of Mob-connected Ruby, how did Jack Ruby get into the heavily crowded Dallas Police Department with a pistol to kill Oswald? Was the Mafia part of this? JFK's brother Bobby had made the teamsters and the Mafia furious by promising to get rid of them. Would there be a WWIII? Was Fidel Castro behind this or was it Russian Premier Nikita Khrushchev? It was common knowledge in Texas that LBJ and his oil-rich cronies never liked the Kennedys. Did he have something to do with it? Is that why the Texas court of inquiry never got off the ground? Were the men behind the assassination living in Texas? Did Edwin Walker have something to do with the assassination? And how come there weren't Secret Service snipers watching the buildings that day? And since Oswald was a known Soviet sympathizer, why didn't the FBI, CIA and Secret Service have him on watch before the Presidential visit? And what about the Dallas Police Department? Why didn't they have more men at Dealey Plaza? Why did they let Jack Ruby roam around their building? And the media? Why weren't we, the American public, allowed to see the whole Zapruder film? Was there something in it that we weren't supposed to see?

Orville had even more questions. He was convinced that his returned film looked changed from the time he had seen it at Dynacolor and then again in New York. Had the FBI done something to it? At that time he didn't realize it, but he would have even more questions several months later. When the Warren Commission convened, the FBI sent a letter asking Nix to give them the camera he had used to take the film.

He asked them no questions and took it to the Santa Fe building in Dallas and gave it to them on January 29th, 1964. He was such a believer in supporting his government, he didn't want them to have to waste the time or manpower to retrieve it; he took the time to take it to them. At that time, the FBI interviewed him, asking pertinent questions as to where he was standing, how he shot the film, and what type of film he was using. He wondered why anyone was just now asking about what he saw. *Hell, the president had been dead for over two months,* he thought.

*****

ORVILLE HAD EVEN MORE QUESTIONS.

HE WAS CONVINCED THAT HIS RETURNED FILM LOOKED CHANGED FROM THE TIME HE HAD SEEN IT AT DYNACOLOR AND THEN AGAIN IN NEW YORK.

HAD THE FBI DONE SOMETHING TO IT?

After that meeting, Orville went home very upset. The agent was so matter of fact; as if Orville were just another bum picked up on Industrial Avenue. The agent, a man whose name he never wrote down, asked him several times how many shots he heard.[237]

"I believe there were at least four shots, maybe five," Orville replied.

"Which shots hit the president?" the agent asked.

"Well, I couldn't rightly say for certain, but I know the third shot hit him because that's when I saw…" Orville struggled for words, "when I saw…the president's head explode and saw the First Lady trying to get out of the car or maybe reaching for something, though I don't know what." Orville looked down into his lap. The agent just stared at him, like a man with no feelings.

Orville later learned this agent's name was Joe Abernathy. Abernathy would be the agent assigned, along with Lyndal Shaneyfelt, to study the camera and determine timing and run speed tests on the Keystone K-810. He also asked Orville how tightly he had wound the spring in an effort to determine timing. Abernathy sent reports through J. Gordon Shanklin from the Dallas office regarding the Nix film to the Warren Commission.

"So I can expect the camera back soon?" Orville asked Abernathy.

"Yessir, you can expect it back when the Warren Commission says they are finished with it," Abernathy assured him.

By March of 1964, he still didn't have it back.

He called his daughter-in-law Elaine knowing that she had a typewriter and could write well and asked her to send the FBI a letter asking when he could expect his camera to be returned. He didn't want to do it himself because he didn't want to misspell words or use incorrect grammar. Elaine had already dutifully typed several letters for him and he trusted his daughter-in-law to be his secretary.

* * * * *

Around the first of March 1964, he got a letter from J. Gordon Shanklin of the Dallas FBI asking to keep his camera for further study until the Warren Commission had finished with it.[238] What Orville did not know at the time was that the FBI was trying to determine timing for the camera, and in doing so, had taken the camera apart - broken it into little pieces.

Why had they not done the same thing with the Zapruder camera? Was there something special about the Keystone camera as opposed to Zapruder's Bell & Howell? Or was there something in the Nix film that couldn't be seen in the Zapruder film?

J. Gordon Shanklin had given Orville no idea as to how long the Warren Commission would need it, but by late March, Orville was beginning to worry about his upcoming vacation. He needed his camera to film his grandchildren.

In April, he asked Elaine again to send a letter. Again, it took weeks to receive an answer.

"Funny thing isn't it, Elaine? These federal boys and the Dallas Police Department can catch Lee Harvey Oswald in a little over an hour, but it takes them months to study my camera." He shook his head as he spoke. It just didn't make sense...even to a man who had never finished high school.

In May, he finally got a letter from the FBI saying he could pick up his camera on June 1st.[239] He was beyond ecstatic. Again, he called his son Orville to go with him to retrieve his precious Keystone camera. As they entered the building on Santa Fe, they stopped at the reception desk to announce their arrival. The kind young woman behind the counter greeted them with a smile.

"May I help you, gentlemen?" she asked sweetly.

"Good morning Ma'am, my name is Orville Nix and this is my father Orville, Sr. We're here to pick up his camera that was used to film the assassination."

Orville Sr. grimaced at his son's introduction. Yes, there was a part of him that liked to let people know he was there. That he had shot the film footage. That he was a part of history. That he had thoughts on the assassination. But there was another part of him that felt guilty for shooting the film; a part that made him feel complicit in the death of the president. He looked down at his shoes as the receptionist excused herself. She came back moments later with a box.

"Here it is, if you could just sign here, Mr. Nix," and handed him a receipt or form. It was on Federal Bureau of Investigation letterhead. There were several numbers he didn't understand and then a line that stated, 'Keystone Camera returned to Orville Nix on June 1st, 1964' then a line for him to sign. He slowly and deliberately wrote his signature as his son held the box.[240] They then thanked the woman and left. When they reached the car, Orville said, "You drive son, I'm going to open the box and look at my camera."

"Dad, did you give them other things? When I was carrying the box I felt something moving inside, like metal or something."

Orville reached into his pocket for his pocket knife to open the package. As he sliced the tightly taped box and looked inside, he couldn't control his anger. There in pieces was his camera. In pieces! The back had been wrought off and the insides were all taken apart. The pressure plate was disconnected from the housing. The aperture plate that held the film in place was also disconnected. The power zoom button and cover lock were removed. The spring was bent. The film speed dial was also removed. The operating lever couldn't be found. This box held nothing more than the skeleton of his camera and parts.

"Goddammit! Goddammit!" Orville screamed.

"What is it, Dad, what is it?" his son peered into the box, his eyes widening. "Good grief, Dad, they've torn your camera up!"

There in the box lay Orville's precious camera: the camera of history...the camera that took an important assassination film... destroyed.

Orville was putting everything back into the box and using curse words his adult son had never heard his dad use.

"I'm going back into that confounded place and asking them what the hell they did to my camera! What makes them think they can give it back to me like this? How the hell am I supposed to use it?"

Orville Jr. felt a cold chill, one he hadn't felt before this moment. "Dad," he whispered, "maybe they did it for a reason, maybe it's a warning," he said quietly.

"A damned warning for what, Junior? To not give the FBI your camera ever again? What would they need to warn me about? You wait here, I'm going in and asking them what the hell they think they're doing."

Orville opened the car door and slammed it shut all the while holding the box that held what was once his camera tightly to his chest. He walked quickly back into the FBI Building and though he felt badly about it, demanded in a loud voice to see the head of the office.

The young receptionist was flustered but made the phone call. She then whispered something into the phone Orville couldn't hear. Within minutes, Mr. Shanklin and Mr. Gemberling were introducing themselves to him, all the while apologizing for giving his camera back in that condition and explaining to Orville how he had helped the Warren Commission immensely by allowing his camera to be studied.

Orville was beyond angry.

"Helped the Warren Commission? Helped? If they were so damned interested in what I had to say, why haven't they contacted me? I was there! I shot the film! I'm the one still having nightmares! Could this camera tell them more than I could? Does this camera dream? I would have liked to take my wife on a trip to Washington, D.C. She's never been there. But instead, you tear up my camera. Now you listen. I may not be rich, but I take care of my things and I did what you asked me to do. What makes you think you can treat me or my camera this way? I want this fixed! I'm taking my grandchildren to White Sands in a few months and I need my camera."

*****

IF THEY WERE SO DAMNED INTERESTED IN WHAT I HAD TO SAY, WHY HAVEN'T THEY CONTACTED ME?

I WAS THERE! I SHOT THE FILM! I'M THE ONE STILL HAVING NIGHTMARES!

Shanklin and Gemberling both spoke at the same time, their words tripping over one another's. "Indeed you shall have your camera and I'm so very sorry we have made this mistake. Actually, we didn't have clearance from J. Edgar Hoover to release it yet anyway, so we will let the Director know how upset you are, find out who did this and have your camera repaired. You should have it before the week is out. Please accept our apologies and my promise."

Orville, satisfied with the man's reply shook his hand and left.

* * * * *

Unfortunately, Orville didn't live long enough to understand the true reason the FBI sent his camera back in pieces. In order to ensure a camera can never again be tested under the same circumstances or to keep it from revealing secrets the future shouldn't find in re-examination, it must be destroyed. That is what the FBI did to Orville Nix's K-810 Keystone camera in 1964.

* * * * *

Within the week, his repaired camera was returned, along with a newer one, a Keystone Capri Model K-27 with a carrying case.[241] Orville had gotten what he wanted and a new camera to boot. He was happy.

Sometimes it was good to lose your temper.

CHAPTER SIXTEEN

THROUGH A GLASS DARKLY

"A man may die, nations may rise and fall, but an idea lives on."

John F. Kennedy[242]

The next week, Orville went into work a more confident man carrying his new Keystone Capri. To most people, this small victory over the powerful FBI would seem inconsequential; but to Orville, it was a coup. He had been intimidated by men of power most of his life, and now he felt what they must feel daily. He liked the feeling.

As he replayed his story over and over to his coworkers, relishing their admiring comments and interest, J.C. Price, one of Orville's supervisors at the Terminal Annex Building called him into his office.

"Orville," he began, "I've been meaning to talk to you about that day… the day the president was killed," he said. "I saw it all too. I was on the roof of the building wearing my new glasses. I saw it all." Mr. Price stared at Orville from across his desk. "I wanted to ask you what you saw."

Orville stared back at him, uncomfortable with being in his office. It wasn't as if the two were friends. This was one of his supervisors.

Noting his hesitation, Mr. Price continued light-heartedly, "You don't have to worry, Orville, I don't work for the FBI, I'm not going to break your camera." He laughed, making Orville feel more at ease. Orville had complained to everyone at work about the broken camera and bragged about how he talked to the FBI.

"Oh, you heard about that, did ya? Yeah, that was sumpin, Mr. Price," Orville replied. "They did a better job of tearin' that camera up than my three-year-old grandson could've done, and that's saying sumpin'. Wanna see his picture?" He reached for his wallet quicker than Price could answer and reaching across the desk said, "That's him, David… but I call him Bubba. Orville beamed with pride and Price reacted courteously.

"That's a fine young man, Orville, a fine young man."

Orville put his wallet back into his pocket. "So what did you want to know, Mr. Price?"

"Well Orville, I wanted to know if you saw what I saw. It seems the Warren Commission isn't calling for my testimony. Did they ask for yours?"

Orville shook his head no.

"Seems odd don't you think, especially since you took that film?" Price replied. "Maybe they just think we're all hayseeds and can't be trusted," he continued.

"Maybe," Orville agreed. "What did you see? One of the boys said you had new binoculars."

J.C. Price continued, "Well, I had just bought me a new pair of high-powered glasses, not binoculars, you know, my older ones were giving me vision problems and I needed new ones to watch the employees in the yard and in the parking lots. We've gotten a lot of complaints about cars being messed with and we can't afford to hire a security guard. Anyways, I was wearing them that day."

Price took them off to show Orville.

"Look at 'em, Orville," he told him, "they're a damned good pair. You can see what color slip a woman is wearing with these if her dress is thin enough," he winked at Orville.

Orville took his own glasses off and put his supervisor's glasses up to his eyes and looked out across the hallway. He could see one of his co-workers James putting sugar in his coffee and could even read the headlines of the paper in the break room. *Maybe I should get a new pair of glasses,* he thought to himself.

"Lord, Mr. Price, this is a damned good pair," he said to his boss as he gingerly gave them back.

"Yessiree they are, that's what I told that deputy sheriff I called on the day of the killing. I also told him while I was sitting up there on the northeast corner of the roof waiting for the president to come by I heard the shots ring out. I saw the Governor Connally slump over and I looked up. That's when I saw a man, younger than us, maybe in his mid-thirties running like all get out. With these new glasses, I could tell he was wearing a cream-colored shirt and khaki pants, and his hair was that beatnik style, kinda raggedy and long and dark. He had something in his hand, but I couldn't make out what it was."[243]

Orville was stunned. *Could his boss have seen someone else shooting at the president?* He hesitated for a moment in that thought, then blurted out, "Where did you think the shots came from, Mr. Price?"

"Well hell, Orville, I don't think… I *know* they came from that little park area in front of the train yards by the Triple Underpass. And that's the direction that man was running from. He was running towards the passenger cars in front of the railroad tracks, between that area and the building that they say Lee Harvey Oswald was shooting from. I heard at least four shots, maybe five. Those FBI boys didn't ask me, so I didn't offer. They said I didn't really see anything pertinent. Where do you think they came from?"

"The same place. And I heard four or five shots too," Orville replied.

"I tell ya, Orville, we're a government agency. But if we had screwed up like the police and the FBI and the Secret Service, hell all of 'em, we'd have our asses at the unemployment office or handout line looking for food. And this Warren Commission thing? What a bunch of hogwash! How can they say they're investigating what really happened when they don't even talk to all the key witnesses? Not me, not you and who the hell knows who else! But you didn't hear me say that. I can't very well be kicking the balls of the government that feeds me." He grinned at Orville again. It was a grin of understanding that quickly turned to a frown as he said, "I have an idea Orville, that there's more to this than we know."

* * * * *

Jesse C. Price made a point in 1964 that wouldn't be revealed until several years later. The Warren Commission failed to call several witnesses who observed the assassination. A partial list includes:

1. Orville Nix: took a home movie of the assassination
2. J. C. Price: witnessed the assassination from the Terminal Annex rooftop.
3. Mary E. Woodward: junior reporter for the Dallas Morning News standing with three other friends on the North side of Elm St.
4. Maggie Brown: with Mary E. Woodward
5. Aurelia Lorenzo: with Mary E. Woodward
6. Ann Donaldson: with Mary E. Woodward
7. Wilma Bonds: took a series of colored slides immediately after the shooting showing the grassy knoll area.
8. Mark Bell: shot movie footage showing the knoll
9. Robert Hughes: shot a film showing the Texas School Book Depository sixth floor at the time of the assassination. No gunman is visible.
10. William and Gayle Newman: the iconic couple seen in movies and pictures protecting their two sons from shots, as they stood on Elm Street in front of Zapruder. They made statements, but not in Washington.
11. Ambulance Drivers: Clayton Butler and Eddie Kinsley of the Dudley Hughes Funeral home.[244]

But the most important witness not called until the Warren Commission had almost completed their work? The head of the Dallas Secret Service office: Forrest Sorrels. As a man who had been involved with the arrival of President Kennedy, the parade route, the Zapruder film, and the questioning of Jack Ruby, why did the Warren Commission wait so long to depose him?

The twenty-six volume *Warren Commission Report* is filled with such anomalies as the partial list above relates. In later years, the public would find that not only did the Warren Commission do a slip-shod job of investigating, but vital information was withheld by a government entity: the CIA. Was John F. Kennedy's assassination the result of a conspiracy? No doubt, if not by assassins, it definitely was by our government. Researchers have known this for years. As Henry Hurt wrote in his 1985 book, *Reasonable Doubt:*

> *"... the political impact of Kennedy's death is why the question of his assassination is as important today as it was decades ago — and as it will be*

> *decades hence, and for all the years of this republic. If the atrocity was the result of a conspiracy, the country and its government, even at this hour are subtly threatened by a cunning invisible enemy as politically potent as the most menacing terrorist or superpower. Moreover, the historical integrity of the whole country remains fractured until the questions are answered."*[245]

Who is this cunning, invisible enemy of whom Hurt speaks? A shadow government within our own? A handful of powerful men with a multitude of "yes" men to carry out their deeds? Or is it the same group of people who in 2013 sent drone strikes, tap American citizens' phones and use technology, the Internal Revenue Service, and the media to ferret out the information they desire? Isn't it strange that of the over eleven hundred documents still being withheld during the Obama Administration's tenure that many are IRS files?

If hindsight is truly clearer, then for over fifty years the American people and the world have been lead through a glass darkly.[246] Isn't it time it stopped?

Shouldn't we care?

CHAPTER SEVENTEEN

A FORREST OF RUBIES

"One man can make a difference and every man should try."

Robert F. Kennedy[247]

Like his friend Orville Nix, Forrest Sorrels kept reliving that day… the first day of the longest, four-day weekend he would ever experience. He still couldn't believe what he had seen almost a year ago. How could he ever tell anyone? He kept asking himself the same questions over and over again. The questions kept running through his mind…all the damned questions. *I should have said something. I should have checked it out. I should have jumped out of the car. But how could I? I would have been insinuating that there was more to this and maybe, just maybe some of the people I was working with were involved. I'm not a young man. I should retire soon. My daughter is ill. Oh God, what kind of man have I become?*

Forrest was riding in the lead car about thirty feet ahead of the Presidential limousine on November 22, 1963. The car held four passengers: Forrest was on the right passenger side in the back seat; Dallas Police Chief Jesse Curry was driving and Win Lawson was in the front passenger side. Dallas Sheriff Bill Decker was in the backseat on the driver's side with Forrest.[248] He had been worried all along about the tall buildings on Main Street and Houston, but as the motorcade got closer to the Triple Overpass, Forrest had begun to relax a bit. He had noticed some black men in the Texas School Book Depository windows as the motorcade turned on to Houston Street, but his worries seem to be unfounded. He stared out the right passenger window; the people weren't as crowded down here at Dealey Plaza. As they passed the Texas School Book Depository making the turn onto Elm, something caught his eye. That was the moment… that moment he saw something he couldn't quit thinking about.

There, behind the crescent shaped pergola was what looked like Honest Joe's station wagon. What the hell was it doing there? The chatter in the car distracted him. Win was complaining that we were running late and radioed to the Trade Mart that we were five minutes out.[249] Then…a sharp sound, not a backfire, not a firecracker. It sounded like it came from the terrace.

Then all hell broke loose. It was gunfire! The president shot! Pandemonium! Were his eyes deceiving him, or was that an officer in the terrace area as well? And there was a policeman on the Triple Overpass.[250] He hadn't placed anyone there. Had Chief Curry? Had Sheriff Decker? Before he could ask them the car radio was crackling with transmissions. *Damned politics have no place in protection,* he thought to himself. Sirens went off all around him. The car sped up and motorcycle cops pulled along next to them. Chief Curry told them to drive quickly to Parkland hospital. The president had been shot. He looked behind him as the cars sped away and looked towards the Texas School Book Depository. There were policemen running towards it. He had to get back there, but there he was heading to Parkland. He felt his chest tightening- a pressure he would feel daily until he died. Those four days were as ingrained in Forrest's psyche as deeply as his wedding day; maybe even deeper. He now knew what it meant to be an island. He now knew from that day forward he could never trust another man.

He quietly began his own investigation; one he would never share with anyone, even his family. For the man who cared more about truth and justice than the government for which he worked, Forrest tried to find answers diplomatically without bringing attention to himself or the many agencies he worked with that day.

He knew the FBI had taken charge of the Kennedy assassination the day it happened. J. Edgar Hoover had investigative tentacles spreading all over the country; in fact, the boys from his branch in DC were already complaining about it. The Dallas Police Department and Dallas District Attorney Henry

Wade were knocking on doors in and around Dallas day and night and not just to investigate; some said to intimidate.[251] They had had their tails handed to them and didn't like it one bit. The Texas Rangers, the Dallas Sheriff's Department, hell, even the Army Reserve were all searching for or covering up evidence, and Forrest had to walk gingerly among the minefields that were government agencies. But the one group that Forrest could never get a clear handle on, the group no one ever heard from until it was too late to protect yourself, was the CIA. It was that group that scared him the most.

To anyone who knew Forrest well, his Warren Commission testimony was the first sign that he had more on his mind than memos, blame for inadequate presidential protection and political correctness. He could give a damn which party was in power. He was to have no part in laying the blame on one agency or person. He knew in his heart of hearts there was much more to this murder than the government wanted America to know. He left the Warren Commission crumbs in which to follow his trail of answers to their questions. How did he do that? He mentioned the Honest Joe's Gun and Pawn Shop vehicle not once, but twice. *Twice!* He also mentioned that he had thought he heard gunshots come from the knoll area as he couldn't see the Texas School Book Depository.[252] Why didn't Messrs. Burr W. Griffin, Leon D. Hubert, Jr., Samuel A. Stern, assistant counsel of the President's Commission, and Fred B. Smith, Deputy General Counsel, U.S. Treasury Department, who were all present pick up the crumbs he put down for them to follow in his testimony? Why didn't they ask the right questions? He was on record with testimony two days in a row: once to Hubert and then again to Stern. When Hubert questioned Sorrels about his activities the day Oswald was shot, this was his direct testimony to the Warren Commission:

> *****
>
> **HE COULD GIVE A DAMN WHICH PARTY WAS IN POWER.**
>
> **HE WAS TO HAVE NO PART IN LAYING THE BLAME ON ONE AGENCY OR PERSON.**
>
> **HE KNEW IN HIS HEART OF HEARTS THERE WAS MUCH MORE TO THIS MURDER THAN THE GOVERNMENT WANTED AMERICA TO KNOW.**

> *I told him I had seen Honest Joe, who is a Jewish merchant there, who operates a second-hand loan pawn shop, so to speak, specializing in tools, on Elm Street, and who is more or less known in the area because of the fact that he takes advantage of any opportunity to get free advertising. He at that time had an Edsel car, which is somewhat a rarity now, all painted up with "Honest Joe" on there. He wears jackets with "Honest Joe" on the back. He gets writeups in the paper, free advertising about different things he loans money on, like artificial limbs and things like that. And I had noticed Honest Joe across the street when I was looking out of Chief Batchelor's office.*

So I remarked to Jack Ruby, I said, "I just saw Honest Joe across the street over there, and I know a number of Jewish merchants here that you know."

And Ruby said, "That is good enough for me. What is it you want to know?"

And I said these two words, "Jack---why? "He said, "When this thing happened"-- referring to the assassination that he was in a newspaper office placing an ad for his business. That when he heard about the assassination, he had canceled his ad and had closed his business, and he had not done any business for 3 days. That he had been grieving about this thing. That on the ...

HUBERT: *Did he at that time, the first interview, indicate anything, or say anything which would indicate what his motive or reason for his act was?*

SORRELS: *Yes; and I might say that it was at that time that I found out his name was Ruby in place of Rubin, and he informed me his name had formerly been Rubinstein, and that he had had his name changed in Dallas. I asked him--after I identified myself, I told him I would like to ask him some questions.*

He said, "For newspapers or magazines?" I said, "No; for myself."

He appeared to be considering whether or not he was going to answer my questions, and I told him that I had just come from the third floor, and had been looking out of the window, and that Friday night he had gone to the synagogue and had heard a eulogy on the President. That his sister had recently been operated on, and that she has been hysterical. That when he saw that Mrs. Kennedy was going to have to appear for the trial, he thought to himself, why should she have to go through this ordeal for this no-good so-and-so.

HUBERT: *Did he use any words or did he say "no-good so-and-so"?*

SORRELS: *He used the word "son-of-a-bitch," as I recall.*

HUBERT: *All right.*

SORRELS: *That he had heard about the letter to little Caroline, as I recall he mentioned. That he had been to the Western Union office to send a telegram, and that he guessed he had worked himself into a state of insanity to where he had to do it. And to use his words after that, "I guess I just had to show the world that a Jew has guts."*[253]

When Stern questioned Sorrels about his interview with Oswald, the last interview Oswald would give, Forrest knew there were concerns about how Jack Ruby had gotten into the Dallas Police building. He didn't want to implicate, but he wanted it on the record as to what he saw. Again his direct testimony the next day to Mr. Stern:

STERN: *And then what happened?*

SORRELS: *He was told that they were going to move him to the county jail, and he requested that he be permitted to get a shirt out of his--the clothes that had* *been brought in, that belonged to him, because the shirt he was wearing at the time he had been apprehended was taken, apparently for laboratory examination. And so Captain Fritz sent and got his clothes and, as I recall it, he selected a dark colored kind of a sweater type shirt, as I recall it. And then he was taken out, and, at that time, as I recall it, Inspector Kelley and I left and went up to---I say up---down the hall to the executive office area of the police department, and to the office of Deputy Chief Batchelor.*

And we remained in that vicinity. I looked out the window, and saw the people across the street, on Commerce Street, people were waiting there. And I saw an individual that I know by the name of Ruby Goldstein, who is known as Honest Joe, that has a second-hand tool and pawnshop down on Elm Street, and everyone around there knows him. He was leaning on the car looking over in the direction of the ramp there at the police station. And we were just waiting around there. And for a few minutes I was talking to one of the police officers that was on duty up there in that area. And he had made the remark, "talking about open windows, I see one open across the street over there" at a building across the street.

I looked over there. I didn't see any activity at the window. And we had walked out into the reception area of the executive office of the Chief of Police there when this same police officer said that he just heard that Oswald had got shot in the stomach in the basement by Jack Rubin, as I understood at that time, R-u-b-i-n--who was supposed to run a night club. Inspector Kelley and I then went just as hurriedly as we could to the basement.

STERN: *As I understand it, Mr. Sorrels, you covered all the relevant information from this point of time on with Mr. Hubert yesterday.*

SORRELS: *Yes. And actually back just a little bit.*[254]

The Honest Joe's Gun and Pawn Shop vehicle sighting was an important one, at least to Forrest Sorrels. To Forrest, it showed that the friendly Rubin Goldstein may have information about the assassination. Of what sort he did not yet know. But that the Honest Joe's Edsel was seen on the day of the assassination, and that Forrest saw Rubin Goldstein in the same car on the ramp entrance of the Dallas Police Department where Jack Ruby entered the day Lee Harvey Oswald was shot could not have been coincidental. He determined to interview the man who knew very well.

Rubin Goldstein, also called 'Ruby' the owner of Honest Joe's Gun and Pawn Shop, was a Jewish merchant who had moved from New York to Dallas in 1931.[255] He and his brothers David and Isaac opened up pawn businesses along Elm Street. His pawn shop catered to poor blacks and whites who would pawn anything from false teeth to prosthetic arms for quick cash.[256] Also, several Dallas Police officers and sheriff's frequented his business, as well as celebrities like Sammy Davis Jr. and Tony Curtis. Honest Joe was also a friend of Jack Ruby, who frequented Honest Joe's often. In later years, Honest Joe would place a picture of Jack Ruby in his store for posterity. When Jack Ruby died, Goldstein was an appraiser for his estate as he was familiar with the .38 revolver Ruby used to shoot Oswald.[257]

Forrest knew of Goldstein from his frequent abuse of the Texas Blue Laws. The Texas Blue Law was a law in force at the time to prevent businesses from being open every Sunday. Goldstein, the ever clever pawnbroker, found ways to circumvent the law, and one way was by buying a shack next to his shop so he could bypass the Blue Law[258] and be open on consecutive Sundays. He called the shack, 'Truthful Joe's'.[259] Forrest had talked to Ruby Goldstein often. He even went to Honest Joe's the day of JFK's assassination and asked to see a Mannlicher-Carcano rifle; one of the two weapons purported to have been used by Oswald. Goldstein happily showed him one, thereby affirming to Forrest that Oswald could have gotten the rifle from Honest Joe's.[260] Goldstein also owned an Edsel station wagon covered with advertising signs and with a nonfunctional submachine gun on the hood. He would often drive downtown in the vehicle as a way to advertise. The submachine gun on the hood was as distinctive as Goldstein; that's why Forrest had recognized it that day in Dallas. It was the only car on the street. He wasn't surprised that the Dallas Police had allowed him access to the motorcade route that day: everyone knew Honest Joe liked to advertise. But that he was there again on November 24th, 1963 made Forrest suspicious. Why wasn't it suspicious to the Warren Commission? Or was this just one more thing they needed to cover up from the American people. The Warren Commission never interviewed Rubin Goldstein and no record has been found of any agency interviewing him after the assassination. The only researcher to interview him was Jones Harris.

It has been well-documented that both the CIA and the FBI failed to inform the commission about their various arrangements with the Mafia, another prime suspect in Kennedy's killing for conspiracy realists. They considerably underplayed Oswald killer Jack Ruby's organized crime ties. "The evidence does not establish a significant link," the commission asserted, but in fact, Ruby was in frequent contact with mobsters, both Jewish and Italian.[261] According to the House Select Committee on Assassinations report, Ruby was casually employed as a provisional criminal informant in regards to those criminal organizations.[262]

Why didn't the Warren Commission enrobe itself in democracy? There was more than enough money to give them everything they needed to get to the bottom of this travesty. Why wasn't honesty upheld? The moral, circumstantial, emotional, and intellectual aspects of the case should have been transparent to anyone reading the final report. During the quick formation of the Warren Commission, several key witnesses were still alive to give testimony. Today that isn't so and vital evidence and testimony has been lost. Unfortunately, in 1964 there was an agenda: and that agenda was to protect the government under the guise of letting the nation heal. With the many mistakes the Warren Commission made in their findings, there would be no way for the nation to heal; the wound would be perpetually opened with each new lie.

Forrest wasn't the only one to see the vehicle that day. Jones Harris saw it in the enlarged frame he had gotten from the camera original Orville Nix film… the one from UPI.[263] The studies he and his friend Bernie Hoffman made with cutting-edge investigative tools would not be seen by the American public until 1965, and even then the lies were still being told. This time the lies would be told by ITEK, a CIA operated photographic lab where Maurice Schonfeld took the Nix film to be properly analyzed.[264]

CHAPTER EIGHTEEN

OF SHADOWS: IN THE NIX FILM, IN THE MIND AND THE GOVERNMENT

"Those who are able to see beyond the shadows and lies of their culture will never be understood let alone believed by the masses."

Plato[265]

In the early versions of the Nix film, there is a car seen in the shadows next to the pergola, between the wooden stockade fence and the low concrete wall. It is Honest Joe's vehicle in plain view. It remains there throughout the entire length of the film.

Jean Hill and one other witness on the north side of Elm Street, a US Marine veteran named A.J. Millican, gave testimony that they had seen the Honest Joe wagon with cardboard-covered windows driving around Dealey Plaza supposedly for advertising purposes before the arrival of the presidential motorcade. Millican gave his testimony to the Dallas Police, and like Orville Nix, he was not called before the Warren Commission.

Jean Hill *did* testify before the Warren Commission, though no mention of the Honest Joe's truck was made. It *would* come later though, during her interview with Mark Lane in *Rush to Judgment* and in an interview conducted by the FBI on March 23, 1964. The report reads:

"Jean again described wanting to take photos and conversing with a policeman near the TSBD entrance. She had noticed a vehicle with "Honest Joe's Pawn Shop" printed on its side, with cardboard windows circling the area, but was told by the policeman that he had been permitted to drive near or through the motorcade route. In regard to the assassination itself, Jean described calling to the President while Mary (Moorman) prepared to take a photo, seemingly not aware that he had already been hit once or possibly twice."[266]

Jean later told Jones Harris that she and her friend Mary Moorman were at the parade to take pictures of their motorcycle policemen boyfriends. This seems strange as Mrs. Hill was married, though Moorman, at the time was not. Harris told the author, "When little Jean Hill told me that story, the motorcycle patrolman she was there to see (J. B. Martin) and was at the interview told her "to never mention publically seeing that car again."[267]

Over the years, whether by aging memory or for some other reason, some of Jean Hill's testimony changed. In fact, she verified the comments she made to author Anthony Summers in his book, *Conspiracy* in regards to her reason for being at the parade:

"...she was paying special attention to the motorcade because one of the police outriders was her boyfriend of the moment. She was sure there were more than three shots." Summers quoted her as adding: "I heard four to six shots, and I'm pretty used to guns. They weren't echoes or anything like that. They were different guns that were being fired."[268]

In 1991 at a conference held in Dallas and in an interview for the *Dallas Morning News*, Hill again talked about the motorcycle policemen whose name was later to be cited as J.B. Martin:

'Well, actually there were a couple (of) cute motorcycle officers that we were interested in, and they couldn't see us if we were in a crowd,' she said.[269]

Though parts of her story changed over the years as to what she did that dreadful day, what didn't change was that she had obviously heeded her policeman boyfriend's advice. She never again mentioned the Honest Joe's sighting that day.

As Hill stated, the Dallas police apparently gave Honest Joe permission to drive behind the pergola, as he was known as the "Mayor of Elm Street", but they waved away other cars from driving into the area.[270]

Though Hill and Millican are the only two witnesses on official record as seeing the Honest Joe's Edsel that day, several people had. His future son-in-law, Marvin Levin, remembers seeing it drive ahead of the presidential parade about twenty minutes beforehand.[271] In fact, when Rubin Goldstein died, his obituary stated "he was part of the presidential motorcade."[272]

Honest Joe's wagon was an Edsel station wagon. It had a mock machine gun mounted on the roof, and Honest Joe's Pawnshop was painted on its sides.[273] Jones Harris related to this author that he has in his possession, a large blown up frame from the camera original Nix film in which the vehicle is visible all through the seven seconds or so of the film; during the frontal head shot to the President, Jackie's climb on the trunk of the car, Clint Hill's run and climb onto the trunk of the limousine, and the acceleration of the car onto the underpass. Generational copies of the Nix film do not show this car. Some believe the Bell film also shows a glimpse of this vehicle on the grassy knoll.[274] Could the Nix film be altered? Could it have been altered so hurriedly that the technicians didn't have time to alter other vital areas? The vehicle Harris sees is prominent. This was not a small vehicle; it was a large and very noticeable one. In fact, the Edsel station wagons were often transformed into use for ambulances; they were that roomy.

In early 1965, armed with the Jean Hill interview and the blow up of the Nix frame, Jones Harris showed Burt Reinhardt and Maurice Schonfeld of UPI his discovery of what he thought suspicious in the Nix film.

"There's nothing there," Reinhardt told Harris. "The Nix film is the runt of the litter."[275]

But not everyone agreed with Reinhardt. As Schonfeld wrote:

> *Word spread fast about Harris's theory of the Nix film. A European journalist wrote an article about a firing from the knoll. Other assassination buffs began to inquire about the film. CBS came over to view it. Nobody knew how to handle the story; nobody wanted to assume the cost of further investigation.*[276]

Schonfeld, eager to make more money and fame, decided to take it to the cutting-edge photographic lab of ITEK. ITEK was a secretive Massachusetts maker of acrial photo gear. Their only customer? The CIA. ITEK was founded in 1957 with seed money from Laurance Rockefeller, that famous family's, most adventurous, venture capitalist. The company's name was a phonetic contraction of "information technology," the sector of the economy that prescient analysts and investors foresaw as America's future.[277] ITEK benefited enormously from their optimism. In just three months, its payroll burgeoned from a handful of executives to over a hundred scientists, engineers, and technicians. After only a year, its revenues and profits soared into the millions. It went public after less than two years in operation, and within 18 months of the initial offering, the price of a share of its stock shot up from $2 to over $200. "ITEK was one of the great glamour stocks on Wall

Street," Lewis writes.[278] "At its peak, ITEK's fame rivaled the notoriety, and the price-to-earnings ratio, of the top Internet stocks of the great NASDAQ bubble of the late 1990s."[279]

ITEK was manufacturing the world's most sophisticated satellite reconnaissance cameras, and the information these cameras provided about Soviet missiles and military activity was critical to U.S. security. So was ITEK. It was contracted by the CIA to help develop the CIA's Project Corona a spy satellite used for national security purposes.[280] Later, ITEK ended up building cameras for the Apollo and Viking space missions, as well as the defective Hubble space telescope mirror. Eventually they ended up building the DB-110 reconnaissance pod. But in 1965, they studied the images Jones Harris saw in the Nix Film for free.

The president of ITEK at that time was Frank Lindsay; the Frank Lindsay of Kim Philby spying fame.[281] Philby was a high ranking, British Intelligence agent who worked as a double agent. He defected to the Soviet Union in 1963. In an interview from Moscow in 1967, Philby claimed his greatest accomplishment was foiling the CIA's Albanian operation. He states in the *Izvestia* interview:

> *As Philby told it, in 1951, shortly after Tito had broken with the Soviet Union, thus geographically cutting Albania off from the rest of the Communist world, the CIA arranged to airdrop anti-Communist Albanians into the mountains of their home country to lead a counterrevolution. Before the drop, the CIA checked out the operation with the great British and anti-Communist spy. From that moment on, the air drop was, of course, a disaster. According to Philby, the CIA agent in charge of the Albanian operation was named Franklin T. Lindsay.*[282]

*****

...AND HE DEFINITELY DIDN'T WANT TO LOOK LIKE A CRAZY CONSPIRACY THEORIST, EVEN IF IT MEANT FINDING ANOTHER SHOOTER ON THE KNOLL. TO ENSURE THAT DIDN'T HAPPEN, HE WROTE OF HIS EXPERIENCE.

How odd that Schonfeld took the Nix film to a CIA company to decipher the shadows on the grassy knoll. Schonfeld swears it was coincidental, though he knew Lindsay's assistant and Schonfeld's contact Howard Sprague worked for the CIA. The fact is, Schonfeld never gave the Nix film the credence it deserved. He just wanted fast fame and fast money for UPI at the least possible expense of time or money…and he definitely didn't want to look like a crazy conspiracy theorist, even if it meant finding another shooter on the knoll. To ensure that didn't happen, he wrote of his experience. In an epilogue to an original essay he wrote concerning UPI's work with the Nix film, Schonfeld wrote:

Of course! I thought. Who else but a former CIA man would head a company 60 percent of whose business came from the government, much of it consisting of analysis of aerial photographs shot for intelligence purposes? Perhaps, then, ITEK's report might not be considered conclusive—at least by those who saw a CIA conspiracy behind every grisly happening anywhere in the world. Of course, ITEK had published, and widely distributed, its report, so that if the results had been fudged, other scientists would have caught it. On the other hand, how many people were there with the scientific ability to challenge ITEK's report—and with no links to the CIA?

Among the people I told my story on myself to was Richard Sprague, one of the most dedicated investigators of the Kennedy assassination—and no, not related to ITEK's Howard Sprague. It was, perhaps, inevitable that Richard Sprague would make contact with assassination buff Jones Harris. Perhaps it was equally inevitable that—given Watergate and the question of whether agents had assassinated (or had tried to assassinate) Fidel Castro and other political leaders—Harris would conclude that UPI and ITEK had engaged in a conspiracy to destroy his theory and cover up the facts of the assassination. In the summer of 1973 he informed Reinhardt and me that he had come to just this conclusion.

The art of electronic analysis had advanced in the more than six years that had elapsed since ITEK had completed its study. So I decided to try one more investigation, this time with a California company called Image Transform.

At this point, in late August 1973, the producers of the film Executive Action inquired about the use of the Nix film. I flew out to the Coast, made a deal—the film would be used only as stock shots, not as evidence of Harris' theory—and then went out to Image Transform's Los Angeles laboratories. There I learned that commercial apparatus could do little to enhance the quality of the Nix film. A technician suggested that, as a last resort, I should take the film to Dr. Kenneth Castleman, a scientist at the California Institute of Technology at Pasadena.

I took a taxi to Pasadena. Dr. Castleman and I viewed the film. He saw the shape. He suggested that more sophisticated digital computer techniques developed by Caltech to reconstruct lunar photographs could, perhaps, solve the riddle of the grassy knoll shadow. He found an interested Caltech graduate student, James Latimer, who did the computer image processing as a class project in a course on digital image processing. The processed images were then analyzed by Alan Gillespie, of Caltech's Jet Propulsion Laboratory.

Fifteen months went by. In February 1975 I received a report marked "PRELIMINARY FOR INFORMATION ONLY." The report concluded:

In this analysis the Nix film fails to support strongly "the grassy knoll assassin" theory. ***No errors were found in the ITEK report and its conclusions remain the most likely. A study of the area between the stairs and the [pergola] found no new evidence of assassins there. However, in the light of the***

> ***poor image quality and the availability of suitable hiding places, a grassy knoll assassin cannot positively be ruled out.***
>
> *The report also states that it is "remotely possible" that certain features are "due to an assassin immediately behind the wall who moved to his right, as Nix moved...." After receiving this report, which I believed to be the nearest thing to a conclusive answer about the film, I learned that assassination buffs have detected three assassins—two of who supposedly bear a resemblance to Watergate figures E. Howard Hunt and Frank Sturgis—in the Nix film, this time on the steps leading down from the knoll. Now Castleman and Gillespie have those frames and this whole this may start up again. God forbid."*[283]

The Caltech findings would have been enough for an interested person to have the Nix film examined further, but Schonfeld didn't. Schonfeld then placed the Nix film back into the safety deposit box at Chase Manhattan Bank never to see it again and never to care. Why, after ITEK offered to analyze the film for free did he not have them look at the trajectory of the head shot like ITEK had with the Zapruder film? Did Schonfeld and Reinhardt know so little about the assassination that they were only interested in a front page news story? Wouldn't an analysis of where the bullet came from be just as profitable and newsworthy for UPI?

Apparently not.

Schonfeld and Reinhardt had produced the documentary, *Four Days in November* that showcased their 'runt films' the Nix and Muchmore films. Though it won an Academy Award for Best Documentary for the director, David Wolper, it was never something Schonfeld bragged about.[284] He was meant for bigger things than purchasing the Nix film and breaching the contract, as well as misplacing the film. He later became the founder of the Food Network after founding, along with Burt Reinhardt and Ted Turner, CNN.[285] What Schonfeld failed to reveal to the public was that ITEK was only given 35mm enlarged black and white copies of selected frames from the Nix film. As Richard Sprague states in his book, "The great amount of detail is lost in going from 8mm to 35mm black and white. UPI only gave ITEK carefully chosen frames from the Nix film that did not show the gunman on the knoll."[286]

Jones Harris wasn't convinced of the ITEK findings. He was sure that the Nix film showed a shooter leaning on or in front of an Edsel with the Honest Joe's writing plainly in view in front of the pergola. He has the enlarged photo to prove it, even today. He believed that the ITEK Corporation, under CIA orders, had removed or smudged the writing on the Edsel so as to make it look like shadows.[287] But if the Honest Joe's signage had been removed, why not remove the image of the shooter?

Coincidentally, several years later, in 1975, an article written about UPI, the Nix film, ITEK, and Jones Harris mentioned that although the men viewing the film all saw 'a shooter leaning against a car' nothing more was mentioned of it as "Frank Lindsay insisted that UPI must prioritize to delay publication of the results, if the shadow proved to be a man, until he had a chance to inform his friends Ted and Bob Kennedy. The stipulation reflected the shared feeling that shape was more than a shadow."[288]

Why did Schonfeld stop there? Was it insistence by CIA and now ITEK president Frank Lindsay? Was proclaiming the figure on the knoll nothing more than shadows another form of propaganda to keep the public in the dark about a second gunman?

Was there evidence of another shooter in that area that day? Could they have been "fake authorities?" According to FBI and Warren Commission testimony, there were plenty. For instance, Dallas Police Department officer J. M. Smith encountered what he described as a "Secret Service Agent" behind the picket fence atop the grassy knoll.[289] He explains to Mr. Leibeler of the Warren Commission that:

> **SMITH:** *I got to make this statement too. I felt awfully silly, but after the shot, and this woman (who had told him they were shooting from the bushes), I pulled my pistol from my holster, and I thought, this is silly. I don't know who I am looking for and put it back. Just as I did, he showed me that he was a Secret Service Agent.*
>
> **LIEBELER:** *Did you accost this man?*
>
> **SMITH:** *Well, he saw me coming with my pistol and right away he showed me who he was.*[290]

Officer Smith wasn't the only official witness that saw 'men in authority' in the area after the shooting, DPD Officer D.V. Harkness saw men who identified themselves as Secret Service agents as well.

> **BELIN:** *Then you went around to the back of the building? (the TSBD)*
>
> **HARKNESS:** *Yes, sir.*
>
> **BELIN:** *Was anyone around in the back when you got there?*
>
> **HARKNESS:** *There were some Secret Service Agents there. I didn't get them identified. They told me they were the Secret Service.*[291]

Of course Officer Harkness would believe there were Secret Service men there. People were running all over the area. The 35th President of the world's greatest nation had just been shot. Why wouldn't he think that all law-enforcement personnel in Dallas that day were trying to find who killed the president? He himself had just radioed to his fellow law officers to seal the Texas School Book Depository off.

In later years, another motorcycle officer, Bobby Hargis, can be heard in a taped conversation admitting to seeing a policeman on the knoll that day. This tape was made many years after the assassination after Hargis had retired from the Dallas Police Department. Jones Harris has a copy of this recording.

Another witness also reported encountering a man who displayed a badge and identified himself as a Secret Service agent. But according to Secret Service Chief James Rowley and agents at the scene, all Secret Service personnel stayed with the motorcade, as required by regulations, and none was stationed in the railroad parking lot [behind the grassy knoll]. It thus appeared that someone was carrying fraudulent Secret Service credentials - of no perceptible use to anyone but an escaping assassin.[292]

The Warren Commission's findings though, were that all the Secret Service, FBI and DPD personnel were accounted for during the motorcade and no officers were on the knoll area or at the Texas School Book Depository. Malcolm Summers disputes this point.

Summers, an eye-witness who can be seen in the Nix and Zapruder films also encountered a man on the knoll immediately after the assassination. Summers states in Jack Anderson's interview:

> *I ran across the--Elm Street to right there toward the knoll. It was there [pointing to a spot on the knoll]--and we were stopped by a man in a suit and he had an overcoat--over his arm and he, he, I saw a gun under that overcoat. And he--his comment was, "Don't y'all come up here any further, you could get shot, or killed," one of those words. A few months later, they told me they didn't have an FBI man in that area. If they didn't have anybody, it's a good question who it was.*[293]

Many years later, Summers was interviewed by Houston Police sketch artist, Lois Gibson. After working with her many hours, he was able to describe enough detail that she sketched a picture of the man Summers said he saw on the knoll. [294]

The questions about gunmen on the knoll and the images in the Nix film didn't stop with ITEK's findings or the *Warren Commission Report*, in fact, they became more pronounced. Orville was receiving phone calls daily and, because UPI was still using his name when the contract he had signed stated it wouldn't, not all the phone calls to his home were reporters or investigators. Seeing how alarmed Orville would become after answering several phone calls a night before he went to work, Ella decided to start answering the phone to shield her husband and allow him to rest.

Orville had become more and more anxious as the months passed, and by 1966 he was smoking even more than he had in the past. Before the threatening phone calls, strange hang-ups and even stranger questions he was asked, he had thought of offering his camera as a commercial idea to the Keystone Camera Company. He had his daughter-in-law Elaine write a letter to the company offering his services and his camera.[295] Keystone politely declined claiming, "The Assassination was too delicate and they didn't want their camera forever associated with the event." It seemed no one was interested in his film, though he felt deeply that it was more important than people thought. He became convinced of the fact when his son also began receiving threatening phone calls. Why would he be threatened if there wasn't something more to the film? Were people just that crazy? And why would his film be a threat? If Lee Harvey Oswald had acted alone, like the Warren Commission said, then his film shouldn't be a problem to anyone. It would be a "nuisance" as *Life* magazine had told him. His film only showed the Texas School Book Depository the next morning; not the day of the assassination. Why was he getting these phone calls?

Though he was convinced of the importance of his film, he also became worried. He didn't want anything happening to his family. One of the latest phone calls was from a man with a foreign accent who told him "to move, your family isn't safe," and immediately hung up before Orville could question him. But the next phone call was from some promoter wanting to put his interview on a vinyl record. There were calls from people writing books, people who were psychics, and people who were just plain mean.

It seems many people were readers of Penn Jones's articles, and his most popular one at that time was of the mysterious deaths. Penn Jones had begun to make a record of witnesses who were mysteriously killed after the assassination and had even called Orville to tell him to "watch himself." Before the assassination, Orville would have laughed Penn's warning off, but now he wasn't so sure. Because of the many strange phone calls, sometimes he chose not to answer the phone at all: a huge change of routine for a man who loved new technology and had never gotten over his amazement at having a phone in his home at all. Growing up poor, Orville's family had never had a phone much less a television; so his movie camera, his television, and his phone were sources of huge delight.

Until the day of the assassination.

Several weeks later, Ella answered a call that she would never forget; and spoke of it until she died. When she answered the phone, the person, a young man with what she thought was a Spanish accent, said in a stern yet authoritative voice, "Ma'am, we know who you are. We know your husband took a film. Do not show it to anyone. Do not talk to the newspapers. Do not talk to the police. Just be quiet and you and your grandchildren will be safe." Ella had hardly ever spoken of her husband's film at all, not even to her co-workers at Wyatt's Cafeteria. But after that phone call, she became cautious of strangers and reporters who asked for interviews from that moment on. Orville had tried to convince her that the calls were nothing more than 'crank calls from touched people' but Ella wasn't convinced.

"Orville, I don't think you should talk to anyone of these news people anymore, it's just not safe. The only way they know you is from the TV or the government."

"Well, Ella, I told you, I think my film is important. People ask me about it every day. Besides, I told that Yankee lawyer, Mark Lane, I would do an interview with him. My boss, Mr. Price, is doing one too. He's not scared, so why should I be? We wouldn't do anything to hurt the government, we work for it!"

*****

MA'AM, WE KNOW WHO YOU ARE. WE KNOW YOUR HUSBAND TOOK A FILM. DO NOT SHOW IT TO ANYONE. DO NOT TALK TO THE NEWSPAPERS. DO NOT TALK TO THE POLICE. JUST BE QUIET AND YOU AND YOUR GRANDCHILDREN WILL BE SAFE.

"Dear Lord, Orville, that's the point! What if someone in the government is trying to scare you? What if one of those FBI guys told someone something? What if you end up on that Jones man's strange death list? I don't like reporters. I can't think of it happening to you. I can't worry about my grandchildren. They killed the president, Orville, they can certainly kill you!" Ella broke into tears.

Orville gathered her in his arms and patted her back. "Ella, Ella, I wouldn't do anything to hurt you or them young'uns. You have to know that. If I'm not worried, you shouldn't be. There, there, stop crying. I promise I won't do any more interviews. Just this one I promised to that lawyer. Okay?"

If you say so, Orville," she said worriedly, "But if you're going to go ahead and do it, then make him come to our house. I don't want you out in the open where someone could do to you what they did to President Kennedy. Promise me?"

Orville winked at his concerned wife and smiled, “I promise, Ella.” But in his heart, he knew she might be right.

The next week Mark Lane and his camera crew came to their home. The interview Lane had with Nix would be on vinyl, in his book, and in his movie, all entitled *Rush to Judgment*.[296] In later years, many of the witnesses he interviewed would proclaim that Lane changed their words and edited out key phrases and manipulated answers. Orville Nix never made that claim, though he did claim Lane was unthoughtful and brash. At the end of the interview, as the cameraman moved the cumbersome equipment through the kitchen to the living room, he accidentally marred Ella’s kitchen wall, leaving a large dark mark. Ella quietly grabbed her weapon of choice, a broom and angrily chased the cameraman and Mark Lane out of her house. That was the last time Mark Lane spoke with Orville Nix. It would be the next to last interview Orville would ever give on camera.

CHAPTER NINETEEN

FIRST GENERATION JFK RESEARCH AND THE SEARCH FOR TRUTH

"Keep up your courage."

John F. Kennedy
On a note written to the mother of a badly burned child in the hospital the night his infant son Patrick died.[297]

Once the conspiracy theories began, they never stopped. Respected researchers from all walks of life like Mary Ferrell, Josiah Thompson, Jones Harris, R.B. Cutler, Penn Jones, Jay Epstein, Jim Marrs, David Lifton, Sylvia Meagher, Harold Weisberg, and Robert Groden became professors of the JFK Conspiracy University that quickly garnered students from all over the world. The Nix film was always key evidence in their theories.

Jack White, a former Navy officer and journalism graduate from Texas Christian University, was one of the first JFK assassination researchers and reporters to follow the findings of Jones Harris.[298] White was a vested conspiracy expert who served as a photographic consultant for the House Select Committee on Assassinations. In his later years, he was vilified by former friends who once believed in the same theories he did, and he was often criticized for embracing any theory he found conceivable. The media had their turn at him as well, branding his theories 'fiction.' White is best known for his belief that the backyard photos of Lee Harvey Oswald were doctored; an argument that is still carried on many JFK discussion forums and conferences. Ironically, a signed copy of this same backyard photo was found in George de Mohrenschildt's belongings in later years.

In regards to the Nix film, White had seen Harris's work and had done much work on another theory he and Sixth Floor Museum curator Gary Mack called, "The Badgeman Image"; an image which they could see in the Moorman photograph.[299] They both believed it showed a man wearing a police uniform and brandishing a weapon that looked to be firing at the moment of the fatal head shot. White and Mack had wondered if the Nix film would verify their findings. Ultimately it did not, but ever the believer in a shooter from the knoll theory, and never thoroughly convinced of ITEK's findings, he wrote the following on a JFK Conspiracy forum several months before he died regarding a gunman on the knoll and Honest Joe's vehicle:

> *Suspend your disbelief for a moment. Suppose there was a car in that location. It is plainly seen in the Nix film. Suppose that the car was connected to the assassination. Suppose the car was the HONEST JOE PAWN SHOP vehicle as some researchers believe, and it was there to supply/hide guns. Suppose retouchers replaced the car with tree foliage, when there is no tree there but railroad tracks. There was testimony that the Honest Joe vehicle drove into the parking lot. OK. Now go back to believing whatever you want.*[300]

Jack White never pushed his views on anyone though he was stalwart in his beliefs and unlike other researchers, apologized when his theories were found to be unfounded.

Other photographs suggested there was a knoll shooter. Mary Moorman took her famous Polaroid at the moment of the fatal head shot. Many of the Dealey Plaza witnesses believed at least one shot came from the Grassy Knoll, which can be seen in her photo.

Closer inspection of the photo shows what appears to bc a man's head looking over the area Orville Nix called the 'stockade fence' on the Grassy Knoll. This figure is at the spot where Sam Holland and six fellow railroad workers observed a puff of smoke where Ed Hoffman saw a man fire a shot at the President, where Lee Bowers noted "some commotion", and where the House Select Committee on Assassinations determined a second gunman fired a high-powered rifle.

Or could it have been a long-barreled revolver?

Films taken in Dealey Plaza shortly after the assassination show police and spectators collectively running towards that same corner of the stockade fence mentioned by the HSCA and Orville Nix. Dallas Police Officer Joe Smith ran to that area after a woman told him "they were shooting the president from the bushes."[301] As he drew his gun, he met a man showing Secret Service credentials as he raised his arms. Officer Smith also claims that he could smell the "...lingering smell of gunpowder...." around the stockade fence.

Two railroad employees who witnessed the assassination from their position atop the Triple Overpass, Sam Holland and James Simmons, raced to the corner of the stockade fence. They found hundreds of footprints in the mud at the exact location of the figure in Mary Moorman's photo. They were interviewed by author Josiah Thompson and even drew a sketch of what they saw.[302] There was mud on the bumper of a station wagon, as if someone had either used it wipe his feet clean, or stood on it to look over the fence. Testimonies of these eye-witnesses was dismissed by the Warren Commission or never studied further. Why?

The 'Classic Gunman' image that Jones Harris and Jack White saw in the Nix film was debunked; not only by ITEK and Los Alamos Scientific Photographic Labs, but by the House Select Committee on Assassinations. Their findings on the Nix film 'Classic Gunman' image stated:

> *...the most probable explanation is that the image is a chance pattern of sunlight on the structure behind the retaining wall. The Panel's conclusion was strengthened by an observation at the Aerospace Corp. that in one frame the "right arm" of the object disappears, only to reappear in the next frame. Such behavior would be virtually impossible for a person, but is conceivable for tree branches casting a shadow pattern on a wall.*[303]

This finding in 1978 didn't stop a documentary being made ten years later that included the Nix film revealing a gunman on the knoll among other conspiracy questions. The documentary was called, *The Day the Dream Died* and aired in Europe.[304] It was filled with distortions and misinformation but it did encourage yet another generation of viewers who knew nothing of the Nix Film to begin questioning the American government again. It also inspired American film director Oliver Stone.

It hadn't stopped Jones Harris either. Still believing in all the testimony he had gathered through personally financed interviews, Harris went to Honest Joe's Pawn Shop to interview Rubin Goldstein. No 'on the record' interview had ever been made with Goldstein. Forrest Sorrels never documented his visit with Rubin Goldstein, though Goldstein's son remembers the visit.[305]

Harris had come from New York and stayed in Dallas with a friend of his, a member of the Masons, who had told him to be very careful as "people disappeared in Deep Ellum all the time." [306] Deep Ellum, as is still called today, is a variation on the street name of 'Elm.' It is the Uptown section of

Dallas today, but in the early 1960s, it was the area of speak easys, pawn shops, and dive motels.

Harris heeded his warning. He went to meet Rubin Goldstein unannounced but before he could begin the interview, Goldstein had to deal with a customer. So Harris began to look around the shop. As he walked towards the back, there he saw on a clothes tree several Dallas Police Department trousers, shirts, and even a white motorcycle helmet. Knowing it was illegal for any pawn shop to sell police uniforms, Harris immediately left without obtaining an interview.[307] Seeing the police clothes was enough for him to know that this wasn't a place in which he should be standing. In later years, another witness, Beverly Oliver, the alleged 'Babushka Lady' (so named because of the scarf she's seen wearing the day of the assassination) offered more to the Honest Joe sighting, though her testimony hasn't always been the most credible.[308] Jones Harris related to Adele Edisen:

According to Beverly Oliver, she said she ran up to the grassy knoll after the shooting and saw "Geneva White's husband there." He was dressed in a dark shirt, no hat, and policeman's trousers and with no gun - pistol. That would be Roscoe White who had been recently hired (in October of 1963) by the Dallas Police Department as a photographer and clerk. He was not yet a policeman, but was in training to become one, and did in 1964. He had no legal right to wear a police uniform, but his getup very much resembled a policeman's uniform. He could have obtained his costume from Honest Joe who bought used uniforms from policemen who were retiring or quitting. Roscoe White, a former Marine, was an expert gunman and is known to have practiced shooting, according to his son, Ricky. It is believed that he was also connected to the CIA, and his proximity to the location of the Honest Joe wagon on the grassy knoll is mighty suspicious.[309]

Oliver's statement reinforces the uniforms Jones Harris saw in Honest Joe's Gun & Pawn Shop. Unfortunately, as the years pass, memories become foggy; the attention some people get from the media is intoxicating, thereby lending fragile egos the impetus to embellish and then, some witnesses are caught in outright lies.[310]

In later years, researcher Dave Perry would find the Roscoe White story bogus, discovering that Roscoe White was in North Dallas at the time of the Assassination.[311] Still, many witnesses claim that Roscoe White was on the grassy knoll. Roscoe White's son, Rickey White said in 1990, that his father was the second gunman on the grassy knoll. Many thought Roscoe White to be the gunman in the classic gunman position of the Nix film.

Of course, the gunman on the running board of the Honest Joe's Edsel could have been someone else, hiding in plain sight: and it could be shadows as has been evidenced. Honest Joe could have been doing what he always did when business was slow: driving around in his unique car to drum up business. But there were other sinister things seen in the Nix film, as well as witnesses who saw shooters, puffs of smoke, and people running away from the knoll. For instance, Ed Hoffman[312] saw someone in a business suit behind the wooden stockade fence. His revelation was later debunked by many including researcher M. Duke Lane.[313] Ironically, DPD officer J.C. White testified before the Warren Commission that he couldn't hear the shots due to a loud freight train. Mr. Lane's article cites the "no train" seen as evidence that Ed Hoffman was lying. If Hoffman was lying, then was DPD Officer White lying as well?

There were other theories of sinister 'shadows' in the Nix film. Among them: Black Dog Man, Running Man, Blue Suit Man, and Shadow Man. There never seems to be an end to the figures in the shadows that can be seen in the Nix film. That so many believe shots came from there is also of great interest. Are there really that many mistaken people in the world? Could one of these sinister shadows actually be the gunman who hit the president with the small throat shot? Or a shot in the right temple that is still debated today?

*****

THAT SO MANY BELIEVE SHOTS CAME FROM THERE IS ALSO OF GREAT INTEREST. ARE THERE REALLY THAT MANY MISTAKEN PEOPLE IN THE WORLD? COULD ONE OF THESE SINISTER SHADOWS ACTUALLY BE THE GUNMAN WHO HIT THE PRESIDENT WITH THE SMALL THROAT SHOT?

Acoustical evidence from witnesses is varied as well. More shots were heard even after the fatal head shot; according to some witnesses there were as many as seven. James Tague was hit by cement or a glancing bullet.[314] Even the House Select Committee found during their hearings that the acoustical evidence pointed to a gunman approximately ten feet west of the southern corner of the picket fence.[315] The irony of that HSCA finding is that this was the last time Orville Nix's camera original film was seen. Some of the HSCA consultants later published books with films that had never been seen by the public. One could question how secure the evidence was as these committees convened.

Or maybe as Orville always knew, his film *did* show there was a gunman on the colonnade area. Maybe it *did* become one more piece of evidence that needed to be destroyed to keep the 'Lee Harvey Oswald acted alone' story going. The truth is that unadulterated photographic evidence does not lie. It has no bias, no agenda, no subjectivity. It is pure.

Moses Weitzman believes this purity is the reason the Nix film is missing. He believes this because in his work with UPI and Reese Schonfeld, he saw an image that has never been discussed. It was an image seen behind the "stockade fence" and was not a visual mirage of shadows and lights. He called this image, "Red Bandana Man."

Could this be a shooter or another trick being played on the viewer's mind by the light, shadows and leaves?

Thankfully, researchers today are still looking at the photographic evidence, including the Nix Film. With technology becoming more sophisticated all the time and easier to obtain, theories that were debunked in the past have proven true. Likewise, truths have been found to be lies. Some of them include:

- A note professed to have been written by Oswald to a "Mr. Hunt" (either Texas oilman H.L Hunt or CIA agent E. Howard Hunt) came to the HSCA's attention. Later, the note was found to be a Soviet forgery in order to promote Kennedy assassination disinformation.[316]
- The Rickey White Story.
- Beverly Oliver's profession of "finding" her original "Babushka Lady's" film. The photos she used as evidence at a 1999 Dallas Conference were of the Nix Film.[317]
- The motorcade route was changed.[318]
- Zapruder was only paid twenty-five thousand dollars in 1963 for his film.

On the other side of the coin, there are theories that were once debunked that have now proven to be true. They include:

- The media was at times and still is manipulated by the government.[319]
- The CIA used mind-conditioning on Americans from 1950-1979.[320]
- The CIA obfuscated records, withheld records, and lied to every committee studying the assassination since 1964.[321]
- Oswald was in Mexico before the assassination.[322]
- The presidential limo *did* slow down during the assassination, as seen in the Nix and Muchmore film.[323]
- US officials destroyed evidence.[324]

We can criticize Oliver Stone for rolling several conspiracy theories into one dramatic piece of entertainment: his movie *JFK*. But the truth is, without his movie, the ARRB would have never been formed and the truth about the CIA would have never been found. Stone made an icon out of Jim Garrison, the District Attorney from New Orleans, though some would disagree with his heroic character. But, like Jim Garrison, even our fallen president had his foibles, as do all humans.

Maybe one of the answers to finding the truth is to be more transparent and fearless in our own lives, thereby forcing our government to do the same. Orville Nix lived by that credo and taught his family to do so, as well. He shared his disappointments, as well as his successes, with his family, thereby living a life of truth. He never faltered from his belief that the shots came from the stockade fence. As I grew older and he shared his fears with me, I'm ashamed to admit that I laughed at him and called him "paranoid." I regret that to this day. He wasn't being paranoid. He was sharing his truth and, in that, his transparency. If we don't care, how can we expect our leaders to care? They are but a reflection of us. Orville Nix was truthful and transparent; but his experience in taking the film of the assassination made him fearful. Fear is a mighty control. Fear is what keeps a person from being all they can be. Fear handicaps a person and stunts their success and happiness. Fear magnified Orville's self-perceived inadequacies. No prisoner at Guantánamo Bay should have been subjected to the fear Orville Nix lived with during the last years of his life. No torturer could have done better. How many witnesses still alive today feel the same way Orville Nix did?

I know a few.

In contrast, John F. Kennedy lived his life fearlessly. He faced health issues that many of us could have never overcome. He wasn't afraid to defy his father's views on World War II and Hitler. After becoming president, he wasn't afraid to bring Jimmy Hoffa and the Mafia to hearings to detail their crimes. He stood up to his one-time friend Allen Dulles and threatened to "splinter the CIA" after the Bay of Pigs fiasco.[325] It wasn't that John F. Kennedy feared his emotions, not at all. He was steeped in them. Kennedy was much like Asquith, a character from one of his favorite books, *Pilgrim's Way*.[326] The author, John Buchan wrote of Asquith, "He disliked emotion, not because he felt lightly but because he felt deeply." [327]

CHAPTER TWENTY

THE MEDIA AND THE LIES

"And so it is to the printing press--to the recorder of man's deeds, the keeper of his conscience, the courier of his news--that we look for strength and assistance, confident that with your help man will be what he was born to be: free and independent."

John F. Kennedy[328]

Who is the keeper of our memories? Who is in charge of writing history? During the late 1950s and early 1960s - print media was. The media developed the 'Camelot' theme of the JFK administration, then sat back and proudly admired their creation and, in doing so, lured the American public and the world into the charming fantasy they created. Readers were eager to enter that realm and bought every magazine and newspaper that showed the Kennedy family. During JFK's administration, Jackie Kennedy graced the cover of *Life* magazine at least three times a year. She was on covers from *Vogue* to *Sports Illustrated* to magazines in Peru. Enduring Cold War school drills, McCarthyism, and the fear of all things 'red', the public needed an escape. Camelot fit the bill. But then, November 22, 1963 happened. There was no escaping the horror of the day, the untimely murder of a beloved young president and the grief of his beautiful grieving wife left to care for two small children. It is well documented that the Kennedy administration would often send letters of 'thanks' to writers of articles in newspapers and magazines that they liked, and letters of "what?" to questionable interviews in the press.[329] As stated earlier, Joseph Kennedy ensured that Henry Luce wrote well of his son John every time *Life* magazine published an issue. But after the assassination, who was in control of the media? Who is in control today? Noam Chomsky states it is the 'corporate media.'[330] What is that? The big corporations, Chomsky says, control our media through their control of advertising. Those corporations, though, should have no particular interest, as a group, in covering up a presidential assassination. But that is exactly what the media has done since 1963.

Operation Mockingbird was a campaign created by the CIA to influence the media.[331] Begun in the 1950s, it recruited leading American journalists into a network to help present the CIA views. It also funded student and cultural organizations, like the one George Joannides funded for the Cuban student newspaper of the DRE after the assassination.332 It also used leading magazines and newspapers as fronts including: *The New York Times, CBS,* and *Time/Life*. Operation Mockingbird worked to influence not only foreign media and political campaigns, but American activities and mindsets as well.

Orville Nix learned how demeaning the media could be in 1967, when, against his wife Ella's wishes, he agreed to do an interview for a national CBS special on the JFK assassination and the *Warren Commission Report*.[333] Always a fan of Walter Cronkite, he had hoped to meet the iconic CBS reporter during the interview. He also was excited to take his grandchildren to the place that had changed his life. By this time, Gayle was almost ten years old and Cindy and David were seven and six respectively. They were old enough to see their grandfather interviewed and enjoy a media experience. When Ella learned the grandkids would be accompanying their grandfather, she happily agreed to let Orville do one last interview.

"What are you going to say to Walter Cronkite?" Ella asked her husband.

"I'm going to tell him what I saw. I'm going to tell him the truth," Orville replied. "I'm going to take my camera too and take pictures of the day."

In May of 1967, Orville Nix and his three grandchildren drove down to Dealey Plaza to meet the press. Orville was chain-smoking and since the author, Gayle was the oldest, she got to ride in the front seat. As we neared the Plaza, Orville reminded us to 'mind our manners' and 'be quiet' during the interview. He then promised us all ice cream if we acted nicely. Orville was wearing another new suit that day; the kind that changes colors from light brown to blue in the light. He also had on a new Fedora and tie. He was quite an imposing site with his 6'6" frame and tailored clothing. As he approached the center of Dealey Plaza, in the grassy part where he had stood when he took the film between Main and Elm, Bernard Birnbaum[334] walked up to greet him.

"Hello Mr. Nix, so nice to see you again." Birnbaum shook his hand. He had met Orville earlier in the year. Orville had allowed Birnbaum to use his camera for the CBS Warren Commission production.

"So these are your grandkids, all blonde, eh?" He smiled at us all and shook each of our hands. We felt quite mature. "If you don't mind kids, I'm going to talk to your grandpa for a few minutes, but you can stand over there and watch how the television cameras work." Mr. Birnbaum was a kind man and he made quite an impression on us, and not just because of his strange accent. My younger brother David was so mesmerized he didn't even run around the grassy area or fight with my sister or me. We noticed there weren't any other children within sight, which made us feel all the more special. Later, before the show aired, he sent each of us a letter telling us how helpful our grandfather was in producing the *CBS Special Report*.[335] None of us had ever received a letter in the mail before, and we all felt quite important.

Orville had noticed there were no other children at the filming as well, and worried that he may have upset the CBS men by bringing his. He worried only for a split-second though…he wanted to share this experience with his grandchildren.

A few minutes later, a lady came and powdered my grandfather's face. He smirked and we laughed. He winked and said, "Don't tell your Granny that I had make-up on." We all laughed at his secret. Just then, a man we recognized from the nightly local news, Eddie Barker, appeared.[336] He too introduced himself and as kids, we felt like movie stars.

One of the key conclusions the 4-part series would confirm was that Lee Harvey Oswald was a lone gunman. The other proved there was no conspiracy, which meant the shots all had to come from the Texas School Book Depository. The series was recorded to ensure the American public believed the Warren Commission's findings and "that there was no evidence that there was a conspiracy."

When it was time for Orville's interview, the interviewer, Eddie Barker, asked his name and then, after asking several questions in regards to his location during the parade asked:

"Where do you believe the shots came from Mr. Nix?"

"From the fence area, over there" Orville replied.

The director immediately yelled, "Cut!"

Orville wasn't sure what it meant, but he knew everything had stopped. "Let's start again," the director barked. "At the time of the assassination, where did you think the shots came from Mr. Nix?"

Orville answered as he pointed, "From that stockade fence over there."

"CUT!" again the director barked.

Orville was baffled. I was a little scared. The director yelled loudly when he said, "Cut". The make-up lady came over again and powdered my grandfather's forehead. I suppose he was beginning to sweat a little from nervousness.

Mr. Barker walked over to the director and they conversed for a moment. I looked at my younger sister and brother who were still being quite still, sitting on the grass. We remained in awe of the whole scene: cameras, police cars, people, men everywhere in suits and a lady who was carrying a bouquet to the grassy knoll. Even at our young ages, we understood the solemnity of the place where we stood.

*****

ORVILLE WAS BAFFLED.

I WAS A LITTLE SCARED.

THE DIRECTOR YELLED LOUDLY WHEN HE SAID, "CUT".

THE MAKE-UP LADY CAME OVER AGAIN AND POWDERED MY GRANDFATHER'S FOREHEAD.

I SUPPOSE HE WAS BEGINNING TO SWEAT A LITTLE FROM NERVOUSNESS.

Just then, Mr. Barker said, "Okay Mr. Nix, we're ready to begin again."

For the third time, the cameras rolled, the clapboard slammed, and Mr. Barker asked, "Mr. Nix, you heard shots. How many did you hear?"

Orville answered, "I heard one… 'Bang,' then a 'Bang-Bang' really fast. Then another loud 'Bang.' I would say four shots."

Mr. Barker then asked, "And where did the shots come from?"

Orville answered, "From the fence area, over by the buildings there."

Again the director yelled "CUT!" and again very loudly, so loudly we all jumped. Mr. Barker went to talk to the director again.

After several more takes, Mr. Birnbaum then came over to my grandfather with a kind smile. He said, "Orville, where did the Warren Commission say the shots came from?"

My grandfather answered slowly, now understanding what they wanted him to say, "Well, the School Book Depository Building."

Mr. Birnbaum said, "Well, that's what you need to say."

Orville frowned, looked down then looked back up. Mr. Barker was again walking towards him, and they began again.

Mr. Barker asked, "Mr. Nix, you were a filmmaker that day, where did the shots come from?"

Orville answered, "The School Book Depository."

That was the end of the filming. That was the last time my grandfather ever gave an interview on camera. I think I saw a bit of his spirit die that day.

On the way home, my brother and sister were in the back seat. Tired from the excitement, they soon fell asleep on the drive home. I could tell my grandfather wasn't happy. He immediately lit a Lucky Strike cigarette and then hit the steering wheel with both of his hands. Startled, I questioned him, "What's wrong, Paw-Paw?"

"Why did they try to make me feel stupid? Why did they make me feel ignorant? I'm not insane," he mumbled as he hit the steering wheel again.

"What do you mean, Paw-Paw? I think you did good!" I assured him.

He looked over at me and I could see a tear in his eye. He just stared at me. I smiled and patted his back.

"Gayle, I want you to know something, I believe you're old enough to understand what I'm saying to you. I was there that day. I know what I saw. The shots came from that fence area. You always remember that, will you?" he said to me solemnly.

"I will, Paw-Paw, I will."

Though I didn't understand it at the time, my grandfather was looking for reassurance. He was looking for validation. He never received it in his lifetime. He had been brow-beaten for so long: from men who were intimidating, like the rich Doctors at Riverlakes Country Club, worry of losing his Governmental job or the words placed in his mouth by the media. He just couldn't take it any longer. He didn't know that CBS was another media front for the CIA. How could he? Few people did. He trusted the government he so loved and would never think they would lie to him or insult him into repeating words they wanted to hear or have told. He didn't know that others were treated the same as he. Many others don't know either. For instance, Kenny O'Donnell, a confidant and adviser to JFK who was in the motorcade suffered the same intimidation as Orville Nix. In former U.S. Speaker of the House Tip O'Neill's book M*an of The House,* O'Neill describes a conversation with O'Donnell, who told him he was sure that two shots had come from the fence behind the grassy knoll. O'Neill said to O'Donnell, "That's not what you told the Warren Commission." O'Donnell responded, "You're right, I told the FBI what I had heard, but they said it couldn't have happened that way and that I must have been imagining things. So I testified the way they wanted me to. I just didn't want to stir up any more pain and trouble for the family."[337]

Whether it was for fear of their jobs, their lives or respect for the Kennedy family, many witnesses were scared to speak the truth, or worse, speak what they were told to speak by the powers that be. These innocent people had no idea that they were part of Operation Mockingbird to the nth degree. They were forced to repeat the governmental story, the truth be damned. I know many witnesses living today who feel the same. I have spoken with them personally. They are afraid to tell their stories for fear their families will suffer.

Later that year, Jim Garrison called Orville and asked him to testify at his now famous trial.[338] Orville refused. He didn't speak of his participation in history for the next five years. He died in January of 1972. Jones Harris worked on the Garrison team. He was never to meet Orville Nix.

Nor did Moses Weitzman. As Orville Nix was taking his last breaths in Oak Cliff, Moses Weitzman was enhancing the Nix film for UPI in downtown Manhattan at his lab, EFX Unlimited. His business was located at 321 W. 44th Street on the 4th floor. UPITN occupied the top floor of the same building. Weitzman had worked extensively on the Zapruder film for years. His clients included Time, Inc. as well as many movie and documentary producers. Since Weitzman was a photographic purist, the assassination of JFK was never of interest to him. He was more interested in the rapidly evolving techniques in regards to photo processing and of course, doing the best job he could for his clients. It is a story that Weitzman knew for years and only repeated two times... Once to the Assassination Records Review Board in 1997 and again to me in 2014. As he explained to the author:

> *"I believe the original Nix film has been destroyed. Here is why I think so. Maurice Schonfeld from UPI brought the Nix film to me in 1973 to see if I could find anything on it. I studied an original internegative. Using a Hazeltine Analyzer, I took it from 16mm to 35mm size. When I did, in it, very plain to me, was the image of a person wearing what seemed to be a red bandana, holding what appeared to be a metallic broomstick type object and the distinct pink flesh tones of hands holding the metallic object. This red bandana image is hidden in the brushy area and clearly moves along the fence after the head shot. It could be seen behind the picket fence area, on Zapruder's right. Schonfeld was so excited; he decided to send it to the Jet Propulsion Lab in California. He paid me a large sum of money to make 24 copies: 12 black and white and 12 color under very hush hush orders. I had a Rolodex with business cards from my contacts at the JPL. I finished the copies and Schonfeld sent a black and white copy to California. Two weeks later, I came into my office to call my contact at the Jet Propulsion Lab and found that my office had been ransacked. Not only were the Rolodex entries missing for the Jet Propulsion Lab, but so was my Nix*

file. I really didn't think much of it until later that day when I noticed many of the employees from the top floor leaving with tears in their eyes. It seemed UPI had gone out of business. I had been paid a nice sum, so that wasn't my worry, but I still found it all odd. The next day, I looked up the number for the Jet Propulsion Lab and was told, 'We are no longer working with you and are unable to answer any questions regarding the JFK Assassination. We are a governmental organization.' As I was not a conspiracy buff, I didn't think this was anything sinister, just strange and I never mentioned it nor saw Mr. Schonfeld again."[339]

Strangely, a report was manufactured by JPL, a copy of which was sent to Maurice Schonfeld. Several years later, Chris Scally, a well-respected and thorough JFK researcher contacted Dr. Alan Gillespie from the Jet Propulsion Laboratory and requested a copy of the report. Dr. Gillespie's reply to him was, "Under our agreement with Mr. Schonfeld we cannot supply you with a copy of that report..." In the letter, Gillespie further goes on to state that the JPL findings parallel the ITEK findings done a decade and a half before. Both reports conclude "it is impossible to use the Nix film to resolve the question conclusively either way."[340]

This statement by Dr. Gillespie and the author's telephonic interview with Dr. Kenneth Castleman confirm that it is imperative to find the original Nix film insomuch that both the ITEK and JPL/Caltech findings don't preclude there is no evidence of a second gunman, rather it cannot be resolved conclusively. Does this mean there is not a second gunman? Absolutely not! In fact, Dr. Castleman told the author that JPL/Caltech didn't study the picket fence area, but rather the pergola area that Jones Harris had initially discovered. In a later telephonic interview with Maurice Schonfeld, he too told me that he had never paid a photographic analysis lab to study anything but the object Harris had pointed out to him, and didn't remember seeing the image to which Weitzman referred.[341]

So now the question becomes, "Why through all the many governmental studies, photographic analyses and viewings of the original Nix film did no one analyze the entirety of the original Nix film?"

* * * * *

In 1988, twenty-five years after the copyright would revert to its original owner as Reinhardt and Schonfeld told my grandfather and dad, I began my quest to get my grandfather's film returned to our family. Not being a lawyer, I waged a one-woman war to get the film rightfully returned. I spoke with a kind man at UPI who was in their legal department. After telling him my story, he agreed to send the film back right away. A few days passed and I didn't hear from him. Like my grandfather, I didn't give up. When I called his number, I was told he was 'no longer with the company.'[342] At that time, UPI was still a powerful force with which to be reckoned and, unbeknownst to the public, on the verge of bankruptcy. Another lawyer told me I would have to wait until 1991 to get the film back. Finally, on June 4, 1991, I received a letter from UPI's general counsel, Frank Kane stating: "UPI agrees that, in accordance with the oral agreement ... UPI hereby releases all rights over the Nix Film to Mr. Nix's heirs and assigns."[343] I felt so victorious! My grandfather's film was now back where it belonged…or at least the rights to it were.

Unfortunately, I could not afford airfare at the time to go to Washington to retrieve my grandfather's films, nor was I educated at the time as to how to distinguish between an original film and a copy. Gary Mack, a friend at the time, suggested I ask Robert Groden to retrieve the films and copies for me as well as inventory them. Since Robert Groden had worked on the HSCA staff as a photographic expert, Gary Mack trusted him. Since I then trusted Gary Mack, I agreed. Groden graciously retrieved the films for me. In the many canisters, strips and folders were frames and copies of the Nix film. But there was no original; at least that's what Robert Groden told me. I called UPI and Worldwide Television News (WTN) to inquire. They were under the impression the original film was there, but could not verify for certain. I became worried. Why would the original film be missing? The House Select Committee on Assassinations had listed in their indices they had examined the original. Unfortunately, later in the back of the book the Nix film is indexed as a copy. I was stunned. Robert Groden seemed to be the answer. Not only had he worked for the HSCA, he had retrieved my films from UPI. I found out later that he also had access to the Nix film while working with Moses Weitzmann and UPI on the film, *Executive Action.*

I wanted to find my grandfather's original film to have it analyzed. I couldn't do that with 100% accuracy because I didn't have the original film. I made up my mind to borrow the money and flew to meet Robert in his home in Boothwyn, Pennsylvania along with his first wife Chris. By the time I had flown to Pennsylvania, many people had suggested that Robert may have kept the original Nix film for himself. I thanked Robert for retrieving my films then asked him eye to eye, "Robert, do you have my grandfather's original film in your possession?" He answered quickly and succinctly "no." I noticed that as he answered, he did not look me in the eye. As a woman who believes one's

*****

CHRIS, PLEASE TELL ME. DOES ROBERT HAVE MY FILM?"

I FELT BADLY PUTTING HER ON THE SPOT.

SHE NEVER ANSWERED ME.

SHE JUST STARED AT THE FLOOR.

I WAS LEFT WITH NO ANSWER AND NO ORIGINAL FILM.

character speaks through their actions as well as their eyes, I was circumspect. I changed the subject and we discussed other things. A bit later, Chris was alone in her dining area. I walked over while Robert was looking at books and said, "Chris, please tell me. Does Robert have my film?" I felt badly putting her on the spot. She never answered me. She just stared at the floor. I was left with no answer and no original film.

When I got back to Texas, I immediately contacted G. Robert Blakey, the head of the House Select Committee on Assassinations. That would be the beginning of many phone calls I have made over the years looking for the original Nix film. I soon received a letter that said the film had gone from the House Select Committee to the National Archives. I called the National Archives. It wasn't there. I then called UPI again only to be told to contact their new owner, Worldwide Television News to see if they had transferred it to their new offices. They had not. The last official place the film was said to have been was in the House Select Committee on Assassinations files, but there was even a question as to whether or not they ever had the original as the indices state 'original' in one place and 'copy' in another. I again called G. Robert Blakey, the Chief Counsel for the HSCA. In his conversations with me, he took full responsibility for the loss of the film because as he stated, "It was his committee that was supposed to assure that all evidence was returned to its rightful owners."[344] He later said in an interview with PBS, "Significantly, the Warren Commission's conclusion that the agencies of the government cooperated with it is, in retrospect, not the truth."[345] Could one of these agencies to which he referred have absconded with the Nix film?

Later, I confronted Reese Schonfeld as to the film's whereabouts. I was nothing more than a bother to him, he didn't show concern about the film's loss at all. He said he had placed the Nix film in a safety deposit box before he left to begin CNN and had given the key to the safety deposit box to the UPI accountant, Alexander Boch. I contacted Boch. A month later, I received a letter from Boch saying he had no knowledge of the film and that the Clinton National Trust Bank was bought by Chase Manhattan and since been demolished.[346] Could the Nix film be under a pile of cement in downtown Manhattan? Or could it have been stolen, as many researchers have thought, by a staff member of the HSCA? Since the HSCA indices mention the use of an "original" film in one place and a "copy" in the other, could the original film have been switched for a copy during that time? No one would have noticed; not even UPI when the film was supposedly returned. Why would they think to check to see if they were receiving the original film back? By that time, they were done with their "runt of the litter" film---the Nix Film.

Undaunted, I chased leads around the world. I spoke with Mexican President Vicente Fox because someone had heard that the Mexican government had

JFK assassination evidence to keep the Oswald in Mexico City event quiet. I spoke with a sheikh in the United Arab Emirates as I was told from someone in Europe that the Nix film had been used as a 'bribe' in some oil negotiation. Because of Oliver Stone's movie and the loss of a key piece of evidence, I begged America to find it by appearing on several national television shows: *Geraldo, Montel Williams*, and even *Entertainment Tonight.*[347] I have always found it ironic that Oliver Stone, the man who was chastised for making a 'fantasy film' of the assassination by the mainstream media, did what the government could not or would not do: force the government to form another committee to find the files; the Assassination Record Review Board. I have since made a point of supporting those who aren't part of the mainstream media. Without readers and viewers, the mainstream media cannot survive. This is one way to make a difference in our society.

As I shared my grandfather's experiences, I found out first-hand how the media and people with agendas work. Many of the original researchers who helped me gave up on finding the film and moved on to proving their own theories, writing new books, and procuring new jobs. The media denied that what happened at my grandfather's CBS interview occurred.[348] I never received threatening phone calls, but I did receive phone calls from strange people who claimed to know where my grandfather's film was, for a price.

There have been people in the past who have had to stop their conspiracy rhetoric for a myriad of reasons. At one time, the former mayor of Dallas (and a frequent visitor to Orville Nix's home) was Wes Wise. He was also a broadcaster for KRLD in Dallas. Wes Wise so strongly maintained his opinion about conspiracy that he broadcast appeals for new photographic evidence over the KRLD local TV shows. This was done against the orders of his boss at the time, Eddie Barker. Wise became Mayor of Dallas, elected in 1971 and defeated the Dallas-established oligarchy. He actually received a new piece of photographic evidence based on his TV appeal from a Dallas citizen named Richard Bothun, who had taken a picture of the grassy knoll a few moments after the shots.[349] But in later years, he found it impractical to discuss conspiracy theories, becoming a champion for the City of Dallas instead. If he ever became part of the Dallas oligarchy, it has only been recently. During the fiftieth anniversary of the JFK assassination events and news, he was front and center in defending Dallas. One cannot blame him; he obviously knew that no one in the city would ever stand up to say, "We could have done better." When I interviewed him in regards to his discussions with my grandfather, he didn't want to talk long though he stated: "Orville Nix truly believed in what he saw that day and I believed him."[350]

Abraham Zapruder never had the problem with his film that Orville Nix did, though both films have been studied by all official committees and both are considered evidence. Why is the original Zapruder film in the National Archives as federal evidence at the cost of sixteen million taxpayer dollars and the original Nix film still remains lost?

Luckily, there are people still today, trying to find the original Nix film as well as all the other missing evidence in the case. These people don't make rush judgments. They don't consider the case closed. They aren't worried about their political careers. They believe that there is truth lying in wait out there to be found. They are the newer generation of researchers, experts and truth-seekers. One of them, Jefferson Morley, has sued the CIA to release information on several key witnesses.[351] Another, Vince Palamara, has studied, researched and written acclaimed books regarding the Secret Service.[352] Others, including author Roger Stone, have spent years finding the Lyndon Baines Johnson connection.[353] Pat Speer offers his years of research freely on his website. None of these men proclaim to have solved the case; rather they offer their work to those willing to listen. They are the future of how history will be recorded in regards to the JFK assassination.

CHAPTER TWENTY ONE

PRESENT DAY NIX FILM RESEARCH: THE JFK ASSASSINATION FORUM

"... what really counts is not the immediate act of courage or of valor, but those who bear the struggle day in and day out - not the sunshine patriots but those who are willing to stand for a long period of time."

John F. Kennedy[354]

When I decided to write this book in 2013, I contacted some of my friends from the past who had been such a tremendous help to me after getting the copyright back from UPI in 1990. It probably wasn't the wisest of timing, since the 50th anniversary of JFK's death was the same year and all of these people were still well entrenched in the JFK community. Many friends, sadly, had passed away. But many were still supportive and encouraging, especially Josiah Thompson, Jim Marrs, David Lifton and the enigmatic Jones Harris. I received a lukewarm re-entry into the fray from Gary Mack of the Sixth Floor Museum but a glowing welcome back from David Lifton. David had been helpful to me during my appearance on the *Geraldo* show in 1991 even going so far as to send me a multiple page fax at the hotel where I was staying so I wouldn't feel uncomfortable as to what I should and should not talk about. I have never forgotten his kindness. He had nothing to gain by helping me and because of that, I will always consider him a friend. I spent much time discussing old times, and new, with Dave Perry. Robert Groden and Mark Lane never returned my calls. Gerald Posner and Mark Zaid were courteous, as were Bill Kelley, Donald Roberdeau, Trish Fleming, Zachary Zendro, Greg Burnham, Bernice Moore, Steve Barber, Jefferson Morley, Vince Palamara, Debra Conway, Clint Bradford, Pat Speer, and Dr. Larry Sabato. Clint Bradford has not only been supportive, but a huge help in helping me chase leads as to where the camera original may be found. I met and became friends with Buell Frazier and his lovely wife Betty; as well as Jim Bowles and his sweet wife Martha. Many delightful and enlightening hours were spent with Jones Harris. When I realized that this time around I would have to make new expert friends to ensure my facts were correct, I spent weeks investigating the newest and brightest researchers. There are many JFK Forums on the Internet, some more well-known than others. I have included footnotes from many of the articles cited on those forums. I read score after score of threads (thoughts) regarding not only the Nix film, but old and new theories. My criterion was simple: find research and opinion that could be documented and explained. After many weeks, I luckily found a bevy of researchers on the Internet at the JFK Assassination Forum.[355]

The Forum began in 2009 and is managed and maintained by Duncan MacRae, a stern but fair man from Scotland who spends much time with this site and its members. He has always answered my questions within a day and intelligently comments on the many debates that are ongoing. The site is dedicated to the debate and inquiry of the JFK assassination and contains a discussion section, but also a photographic/film section that is astounding in its findings. There is also a separate panel for discussions involving video and audio. Mr. MacRae doesn't take a side when commenting on his forum and allows equal time to Warren Commission defenders, as well as conspiracy realists. It is quite the amalgamation of perception, personalities, and passion; three of the reasons I was drawn to it. His moderation of the site is democratic: he doesn't impose censorship, disallow people who don't agree on a topic point, or put limitations on anything but nonsense: he's a first amendment moderator in that he adheres to "freedom of speech." He also hosts a YouTube channel[356] that is encyclopedic in its scope and wildly popular, as well as hosting the incomparable Robin Unger's Photo Gallery of literally every key photograph any researcher could want, complete with credits and dates.[357] Mr. Unger has spent much of his own money buying critical film prints from auctions and owners from all over the world at a considerable cost. He charges nothing for his research and asks nothing but credit for his photos. Robin's photo gallery is like having a complete JFK museum of photographs online. MacRae realized early on, in this age of videos and the partial demise of news print, that having visual reminders of the JFK assassination would appeal not only to older generations, but newer ones as well. His site is cutting-edge, democratic, and a mother lode of information. With thousands of members from all over the world, there are many who feel the same as I about this treasure trove of JFK information.

When I joined this site, I tentatively introduced myself and explained I was doing research for the book I was writing about my grandfather. I was instantly welcomed and treated as if I were the one who shot the film: there was that much interest and kindness shown to me. Mr. MacRae welcomed me personally and quickly suggested many places for me to look, as well as making my initial introduction about trying to find my grandfather's film a "sticky" topic; which means it would always stay on top of the recently discussed threads. As I swam slowly through the sea of information regarding Forrest Sorrels, Honest Joe's, and of course my grandfather, Mr. MacRae always navigated when I began to falter and offered suggestions, ideas, and support. I will never be able to thank him enough for all the many questions he answered and advice he has given me in continuing my quest to find the camera original Nix film; a quest he has joined.

*****

NO ONE IN FIFTY YEARS HAD SEEN THAT EXCEPT RICK NEEDHAM. IT WAS A MEMORABLE DAY FOR ME AND FOR RICK TO SAY THE LEAST, BUT AN IMPETUS FOR OTHERS TO REALIZE THAT THINGS COULD STILL BE FOUND IN THE PHOTOGRAPHIC EVIDENCE FROM THE JFK ASSASSINATION.

Early on, I was introduced to the meticulous work of Rick Needham. Fortunately, when I first joined, he was working on researching and stabilizing a portion of the Robert Hughes film - the aftermath of the assassination. In it, he thought he had glimpsed at who he thought might be my grandfather, seen while shooting part of his assassination aftermath footage. Initially, I thought it wasn't him. But I was wrong. In speaking with my father Orville Jr., and going over family pictures, we realized that Rick had found my grandfather while in the act of shooting his own aftermath footage of the assassination.[358].

No one in fifty years had seen that except Rick Needham. It was a memorable day for me and for Rick to say the least, but an impetus for others to realize that things could still be found in the photographic evidence from the JFK assassination.

Rick then pointed me to the research he was doing on stabilizing a portion of the Nix film. What he had directed me towards was a re-posting that he had made in 2009. But in fact, Rick informed me that he had first begun stabilizing this portion of the Nix film way back in 1999 or 2000, and that he had first posted this back then on a JFK forum that was owned and operated by another JFK researcher, the late Rich Della Rosa. His quote:

> *"I have spent a great deal of my time studying the Nix film, for it offers the best view of the grassy knoll and stockade fence area of all the films taken that day. Why look there for a shooter? Because so many of the witnesses feel a shot or shots came from there/that direction... myself included. So I will push on studying the film. If you choose to believe no one was behind the fence that day, that's fine then. We are all entitled to our own opinions."*[359]

In his work, Rick Needham has found an image near the stockade fence...the same place Orville Nix maintained he thought the shots came from. Like Jones Harris, Rick Needham is tenacious and resolved to discover what the movement is that he sees in the Nix film. As he states in explaining a .gif he stabilized from the Nix film:

> *"Are we seeing a shooter quickly packing away a rifle... ready to flee the area while the confusion and chaos is just beginning to unfold as the witnesses' attention is drawn towards the passing motorcade below him? The "cut outs" from each individual frame were slightly enhanced in brightness and contrast only before I constructed the animated gif. The real beauty of this animated gif is that the panning motion is eliminated, allowing the eye to detect which is almost impossible to see when watching the Nix film full frame and with the panning of the camera."*[360]

In the animation, movement can be seen in the same area Orville Nix said the shots came from. Another member of the Forum, Craig Carvalho writes, "Rick was able to produce the animated picture without the distraction of the panning motion of the camera which allows the eye to remain focused on the movement behind the fence."[361]

The photographic panel of the House Select Committee on Investigations examined the Nix Film. Though they basically agreed with ITEK*'s* findings, they did concede to something else. Because the ITEK report only studied the image Jones Harris saw, it didn't take into consideration the rest of the grassy knoll area. The HSCA studied these areas captured in the Nix Film, especially one area near the darkened end of the retaining wall where the steps lead down to Elm St. The panel agreed to study it as there appeared to be movement there. Could this quick movement still be seen?

What is the movement Rick sees behind the fence in the Nix film? That he's seen something without the advanced tools of a CIA fronted ITEK or a government funded photographic lab speaks volumes.[362] Rick's only agenda is to find the truth in the hard evidence. His work has been done on the same kind of computer any of us could use; the difference is, he doesn't quit or give in to the naysayers. Could Rick have found the elusive "Hat Man" that Josiah Thompson wrote about in 1966?[363] Rick states:

> *It should be noted this movement behind the fence is seen less than 5 seconds AFTER the fatal head shot (maybe more like 3-4 seconds)... and where many have approx. put a grassy knoll shooter. This is NOT in the Badge Man position.*[364]

Duncan MacRae doesn't see a person in Rick's enhancements, but he does see Rick's "object" as being a car wheel further back in the parking lot.[365] The point is there are still 'objects' being found in films from fifty years ago. If we could find the original Nix film, what more could be found?

In tandem with Rick's work, Martin Hinrichs from Germany has spent many hours reviewing and enhancing the Nix Film and sharing his findings on the JFK Assassination Forum. He is now in the process of time-stamping the Nix film: a huge undertaking that no one has ever done. He also believes he can see a figure, possibly two, on the knoll area, and he believes one of them could be a gunman. His current study is on Nix frames 50-60. His studies show movement above the retaining wall where the "Black Dog Man" stood. Hinrichs believes he sees the "Black Dog Man" behind the fence and believes this person to be either a signal or protection man for the assassin behind the fence. His beliefs are based not only on the work he and Mr. Needham have done, but on the testimony of Lee Bowers who saw two men behind the fence. This could be the same movement the HSCA saw. Their findings stated: "The enhanced Nix Film shows an object that can be construed as having a shape similar to that of a person."[366] This movement still remains unresolved. Could Martin Hinrichs be the person to solve it? Mr. Hinrichs states:

> *There is a bright static point in the location where maybe the cola bottle stands on the wall. As you can clearly see, there is a bright point moving towards this white point downwards. The frames are taken from Orville Nix showing this area a moments after the headshot. If you can't get a logical explanation for this... please feel free to send this GIF to others who may be interested to watch it. This GIF is for free. You can post it on Facebook either if you like.*
>
> *Again, nobody til today can conclude what it is, but it's so important because it is hard photographic evidence. It is definitely out of the ordinary. It can even have something to do with the shooting. It's not natural. It's caused by human action. I'm very sure that this figure is responsible for the white moving dot seen in Nix frames 50-60. Maybe it was something he caused to distract from the loud*

shot from behind the fence. At that time, he must be on the way back into the parking lot to disappear forever.[367]

What is again notable in Hinrichs's research, and in its sharing with the JFK Assassination Forum, is the atmosphere of collaboration. There are no agendas here, just a search for the truth. That these men are trying to find it in the Orville Nix film would make my grandfather so very proud. These men, and many others, no matter their viewpoint on the JFK assassination, are pure researchers. Chris Scally is also one of these men. His pain-staking work on the Zapruder film chronology has been referenced in many books, including this one. He has done much detailed and exacting research on the Nix film and I am happy to say this work is featured at the end of this book. They are not trying to get rich and not looking for fame; in fact many of them were reticent to have me applaud their help. They consider themselves true seekers of the truth, and they come from all over the world.

*****

ROBIN UNGER'S EAGERNESS TO HELP ME FIND MY GRANDFATHER'S ORIGINAL CAMERA FILM RESULTED IN HIS SHARING MY QUEST WITH OTHER FORUMS AND RESEARCHERS.

LIKE A VERITABLE VIRTUAL ARMY, THANKS TO ROBIN, PEOPLE WHO FREQUENT THE JFK FORUMS NOW ARE AWARE THAT THE ORIGINAL IS MISSING.

So often we think of the JFK assassination as an 'American' catastrophe. That is where we are wrong. JFK's death was a worldwide event that affected everyone. People like Steve Barber, Jeff Shaw, Ray Mitcham, Calli Robertson, Jim Ostrowski, Jim Hess, Anthony Fratini, Bill Brown, Mark Dancer, Martin Weidmann, Matthew Scheufele, Denis Morrissette (who has a fantastic website),368 Robert Caprio, George Sawtelle, Anthony Marsh, Martin Mizzi, Jimmy Dace, John Mytton, Mike Orr, Herbert Blenner, Michael Daly, Chris Scally, Craig Carvalho, and Gert Kuiper have all taken the time to either support, suggest, or answer questions in my search for the camera original Nix film. They don't all agree with the findings of the Warren Commission, but they do all agree that finding the Nix film is of the utmost importance.

Throughout my research, I often asked Robin Unger for help when it came to finding photos or looking for people or things in photos. My photographic eye sees the photograph; Robin's photographic eye seems to have a photographic memory. He can remember things from every picture he's examined, which is a testament to his research. Robin, even without my grandfather's original film, tenaciously watched the Nix film frame by frame and found a splice in it at the very beginning.369 From which version, we don't know as there are so many circulating today.

Robin Unger's eagerness to help me find my Grandfather's original camera film resulted in his sharing my quest with other forums and researchers. Like a veritable virtual army, thanks to Robin, people who frequent the JFK forums now are aware that the original is missing.

The ever charitable Robin Unger says, "For JFK Assassination Researchers like me, the NIX film is one of the MOST important historical films, covering the assassination of President Kennedy."[370]

Martin Hinrichs says, "The Nix film is the Holy Grail of the assassination films."[371]

Bruce Marshall, another researcher and friend I met on the JFK Assassination Forum has been a huge help to me. He has been a trusted business adviser, editor and more importantly, a friend. As he commented, "Finding the original Nix film would be one of the most important finds the research community could make. It is evidence and should have been treated as such."[372]

Comments like these give me hope and ensure that my grandfather's place in history will never be forgotten. It is imperative that we find the camera original Nix film. If we don't, in Jim Marrs' words, "there is little likelihood that the originators of the plot (to kill JFK) will ever be identified or brought to justice."[373] I have included pictures and descriptions of the work these men have done at the end of this book. I hope you find, as I have, the Nix film still has many secrets to tell.

Unfortunately, until we find the original Nix film, these secrets may never be revealed.

CHAPTER TWENTY TWO

FIFTY QUESTIONS OF CONSPIRACY

"Let us not despair but act.
Let us not seek the Republican answer or the Democratic answer
but the right answer.
Let us not seek to fix the blame for the past -
let us accept our own responsibility for the future."

John F. Kennedy[374]

1. Where is the Nix film and who has it?
2. Why did the FBI keep the Nix camera for over five months and send it back in pieces?
3. Why has there been a delay and difficulty to get all the JFK files released since the passage of the JFK Record Act of 1992?
4. Why was Jean Hill warned to never speak of seeing Honest Joe's Edsel?
5. Why was JFK's body forcibly removed from Texas by the Secret Service before the legally required autopsy could be performed?

6. Why did Kennedy's body show up in Bethesda with head wounds that contradicted Dallas medical personnel reports?
7. Why was the Zapruder film concealed from the Warren Commission, the American public and researchers until Jim Garrison subpoenaed it in 1967?
8. Why are the files on George Joannides, the CIA liaison between the Warren Commission and the CIA, still classified?
9. Why were so many eyewitnesses, including Orville Nix, never asked to testify before the Warren Commission?
10. Why did George Joannides fund the publishing of a special edition of the CIA-backed Cuban Student Directorate magazine on November 23, 1963 linking Lee Harvey Oswald to Fidel Castro?
11. Why does Dr. Don Teal Curtis, a physician in the Parkland Trauma room state he loudly declared that as the President's head was raised, all life-support procedures should stop as the back of the president's head was missing, clearly indicating an exit wound.
12. Instead of being located where it had always traditionally been, in front of the presidential limo, why was the press car moved further back in the motorcade?
13. Why was the military Aide to the President not sitting where he had always sat in the past, in the front seat of the presidential limo?
14. Why was Clint Hill the only Secret Service agent to react in a protective manner once the shooting began?
15. Why didn't the FBI and CIA warn the Secret Service and the Dallas Police of their knowledge of Lee Harvey Oswald if he was considered a threat?
16. Why did the Secret Service not allow the public to see the Dallas doctors' JFK news conference?
17. How can a 6.5mm bullet create an entrance wound measuring 6.0mm?
18. Who really owned the wallet with the Oswald and Hidell identifications reviewed by FBI Special Agent Westbrook?
19. Why did communications between the Pentagon and all other agencies go dead at the moment of the assassination for two hours?
20. Why did the HSCA close their investigation without demanding access to secretive evidence?

21. Why were witnesses intimidated not only by the FBI and the Warren Commission Counsel, but also by the media?
22. Why has President Obama chosen to keep the remaining declassified CIA and evidence files sealed until 2017?
23. Why was the presidential limo cleaned at Parkland Hospital?
24. Why was the cleansed limo quickly sent back to Hess & Eisenhardt of Cincinnati, Ohio, before a forensic examination could be completed, and who ordered it done?
25. Why was Lee Harvey Oswald's clothing not examined for blood spatter after killing Officer J.D. Tippit?
26. Where are the records or transcripts of conversations during the presidential motorcade on radio stations "Charlie" and "Blade" that are normally kept by the White House Signal Corps?
27. Why was the Zapruder film purchased by the American taxpayer for an estimated $16+ million dollars as evidence, yet none of the other films of the JFK assassination were treated as such?
28. Why was the Zapruder film not treated as evidence for 14 years after the assassination?
29. Why did the Warren Commission ignore the ear witness testimony of over twenty-one policemen and thirty three witnesses who heard shots from the Dealey Plaza colonnade area?
30. Why did the president's brother, U.S. Attorney General Robert F. Kennedy, ask CIA director John McCone if the CIA was involved in his brother's death?
31. Lee Harvey Oswald's "Historic Diary" has all the markings of a KGB plant. Why was the diary not examined more fully?
32. Which stretcher did WC Exhibit #399, the nearly whole bullet found at Parkland Hospital come from? Connally or JFK's stretcher?
33. Why was someone impersonating Lee Harvey Oswald in Mexico City?
34. Why was the command "Black Box" missing for a period of time following the assassination?
35. Why did witnesses testify seeing Secret Service men behind the stockade fence and in the plaza area immediately after the assassination, yet the Secret Service said all agents were accounted for and "none remained at the scene of the shooting?"

36. Why, as the FBI report showed, did the three shells found near the sixth-floor window indicate they had been loaded twice, and possibly once in another rifle?

37. The "Babushka Lady" is seen clearly in the Nix film with a camera. Where are her pictures?

38. Why weren't Oswald's fingerprints found on the trigger, barrel, shells, or remaining ammunition in the rifle, but were found as a palm print that would normally be found during disassembly?

39. The Warren Commission was given the responsibility by President Lyndon Baines Johnson of answering six questions – What did Oswald do on November 22, 1963? What was Oswald's background? What did Oswald do in the US Marine Corps and in the Soviet Union? How did Jack Ruby kill Oswald? What was Ruby's background? And what efforts were taken to protect the president on November 22? Yet, the commission was never asked to answer the questions of who killed President Kennedy, and how.

40. Why did two Dallas police officers say that the rifle found on the sixth floor of the Texas School Book Depository was a 7.65mm Mauser – only to be contradicted later by the official Dallas police department statement saying the rifle was Oswald's rifle, a 6.5mm Mannlicher-Carcano?

41. Why does Jeremy Gunn, former general counsel for the ARRB and a man who had first-hand access to assassination documents released by the government after 1992, say: "There's also rather important exculpatory evidence for Oswald, suggesting he didn't do it, and that he was framed... there are serious problems with the forensics evidence, with the ballistics evidence, with the autopsy evidence."

42. Why, if Oswald used either the Mannlicher-Carcano or Mauser, is there no evidence or testimony that either rifle was given a "sniff" test? A sniff test was the way in the Sixties that law enforcement could detect whether or not a rifle had recently been fired.

43. Why were people posing as Secret Service agents seen confiscating and removing evidence from the Dealey Plaza crime scene?

44. What did CIA agents David Atlee Phillips, Anne Goodpasture, E. Howard Hunt, and Bill K. Harvey know about the assassination and Oswald's activity in Mexico City?

45. What happened to JFK's brain?

46. Why did James Joseph Humes, one of the autopsy doctor's burn his original, blood-stained autopsy notes?
47. Why did SAIC Gordon Shanklin order FBI agent James Hosty to destroy the note from Oswald?[375]
48. What was George de Mohrenschildt's role in the JFK assassination? He was friends with Lee Harvey Oswald and his wife Marina; he was married to Abraham Zapruder's former co-worker Jeanne LeGon, and sent letters to former CIA director and later U.S. President George H.W. Bush asking for his help with all the questions he was getting before he allegedly committed suicide during the HSCA hearings.
49. During the HSCA investigation (1978), why did the CIA find it necessary to have one of its employees, Regis Blahut, break into a safe containing JFK autopsy photos?
50. Why would our government lie to us?

The biggest questions still remain and save for question 50, they are not listed above. They are too large and too terrifying to answer. But they are the questions that will one day answer the truth as to what happened on November 22, 1963.

Who could orchestrate something like this? Who could exert power to conceal from the world what really happened, and why? Only a few had to know the truth. Others, the patsies and the unassuming, were unknowingly manipulated to comply with direct commands. A conspiracy was created to hide the truth and to ensure a successful assassination. So why haven't these questions been addressed? The answer is obvious to many: because very high-level government officials were complicit in organizing, concealing, and promoting falsehoods to cover their participation in the assassination plot. Various government intelligence, security and military agencies went along because they were told to do so. But who told them to do this? Will we ever find out? Or is it like Oliver Stone wrote in his screenplay from a quote from Winston Churchill for his 1991 movie *JFK,* "It's a mystery wrapped in a riddle inside an enigma."[376]

These are the *real* questions, the ones that no amount of time, cover up, death, and propaganda can conceal as long as people continue to search for the truth. And we're still out there - the truth seekers. Without answers for the horrible murders in Dallas that four-day weekend in November of 1963, the scar over our belief in our government will keep opening. Lies ooze, truth heals. In writing this book and doing extensive research, my idealism and optimism were shaken from time to time when reading how the news media and the people we trust- our protectors, our intelligence agencies, our elected officials have chosen to treat us as uneducated people who cannot handle the truth of what really is happening not only in this case, but in our own country and the world.

It is my greatest hope that after reading Orville Nix's story you choose to do something. Choose to ask questions. Choose to find the truth. Demand it of your government, of *our* government.

We are still the people... for now.

APPENDIX A

"I was there that day. I know what I saw. The shots came from that fence area. You always remember that, will you?"

Orville Nix, the man who took the second most important film of the JFK assassination, to his then ten year-old granddaughter Gayle Nix-Jackson

I have just reread this book about my grandfather. In doing so, I felt something might be missing. No, not missing. I felt something needed to be underscored. I find myself unsure if fully expressed the importance in finding the original Nix film and in understanding how horrendous his treatment was by the media and the government. Remember these vital points:

- He was not asked to testify before the Warren Commission.
- The only "evidentiary" statement given to an investigative authority was the statement he gave in January of 1964 to a newly-hired agent at the FBI office in downtown Dallas almost three months after the assassination, and even then it was if it were an after-thought…they wanted his camera.
- *Life* magazine, one of the biggest pimps the CIA and often times the government utilized was totally disinterested in a film that showed the opposite side of the Zapruder film. Why would they call it a nuisance film? Why wouldn't they want it to bolster the almost million dollars they invested in the Zapruder film? That's good business sense right? But they didn't use it. Why?

- His camera was kept by the FBI for over five months and when returned to him, returned in pieces. Why? So no one could ever recreate what he filmed on November 22, 1963.
- If his testimony wasn't important enough to be heard by the Warren Commission, why was his film used as the measurement standard for the Warren Commission recreation of the assassination.
- Why did Orville Nix believe his film was "different" after its return from the FBI?
- Why was he told to say "the shots came from the Texas School Book Depository" by CBS?
- Why, after speaking with two members of the HSCA committee, did I find out that they never studied the Nix film in its entirety: only 8 select frames?

These are but a few of the many inconsistencies in how the Nix film was treated during Orville Nix's lifetime. Could all these things be coincidental? Do you, the reader, have an answer to all the 'whys' posed in this book?

Rick Needham and Martin Hinrichs have answers. They've found some in the Nix film. These are not the images that have been dismissed by ITEK, Los Alamos, The Warren Commission and countless others. No, these are the images they have found with technology afforded to them in today's time. These are not images you will find in the Sixth Floor Museum at Dealey Plaza. Fifty years ago Jones Harris found the classic gunman and the Honest Joe's car. Fifty years later, here is what Rick Needham has found.

Marked with red arrows, Rick has found what can better be seen in a moving file as human movement behind the picket, or as Orville Nix called it, the stockade fence. The static frames shown here are hard to detect, but upon close investigation, look like a person moving among the shadows. As Rick states in regard to his findings in the Nix film:

> *I believe it to be the very top of a man's head… or a hat on top of his head.*
>
> *I can also spot an elongated "object", which when viewed in motion within these frames, is seen in the 10:00-11:00 o'clock position. My best guess is that we ARE seeing a shooter… in the beginning process of breaking down/storing a rifle. This "movement" is seen 3-4 seconds AFTER the fatal head shot.*

Though to many what Rick sees could look like a Rorschach test of light and shadow, upon further investigation, this image doesn't show up in one frame, but in many. Since the frames are moving at approximately 18.5 seconds, Rick's finding is significant.

Here is a map Rick diagrammed showing the Orville Nix camera field of view in Dealey Plaza.

Note in the above aerial view, taken in 1967, the placement of the picket fence and railroad tracks between the parking lot and fence. Many have said this would not be a good place to hide. Do you agree?

Rick describes further:

> *Below is a cutout portion of Nix frame 093... seen as the last frame in my animations before they loop over and begin once again. This cutout has been increased 6X from its normal size. Nothing more. No sharpening to the focus or anything. Note the color textures seen in the "top of the head" of the person who pops his head up in Nix frame 093. Now... note the color textures of the tree/branches just to the right of the "top of the head". I see no colors that look like the continuation of even the nearest tree branch.*

Below is frame 93 from the Nix film by Rick Needham

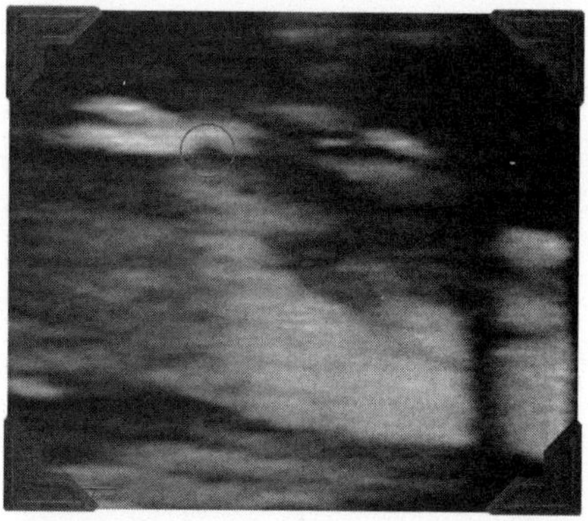

The area shaded with red and yellow circles is where Rick sees human movement.

Rick says, "I truly do believe this to be the one hidden gem in the Nix film. Possibly more could be found if you can locate your grandfather's camera original film. I think this is the best supporting photographic evidence for another shooter in Dealey Plaza that day... coupled with witness accounts from that day. We don't know who this person was, or which shot(s) he fired. But I am quite confident your grandfather shot the most important film that day... possibly the most famous in the history of this country. Hopefully someday soon the original will be located and subsequently returned to you and your family... so it too will have its chance to be digitally enhanced."

Martin Hinrichs's work shows a small white dot in frames 51-57. What is this suspicious white dot that changes position each frame?

See the frames circled below:

Nix frame 51, enhanced by Martin Hinrichs

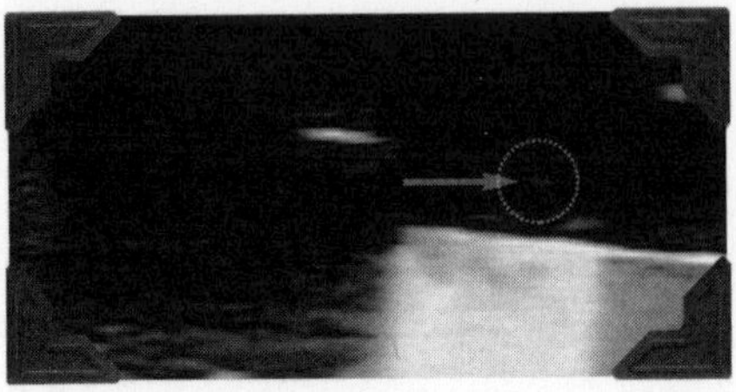

Nix frame 55, enhanced by Martin Hinrichs

Nix frame 57, enhanced by Martin Hinrichs

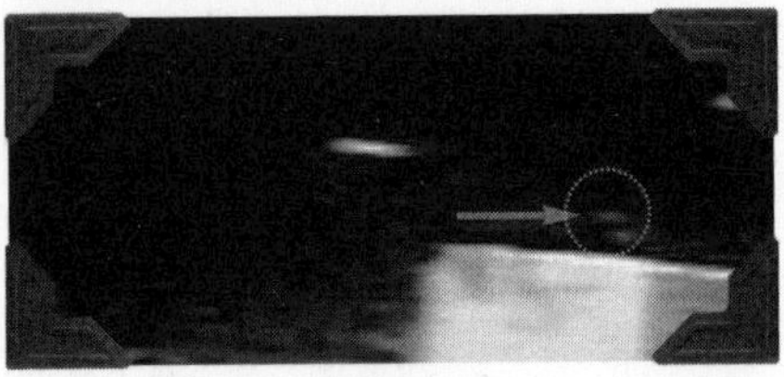

To see more of Rick's work and descriptions on the Nix film, please visit the JFK Assassination Forum online. Martin Hinrichs's work on the Nix film can be viewed there as well.

You can also view Rick Needham's animations on the Nix film here: www.mejuba.com/albums/Rick1960/119522/9562192/show/original

I hear my grandfather's words to 'always remember' often.

I hope you will as well.

APPENDIX B

THE ORVILLE NIX FILM: A CHRONOLOGY BY CHRIS SCALLY

INTRODUCTION:

This paper is a work-in-progress, the objectives of which are twofold: first, to document as completely as possible the chronology of the Orville Nix 8mm film of the assassination of President John F. Kennedy in Dallas on November 22, 1963, from the time of the assassination until the last known confirmed sighting of the film; and second, to serve as a research aid to Ms. Gayle Nix Jackson, the granddaughter of Orville Nix, to assist in her search for the current whereabouts of her grandfather's film.

FRIDAY, NOVEMBER 22, 1963:

Orville Orhel Nix (April 16, 1911 – January 17, 1972)[1], of 2527 Denley Drive, Dallas, an employee of the General Services Administration based in the Terminal Annex Building, Dallas, filmed the presidential limousine on both Houston and Elm Street with his Keystone Auto Zoom 8mm home-movie camera, Model K-810, Serial Number 5094T, using Kodachrome II Type A indoor film, with the camera speed set to 'normal' (the FBI later determined that the average film speed was 18.5 fps).[2] He returned to the Plaza the next morning, and filmed in the area again around 7:28 am.[3]

Saturday, November 30, 1963:

Nix's son Orville Jr., asked him to drive to a South Oak Cliff High School football game, where a girlfriend of his daughter-in-law's brother was a majorette leading the school band during half-time of the football game.[4] On the way home, Nix dropped off his film for processing overnight at the Dynacolor photo lab at 3221 Halifax Street, near Love Field airport in Dallas.[5]

Sunday, December 1, 1963:

Dynacolor called Nix in the middle of the night to inform him that he had captured the shooting on film. Nix called his son in the early morning hours of December 1st and they both drove to the plant. There Orville Nix, his son and two technicians viewed the Nix film for the first time against a white wall. They replayed it over 20 times. Dynacolor informed Nix that the FBI had issued an edict to all the photo labs in Dallas to turn over any film they processed that captured the JFK assassination. Nix contacted the local FBI office that same morning, as a result of which he was interviewed by SA Joe B. Abernathy, to whom he handed over his 8mm camera-original film.[10] Nix wanted his film returned to him as soon as possible, so the Dallas FBI office had a copy of the film made at the Jamieson Film plant in Dallas, and that copy was later sent to the FBI Lab in Washington.[11]

Wednesday, December 4, 1963:

Nix's original film, now said to be badly scratched, was returned to him.[12]

Thursday, December 5, 1963:

According to an unpublished FBI file located at NARA[13], SA Barrett got the film from Nix on December 5 – it is probable that Barrett got the copy made for the FBI by Jamieson between December 1 and December 4, and sent it to headquarters on December 5, rather than he 'got the film from Nix' on December 5.

Friday, December 6, 1963:

Nix and his son flew to New York where, having been rejected by *Life*, the original film was sold for $5,000 to UPI, in the person of Burt Reinhardt and Maurice Schonfeld. Nix asked Reinhardt if the family could have the film back in, perhaps, 25 years or so. Reinhardt agreed, and the two men sealed the deal with a handshake.[14]

Tuesday, December 10, 1963:

Nix received a copy of his film, a check for $5,000 and a new hat from UPI. That copy of the film was the copy held by the family throughout the years, and eventually exchanged with the Dallas FBI office in 1991 for their superior copy.[15]

Thursday, December 19, 1963:

FBI headquarters sent a copy of the Nix film back to their Dallas office.[16]

Wednesday February 26 – Tuesday, March 3, 1964:

Secret Service agent John Howlett asked the FBI's Lyndal Shaneyfelt if the FBI could let the Secret Service have a copy of the Nix film. According to Howlett, he had "requested a copy of the film from Mr. Nix and found Mr. Nix's copy is very poor". On March 3, 1964

Orville Nix asked the Dallas FBI office if it would be possible to get a "more clear copy" of his film from them, as the copy of his film which he had originally received from the Bureau "does not appear as clear as his usual pictures and that it may be partially due to the fact that in viewing his present copy he had frequently stopped the film in the projector." A "copy of the film originally furnished (to) the Bureau" was sent to the Dallas FBI office on March 24, to be given to Mr. Nix.[18] (Was this the copy of the film which was exchanged with the Dallas FBI office in 1991?)

Thursday, March 26, 1964:

The copy of his film requested from the FBI by Nix on March 16 was sent by the Dallas office to his home address via registered mail.[19]

Wednesday, August 12, 1964:

John F. Novatney, Jr., of the Cleveland Law firm of Baker, Hostetler and Patterson, wrote to Edward C. Kemper Jr. of the FBI regarding the protection by the FBI and Warren Commission of UPI's copyright over the Nix film. Novatney wrote that his notes of their meeting the previous day indicated that the FBI/Commission were in possession of at least six copies of the Nix film, including the copy given to the FBI by UPI. Novatney also noted that a single print of the film had recently been given to Mr. Nix, but that "the FBI has no intention of giving Mr. Nix any further prints".[20]

1964/1965:

When the Warren Commission ceased to exist, the copies of the Nix and Muchmore films which UPI had given to the Commission were turned over to the National Archives under a special agreement with UPI, which prevented anyone from obtaining copies of the films, or slides from individual frames from the Archives for any purpose, commercial or otherwise.[22] Indeed, until researcher/author Harold Weisberg obtained written permission from UPI in 1966, nobody was even allowed to see the Nix or Muchmore films at the National Archives.[23]

Meanwhile, UPI made a composite 35mm movie film from the original 8mm original Nix and Muchmore films, and this composite film (which used a technique of repeating a frame several times to give the impression of slow-motion or stop action during key sections of the films) was shown to researchers by Maurice Schonfeld, Burt Reinhardt and Jack Fox at UPI's projection studio in New York.[24]

WINTER 1965:

Jones Harris and Bernie Hoffman worked through the winter of 1965-66 with Maurice Schonfeld in an effort to determine if a gunman on the grassy knoll was visible in the Nix film. According to Schonfeld, UPI "produced the original" film, so that Hoffman "could make the best possible reproductions." Harris and Hoffman discovered what they believed were "the head, shoulders, arms and gun of (a) rifleman" leaning on a station wagon which was parked some distance behind the retaining wall to the west of the pergola, on the north side of Elm Street.[25] UPI was unwilling to pay for further research, on the grounds that it could potentially prove very costly, might turn into an "epic nonstory", and would provide no immediate financial return.[26]

JAN-MAY 1967:

Arising from the Harris/Hoffman research, a study of the Nix film was carried out for UPI by ITEK Corp., Lexington, MA. Maurice Schonfeld of UPI personally carried "the original Nix 8-millimeter color motion picture" film, which was described as being "31-foot long", taken by Orville O. Nix and owned by UPI, to Lexington from its vault location at New York's Chase Manhattan Bank.[27] The photographic source data for this study reportedly included the original film, as well as "black and white 13x enlarged negatives made from all colour frames of the original Nix film"; "black and white 13x enlarged paper prints" made from those negatives; and "color transparencies of selected frames of the original film, enlarged 13x".[28] ITEK concluded that the unidentified 'shape' in the vicinity of the concrete wall was "shadow and highlight details created by the sun casting shadows of tree branches on the wall".[29]

Friday, June 2, 1967:

The Emilio De Antonia/Mark Lane film "Rush to Judgement" was released. The film included an interview of Orville Nix by Mark Lane, in which Nix – when answering Lane's question about the film being handed over to the authorities more than a week after the assassination - said that his film was "lost" at the processing plant. With regard to the film he now had in his possession, Nix said that some frames may be missing - "some of the frames were ruined".[30] There is, however, no credible evidence to hand at this time to support either of these assertions.

Early 1969:

Robert Groden first approached Moses Weitzman, owner of EFX Unlimited, a NY photo lab, seeking employment.[31]

1971:

According to Richard E. Sprague, UPI offered "to make the (Nix) film available for a very large sum of money" while at the same time refusing to make copies available for research.[32] Unfortunately, as Mr. Sprague is now sadly deceased, it has not been possible to get further clarification of what was meant by 'making the film available for a large sum of money' – were UPI considering the sale of the film at that point in time?

August 1973:

The producers of the film "Executive Action" approached UPI regarding the use of the Nix film in their movie.[33] Robert Groden confirmed this in his deposition before the ARRB, when he explained how he subsequently got Wakeford-Orloff Productions and Moses Weitzman's company, EFX, together.[34]

October 1973:

Still unconvinced about whether or not the Nix film contained definitive evidence of a gunman in the area behind the retaining wall to the right-front of the presidential limousine (the area in question is circled in the photographs below), Maurice Schonfeld looked into the possibility of enhancing the imagery in the film. Digital enhancement was carried out between October

1973 and February 1975 on "a copy of the Nix film supplied by Mr. Maurice Schonfeld" by James Lattimer, a student of Dr. Kenneth Castleman, a scientist at Caltech's Jet Propulsion Lab.[35] Dr. Castleman has recently confirmed that only one copy of the Nix film was provided for study, and that this colour copy was provided to him by to Maurice Schonfeld. Dr. Castleman also confirmed that the Caltech/JPL study was focussed only on the area behind the wall which had been first identified by Jones Harris and Bernie Hoffman in 1964-5.[36] The study concluded that while "the Nix film fails to support strongly" the theory of a grassy knoll gunman, "it cannot be positively ruled out". The report added that it was "remotely possible" that what was shown in the film might be "due to an assassin immediately behind the wall who moved to his right, as Nix moved".[37]

According to Moses Weitzman, "Mr. Schonfeld contracted with Effects Unlimited to make 35mm blow-ups with six or eight copies, three or four in colour and others in black and white." Weitzman "believed the black and white prints were for Caltech's Jet Propulsion Laboratory analysis. When Robert Groden showed digital black and white "JPL copies" to him, Weitzman did not recall seeing the same detail in the knoll area that he remembered. In an earlier study of the Nix film, on a Hazeltene (sic) Color Analyzer, the original film purportedly revealed more background details and a possible flash or other clue in the background."[38] Mr. Weitzman has recently told Gayle Nix Jackson that this work for UPI was carried out in 1972 (although he almost certainly meant 1973), and that Schonfeld had asked him to "enhance" the classic-gunman image on the film, which he did using a Hazeltine Analyzer.[39] Therefore, in this author's opinion, Weitzman's reference to an "earlier study" is probably in error – the examination of the material with the Hazeltine Analyzer was clearly carried out during the early stages of the Caltech/JPL project.

In his deposition before the ARRB in 1996, Weitzman referred to what he perceived to be the very clear presence of a man in the colour photographs which he made for UPI at this time.[40] He repeated this in a recent telephone conversation with Gayle Nix Jackson, when he described more clearly what he saw as "the image of a person wearing what seemed to be a red bandana, holding what appeared to be a metallic broomstick type object and the distinct pink flesh tones of hands holding the metallic object. This red bandana image is hidden in the brushy area and clearly moves along the fence after the head shot. It could be seen behind the picket fence area, on Zapruder's right."[41] Moses Weitzman explained why the 1975 Cal Tech/JPL study did not appear to see the same imagery that he described, when he told the ARRB: "In fairness to them, they didn't see what we saw – they saw a black-and-white image, they didn't see colour - and colour made the difference."[42] Weitzman has also recently claimed that UPI subsequently paid him (through Maurice Schonfeld) $100,000 to make 24 copies of the Nix film, 12 in colour and 12 in black-and-white, which were then sent to Caltech under very clandestine terms. He also expressed the view that the camera-original film was destroyed around this time.[43]

There also appears to be a discrepancy between the locations in which the suspect images were seen by Caltech/JPL and Moses Weitzman. The Caltech/JPL study was focused on the 'classic gunman' image behind the wall very close to when Abraham Zapruder was also filming at the time of the assassination; Weitzman, however, claimed to have seen 'bandana-man' in the bushy area behind the picket fence, which would suggest a location somewhat further to the west of the Caltech/JPL location. A satisfactory resolution to this apparent difference may never be found – are the parties involved referring to two entirely different images, or is it simply a case of a faulty recollection after more than 40 years?

1973 (PRE-NOVEMBER):

Robert Groden allegedly obtained a 16mm or 35mm (his ARRB deposition indicates it could have been either[44]) colour second-generation copy of the film from Mo Weitzman, whose EFX lab had done work on the film for the movie "Executive Action", which was released on November 7, 1973.[45] Groden also got a fourth-generation 35mm copy (unsure whether it was negative or a print) of the film from David Lifton, who had also obtained it while working on "Executive Action".[46]

THURSDAY, NOVEMBER 22 - FRIDAY, NOVEMBER 23, 1973:

Groden's deposition says he screened a 16mm copy of Nix film at a symposium in Georgetown University.[47] As noted above Lifton only had a 35mm copy of the film. Therefore, this could not have been the Lifton copy, so where did it come from? Could it have originated from the work done by EFX for the producers of "Executive Action" earlier in 1973?

1974:

Maurice Schonfeld left UPI in 1974. Prior to his departure, he accompanied Burt Reinhardt as a witness while Reinhardt placed the original Nix film in a safe deposit box at a New York branch of Chase Manhattan bank (now demolished, the branch was formerly the Clinton Union Trust Bank) and sent the key to the box to Alexander Bock, UPI's chief accountant, a claim subsequently denied by Mr. Bock.[48] Burt Reinhardt also subsequently left the company (he joined CNN in 1979 after leaving UPITN[49]), and UPITN (the successor to UPI Newsfilm) eventually closed its offices in New York in the late 1970s.[50]

APRIL 1977:

A Canadian research group made available a Super-8 colour copy of the Nix film, which included "complete footage shot of motorcade". A description of the film which was circulated to potential purchasers said that there were no frames missing from the film "as we now have the complete print of his footage (from the original) and there is nothing missing. Nevertheless it would seem that a hoax of a kind was created with regard to the Nix film being of little use due to poor quality, etc. This is not so. As we now have the 2nd generation copy – his film is of superb quality and is possibly as good as the Zapruder original." It is believed that this film, along with the Muchmore film, which was also owned by UPI, was made when the original was being prepared for the use of the House Select Committee on Assassinations (HSCA).[51] [In an effort to elicit any information regarding the source of a splice in the copy of the Muchmore film, the author contacted UPI in London by letter in June 1977. In the absence of any response, I contacted UPI in London by telephone. Unfortunately, no effort whatsoever was made to assist, and it was suggested that I contact the Head of their Newsfilm department in their New York office, which I did on July 12.[52] No response was ever received to either letter.]

1976-1978:

The HSCA subpoenaed (and received) the original Nix film from UPITN; however, two members of the HSCA's photographic panel (Drs. Clyde Snow and Paul Roetling) told Nix's granddaughter, Gayle Nix Jackson, in March 2014 that "they had never studied the film, only frames… Eight frames were shown to them and those were the eight frames studied".[53]

The HSCA used the film as part of their overall "grassy knoll" photographic evidence study. Several frames of the Nix film were scanned at Los Alamos Scientific Laboratory, and the scanned frames were then computer-enhanced at the Aerospace Corp., resulting in images which appeared to be more 'in-focus' than the original frame. The HSCA's attention was focussed on the 'classic gunman image' behind the retaining wall, the same area which was first highlighted by Jones Harris and Bernie Hoffman nearly 15 years earlier. The Committee's photographic panel concluded that while the object in question could be "construed as a shape similar to that of a person", the absence of detectable flesh tones in either the original or enhanced Nix frames indicated that "the most probable explanation is that the image is a chance pattern on sunlight on the structure behind the retaining wall", endorsing the findings of the 1967 ITEK study of the film in the process.[54] According to Robert Groden, "the original (Nix) footage disappeared in 1978 after it was returned to UPI by the House Assassinations Committee."[55]

1979:

Sixth Floor Museum Curator Gary Mack notes that Gayle Nix Jackson was in possession of documentation from the HSCA showing the original 8mm Nix film was returned to UPITN and a signed receipt was obtained.[56] However, according to Maurice Schonfeld, it was Gary Mack who confirmed that the original Nix film was returned to UPITN in 1979, not Gayle Nix Jackson. Mack had allegedly found a receipt for the film at UPITN, signed by two UPITN employees, one of whom is deceased and the other's signature is unreadable.[57]

1982:

Evidence originating from a senior level within UPITN indicates that the original Nix film might have been among the material in the UPI film library when it was sold to ITN (Independent Television News) in London in 1982, although ITN subsequently claimed not to have the film in their possession.[58]

Also in 1982, the Western New England College, Springfield, Mass. (WNEC) Center for the study of American Political Assassinations produced a videotape called "The Assassination of President John F. Kennedy", which contained a number of assassination-related films, including the Nix film.[59] Study of this tape seems to indicate that two versions of the Nix film were included – one with the hair, and the second without the hair. Although not identified, the narrator on the latter half of the videotape (which includes the version containing the hair) is clearly Robert Groden. This is the first reference I can find to a copy – described in 1995 by Groden as having been "made from a duplicate negative" - in the public domain, which does not contain the hair! Prior to this, the only confirmed public domain copy I can find is from "Executive Action" (1973), which contains the hair. Is there any possible link between the appearance of this 'hairless' copy of the film and the alleged transfer/sale of the original film to ITN in London?

1988:

A British TV documentary, "The Day the Dream Died", included a showing of the Nix film. This copy of the film contained the "hair" in the lower part of the frame.[60] In the course of the program, it was stated that Belgian-born film producer Jean Michel Charlier had obtained a copy of the Nix film from Nix's son, Orville Nix Jr., and that the copy was made "before the original was given to the FBI". An Internet search has revealed that M. Charlier is now deceased.[61] The Nix family has no memory or contract of ever allowing or giving Charlier a copy of the film.

Circa 1990:

In a letter to Rollie Zavada, published as part of the Kodak/Zavada Report for the ARRB, Mo Weitzman claimed than an exchange of correspondence between himself and Robert Richter (a NY film producer) in 1990 arose out of a claim by Groden that Richter and David Lifton were using material loaned to WGBH (Boston public TV station) for the production of a "Nova" Special program.[62] According to Weitzman, "the negative was obviously copied, an interpositive made and a duplicate negative struck. I received the negative and interpositive (presumably the negative I originally supplied) which I gave with all prints that I had made to Robert Groden for safe keeping". In a summary by Rollie Zavada of his dealings with Weitzman, Zavada wrote: "Mr. Weitzman recalls that in 1990 or 1991, Mr. Groden rented printing time from Eastern Optical Effects, and this may have represented the time period that the 35mm contact prints supplied to NARA were made by Mr. Groden".[63] [Note: Eastern Optical Effects was a company owned and managed by Mr. Weitzman from 1989 to 1997 (and possibly beyond that date); also, the reference to "NARA" should probably read "ARRB". As Weitzman does not specify exactly when the Richter/Lifton use of the material loaned to WGBH allegedly took place, his explanation is possibly inconsistent with my discovery that Groden had a copy of the film without the hair as early as 1982.

1991:

Gayle Nix Jackson, the daughter of Orville Nix Jr. who had heard the story from her father, sought to get the film back from UPI, as her grandfather had agreed with Burt Reinhardt on December 6, 1963. She contacted Worldwide Television News (WTN), the successor company to UPITN since 1985, and they contacted Reinhardt (who had left UPI many years earlier and became one of the founders of CNN), who promptly confirmed the 1963 oral agreement. WTN ultimately returned all copies of the Nix film they could find to Ms. Jackson, with the exception of the 8mm original, which could not be located.[64]

Prior to Friday, June 28, 1991:

Ms. Nix Jackson mentioned to Gary Mack that the family only had a well-worn 8mm copy of the film which she thought came from UPITN many years before. Unfortunately, it was in terrible condition, was badly scratched and had been broken and repaired by splicing. At Mack's suggestion, Ms. Nix Jackson contacted the Dallas FBI office, where a female agent told her that they had a copy of the film which had been in their files since 1963 (presumably the copy made by Jamieson in Dallas, sent to Washington and later returned to Dallas). The FBI copy, which was "in near-pristine, beautiful condition" was given to Ms. Nix Jackson the next day, in exchange for the Nix family's copy. According to the Sixth Floor Museum website 'Collections' section, their copy of the film is a "First-generation print of an 8mm color home movie by Orville Nix showing the presidential motorcade in Dealey Plaza... This first-generation print of the original home movie was originally made for the FBI."[65]

FRIDAY, JUNE 28, 1991:

According to Gary Mack, Robert Groden drove from his home in New Jersey to New York City to collect all copies of the Nix film from WTN, and then flew to Dallas to deliver the reels to Ms. Nix Jackson. In his ARRB deposition, however, Groden said he took the material home, wrapped it up, and shipped it to her within three days – he denied making any copies of the material, saying that his copy was "far superior".[66] An effort to determine if a complete inventory of the material obtained from WTN is contained in the files of the ARRB is ongoing as of April 2014. The possible existence of a complete inventory of the material obtained from WTN was raised in Robert Groden's deposition before the ARRB, and the author is currently engaged in e-mail correspondence with NARA regarding its possible existence within the records of the ARRB.[67]

1991:

Gayle Nix Jackson was asked to provide a videotape copy of the Nix film for a TV production. She asked Gary Mack for help and he took the reels to 'Filmworkers', a Dallas film post-production company founded in 1991. The best copy was a print made by UPITN in 1964, according to the film's date code, that included slow motion and blow-up scenes (this could very possibly be the copy referred to by Richard Sprague in his 1973 "Computers and Automation" article – see earlier entry under "1964/1965"). The videotape was licensed to Oliver Stone for his movie, "JFK" (released in the USA in December 1991), and Ms. Jackson loaned the best reels to his production team. Stone later returned the films, with at least one new 35mm copy for Ms. Jackson's own use.[68] In the narrative on the 1995 "The Assassination Films" (15:20), Groden says: "This is the only known copy of the Nix film made directly from the original. The original is now lost. The copy negative this was made from unfortunately picked up a hair at the lower left-hand corner. It is included here because of its historic value. [A second version is now shown, as Groden continues to narrate…] This version is slightly slowed down, and is made from a duplicate negative that does not have the hair". [These are similar to the words used ("a print of the copy negative") in Groden's ARRB deposition to describe the copy he got from David Lifton in 1973.] I have subsequently been told that Groden now admits that the hair in his copy of the film got there while he was copying a 16mm print.[69]

Thursday, December 21, 1995:

Charles Mayn of NARA reported that the copy of the Nix film stored at NARA "is not an out-of-camera film".[70]

Tuesday, July 2, 1996:

Robert Groden turned over what he described as a second-generation 35mm colour print of the Nix film to the ARRB. Groden described this as the copy he received in 1973 from Mo Weitzman, and which he said was a copy made from a negative, which was made from the camera-original film, and to his knowledge it was the only surviving copy of the film made directly from the original.[71]

Friday, September 25, 1998:

A Kodak Technical Report (commonly referred to as the Zavada Report) revealed that the 35m copy of the film given to the ARRB in 1996 by Robert Groden was printed on 1992-manufactured Eastman colour print film stock, and the 35mm laboratory intermediate film from which it was printed was of 1991 manufacture.[72]

1999/2000:

The Nix family transferred ownership of the Nix film to The Sixth Floor Museum. The acquisition included the Nix film copyright along with all known copies of the film, including the FBI's 8mm print, Oliver Stone's 35mm copy, and the video tape transfer.

2011

Frames from "The Lost Bullet" (National Geographic, 2011), which also contain no 'hair-like' artefact, and which Gary Mack says are "HD scans of the first generation 8mm FBI print and a 16mm second generation copy print."[75] Mack also confirmed that "a first generation 16mm negative has not yet been scanned" - presumably by the Sixth Floor Museum?[76] I suspect this could be the 'missing' first-generation negative from which Robert Groden claims to have received (through Mo Weitzman) his alleged second-generation print of the film in 1973.

NOTES

1. http://en.wikipedia.org/wiki/Orville_Nix. Corrected by Gayle Nix Jackson's "Orville Nix: The Missing Film of the JFK Assassination." April, 2014.
2. See Sixth Floor Museum "Orville Nix Film Overview and Time Line" and "Curator's Notes" relating to the Nix film, at http://www.jfk.org/go/collections/about/orville-nix-film-interview and http://emuseum.jfk.org/view/objects/asitem/search@/3/title-asc?t:state:flow=833edea1-cff8-4463-ab80-f06ad6f52ea8 respectively; see also CD 385, p. 70 – FBI lab report dated February 4, 1964.
3. "The Shadow of a Gunman", by Maurice W. Schonfeld, published in July/August 1975 issue of the Columbia Journalism Review , available on-line (with an additional Epilogue dated November 22, 2011) at http://www.cjr.org/fiftieth_anniversary/the_shadow_of_a_gunman.php?page=6
4. Schonfeld, op cit.; Richard Trask, "Pictures of the Pain", citing Richard E. Sprague notes of telephone interview with Mrs. Orville Nix Jr., in 1968.
5. Schonfeld, op. cit.; SFM Curator's Notes, op. cit.; see http://www.city-data.com/zips/75247.html for reference to 3M/Dynacolor on Halifax Street, Dallas.
6. Trask, "Pictures of the Pain", pp. 620-1;
7. Dale K. Myers, "Epipolar Geometric Analysis of Amateur Films Related to Acoustics Evidence in the John F. Kennedy Assassination", Second Revision, November 1, 2010, Appendix III, pp. 135-6
8. "JFK Assassination: The complete Orville Nix film" on the JFK Assassination Forum website

9. Author's calculations on April 14, 2014

10. See SFM Curator's Notes, op. cit.; Warren Commission Exhibit 2109 (also CD 385) - FBI interview by SA Joe B. Abernathy with Orville Nix on December 1, 1963. Warren Commission Hearings, Vol. 14, p. 539

11. "Pictures of the Pain", by Richard Trask, p. 183; FBI Airtel dated December 5, 1963 from SAC, Dallas to Director, J. Edgar Hoover, marked "Attention FBI Laboratory, #62-109060-2063"; FBI Memorandum from Cartha DeLoach to A. Rosen, dated November 18, 1966 in FBI headquarters file, 60-109060-4275.

12. See Schonfeld, op. cit.

13. NARA FBI file 89-43-271 (or 1A271), dated January 11, 1968, which purports to be a "list of alleged photos pertinent to assassination and pertinent comments re each of those accounted for." The list was compiled "By SA F.F. John".

14. E-mail from Gayle Jackson, March 24, 2014; Schonfeld, op. cit.; SFM Curator's Notes, op. cit.

15. Gayle Jackson e-mail, March 24, 2014; Sixth Floor Museum, op. cit.

16. FBI Memorandum from Director to SAIC, Dallas dated November 18, 1966, summarising the handling of the Nix film and camera – in FBI headquarters file 62-109060-4265

17. FBI Memo from Mr. Conrad to W.D. Griffith dated March 26, 1964 and letter to Kelley from Hoover dated March 3, 1964, in FBI headquarters file, 60-109060-2519

18. FBI Airtel dated March 17, 1964 to Director from SAC, Dallas, in FBI headquarters file – 105-82555-2722; Airtel from Director, FBI to SAC, Dallas dated March 24, 1964; see also Richard Trask, "Pictures of the Pain", pp. 183ff

19. FBI Memorandum from Director to SAIC, Dallas dated November 18, 1966, summarising the handling of the Nix film and camera – in FBI headquarters file 62-109060-4265.

20. Letter to Edward C. Kemper Jr., FBI, from John F. Novatney, Jr., Baker, Hostetler & Patterson dated August 12, 1964, in FBI headquarters file 60-109060-3646

21. Commission Exhibit 885, in Volume 18 of the Warren Commission Hearings, pages 81-3

22. Richard E. Sprague, "The American News Media and the Assassination of President John F. Kennedy: Accessories After The Fact", in Computers and Automation, July 1973, p. 34. This article subsequently appeared in Sprague's

book, "The Taking of America 1-2-3" (1976 and 1979, Private Publication), pp. 115-120 and 100-103, respectively.

23. Harold Weisberg, "Photographic Whitewash" (Private publication: Hyattstown, Md. 20734; 1967), p. 296
24. Sprague, op. cit.
25. Schonfeld, op. cit.
26. Ibid.
27. "Nix Film Analysis", dated 18 May 1967, produced by ITEK Corporation, Lexington, Mass. 02173, in author's files.
28. Ibid. The manufacturer of the black and white negative and prints, and/or the colour transparencies is unclear – were they made by ITEK in 1967, or were at least some the work of Jones Harris and Bernie Hoffman, who studied the film in 1965/6? And was Moses Weitzman involved in the process in any way?
29. Ibid.
30. "Rush to Judgement", starting at approx. 43 minutes into the film
31. Moses Weitzman ARRB interview, July 19, 1996 at 6 mins. 30 secs. into Side 1a of recording in author's files
32. Sprague, op. cit.
33. Schonfeld, op. cit.
34. Groden ARRB deposition, p. 238
35. Schonfeld, op. cit.; Author's correspondence with Cornell University and Caltech's Jet Propulsion Lab from February through October, 1976; also referenced at 10:55 into Side 1b of recording in author's files of Weitzman's ARRB interview, June 19, 1996.
36. Dr. Castleman telephone conversation with Gayle Nix Jackson, April 11, 2014
37. Schonfeld, op. cit.
38. Kodak Technical Report 318420P, "Analysis of Selected Motion Picture Photographic Evidence", dated September 25, 1998, authored by R.J. Zavada, on behalf of the Assassination Records Review Board (ARRB), Study 2, Attachment 2-8. Note that Effects Unlimited (EFX) existed from 1968 to 1989, also according to this Zavada Report attachment. Note: Internet research (see http://ebookbrowsee.net/hazeltine-color-film-analyzer-brochure-sep69-pdf-d438393941) indicates that the correct spelling of the Analyser name is "'Hazeltine", and it operated with 16mm and 35mm film – the original Nix film was in 8mm format since the day it was processed, I believe.

39. Moses Weitzman telephone conversation with Gayle Nix Jackson on April 10, 2014.

40. Weitzman ARRB interview on July 19, 1996, starting at 39 minutes into Side 1b, and again at 25 minutes 13 seconds into Side 2b of recordings of the interview in author's files.

41. Weitzman telephone conversation with Gayle Nix Jackson, April 10, 2014.

42. Weitzman ARRB interview on July 19, 1996 (beginning at 25 mins 13 secs into Side 2b of recording in author's files)

43. Weitzman telephone conversation with Gayle Nix Jackson, April 10, 2014.

44. Robert Groden deposition before the ARRB, July 2 and August 20, 1996 – available on-line at http://www.aarclibrary.org/publib/jfk/arrb/medical_testimony/pdf/Groden_7-2-96.pdf

45. Weitzman denied during his ARRB interview on July 19, 1996 (at 9 min 30 secs into Side 1b of recording in author's files) that Groden ever got the 'copy of a negative made from the camera-original Nix film' from him

46. In a letter to me in August 1978, Lifton confirmed that he had received a 35mm copy of the film while working on "Executive Action". See also "Pig On A Leash", by David Lifton, in the compilation book "The Great Zapruder Film Hoax", James H. Fetzer (ed.), (Catfish Press, 2003)

47. Groden ARRB deposition, op. cit.

48. Schonfeld, op. cit.; Gayle Nix Jackson e-mail to author, December 4, 2013; Schonfeld telephone conversation with Gayle Nix Jackson on April 16, 2014.

49. Burt Reinhardt (1920-2011) - see http://en.wikipedia.org/wiki/Burt_Reinhardt

50. For a brief history of UPITN, see http://en.wikipedia.org/wiki/United_Press_International_Television_News

51. Letters to the author from researcher Harry Erwin, dated April 8 and May 26, 1977, with an attachment dated April 3, 1977

52. Letters to UPI dated June 19 and July 12, 1977

53. http://gaylenixjackson.com/uncategorized/not-in-the-book-the-photographic-panel-of-the-hsca/

54. 54 HSCA Photographic Panel Report in HSCA Appendix to Hearings, Vol. 6, pp. 121, 126, 130-131

55. Robert J. Groden, "The Killing Of a President" (Viking Penguin: 1993), p. 32

56. Sixth Floor Museum Curator's Notes, op. cit.; these notes must have been written after the Museum obtained the Nix material in 1999/2000

57. Schonfeld, op. cit. (only included in the November 2011 Epilogue, in the on-line version of the article)

58. UPI/Gayle Nix Jackson correspondence , 1981, referenced in Gayle Nix Jackson e-mail to the author, April 10, 2014

59. http://www.worldcat.org/title/assassination-of-president-john-f-kennedy/oclc/8551687 or http://www.worldcat.org/title/assassination-of-president-john-f-kennedy/oclc/9544941

60. http://www.youtube.com/watch?v=j35UxRKDW-s

61. http://en.wikipedia.org/wiki/Jean-Michel_Charlier M. Charlier was born on October 30, 1924, and died on July 10, 1989.

62. Moses Weitzman ARRB interview, July 19, 1996 at 13 minutes into Side 1a recording in author's files

63. Zavada Report, Study 2, Attachments A2-7 and 2-8

64. SFM Curator's Notes, op. cit; Schonfeld, op. cit.

65. SFM Curator's Notes, op. cit

66. SFM Curator's Notes, op. cit; Groden ARRB deposition, op. cit.

67. Author's ongoing e-mail correspondence with NARA, which commenced on April 9, 2014.

68. SFM Curator's Notes, op. cit; https://www.facebook.com/pages/Filmworkers-Dallas/339980002692629?sk=info

69. Gayle Nix Jackson e–mail to the author, April 4, 2014

70. James Fetzer, "Assassination Science" (Catfeet Press: 1998), p. 303

71. Groden ARRB deposition, op. cit.

72. KodakZavada Report, Study 2, pp. 1-9

73. SFM Curator's Notes, op. cit.

74. http://www.jfk-online.com/1nix.html. My e-mail to Dave Reitzes of March 31, 2014, requesting any information he might be able to share regarding the source of this copy of the film has remained unanswered.

75. Gary Mack e-mail to Robin Unger, March 24, 2014

76. Ibid

AFTERWORD

A FEW LAST WORDS

"Dante once said that the hottest places in hell are reserved for those who in a period of moral crisis maintain their neutrality"

John F. Kennedy

This section of the book is one I debated on including. Many told me to include it, others said not to. What good would this part do? How would it help find the film? I wrote this book as a testament to the life my grandfather lived after taking the film of the JFK assassination. I shared his foibles; I felt it only right to share mine. I have witnessed and been victim to many shameful acts regarding the Nix film. In the vein of true transparency, I have chosen to share my experiences and decisions regarding my grandfather's film.

The first one was in 1988, when I began negotiating with UPITN to get the rights back to the Nix family. My own family thought I was chasing a lost cause. How could someone like me, without a law degree, without even the benefit of a lawyer get them back from such a huge company? I have always thought, and still believe, that the truth will ultimately overcome the biggest of obstacles. Michael Veve, the lawyer for UPITN who was unjustly fired for agreeing to return the rights to my family was a kind man doing the right thing. Unfortunately, in business negotiations, doing the right thing doesn't get you promoted. Though the agreement to return the rights was nothing more than a handshake between my grandfather and Burt Reinhardt, at one time, a handshake meant something...just like a promise used to mean something.

Michael Veve knew this. It also helped, of course that copyright law before 1978 was written in such a way that the original owner's copyrights were renewable after twenty-five years.

After consulting with Reinhardt, who was no longer with UPITN, Veve agreed to return the rights to me and my family and was fired by UPITN. I soon got a letter from his successor saying Veve was wrong and that I would have to wait an additional two years. I am not a wealthy woman. I am not from a wealthy family. I could not afford to hire an attorney, yet I called one, Howard Key, and pleaded my case with him. For a small sum, he sent a few letters to UPITN on my behalf to request the film and copyright be returned. I still had to wait for several months.

When the film was finally returned, I then had the burden of retrieving all existing copies. Again, finances became an issue. By this time, the local newspaper had heard my story and the wire picked it up. I was interviewed by several daily newspapers and eventually met Gary Mack. At that time, he was working for the local NBC affiliate as a voice-over man with a penchant for the JFK assassination. He had gotten a copy of the Moorman photo from Robert Groden. Since he and Groden were friends and Robert lived near New York where the UPI offices were, he suggested I have Groden not only pick up my copies from UPITN, but also check to see if the original Nix film was housed at the National Archives. It wasn't. In fact, the copy at the National Archives wasn't even as good as the copy Groden owned. How could that be?

One reason is because UPITN, unlike *Life* Magazine, wasn't diligent in their safe-keeping of the Nix film. During his tenure at *Life*, one of the jobs James Wagenvoord had was ensuring the safety of the Zapruder film. He knew where it was at all times and who had access to it. That wasn't the case for the Nix film. In 1971, when the movie *Executive Action* was made, the Nix film was sent to Moe Weitzman's studio, Manhattan Effects, later called EFX Unlimited. Weitzman used a liquid gate to get high quality 35mm images that were quite ahead of their time. It just so happened that Robert Groden worked there as well. He testified to the ARRB that he never made copies of the Nix film and that the copies he owned and gave to me were second and third generation copies, but many researchers, including David Lifton, disagree with this.

In hearing these stories of how Groden had several 'missing' pieces of photographic evidence in his possession, I became worried. Not only had he worked for EFX where he had access to the camera original film, he was also the photographic consultant for the HSCA. Then, I trusted him (on Gary Mack's advice) to retrieve my copies from UPI. He had three different shots at taking the original Nix film, one of which I personally gave him. Worried, I gathered the funds to meet Groden and his late wife in Boothwyn, Pennsylvania. I asked him face to face if he had the original, assuring him I wasn't the litigious type and just wanted the film back. He swore to me he didn't have it. Later in the day I asked his wife. She never answered me; she just looked down at the floor. I left Pennsylvania still unsure.

I decided to hire a copyright attorney. I wanted one that was familiar with the JFK assassination and knew how often the footage was used worldwide. I came upon Jamie Silverberg.

Silverberg was the attorney for the Zapruder family (one of many). After speaking with him and believing in his assurance that in no way would his representation of the Nix film be a conflict of interest with the Zapruder film, he became the Nix film representative. I will say, my little voice told me I probably shouldn't do this, but since I was becoming jaded by all the dishonesty I was finding within the JFK community, I silenced the little voice by reasoning it was just my neuroticism. The Silverberg relationship didn't last long due to this and his fees were a little higher than most copyright attorneys charged. No matter, I was fine with it as I was in graduate school and I didn't have to put money upfront. Silverberg was paid from the proceeds of the royalties.

By 1999, I was over forty and pregnant with my son. I was forced to quit work on my PhD as my pregnancy was considered high-risk due to my age. My parents decided that they and my growing family should buy a country estate in East Texas and raise my children the Emersonian way—near nature. My husband and I put in all our savings for the down payment as did my parents. Fate had other plans. Unfortunately, the owner decided she needed an additional sum of money down before we could purchase the home. My mother, who I believe knew she was terminally ill, was very upset. Her dream of living where she could raise a vegetable garden, have goats and enjoy the pine trees of East Texas was fading quickly. She loved this property with its 20+ acres, 3 homes and a pool house with a cabana. She envisioned having her children and grandchildren there during vacation times while enjoying the new lives of her two youngest grandchildren; my daughter and son. My father wanted to ensure my mother could realize her dream, as did I. So he suggested I sell the film. As much as I love my mother, I knew it was the wrong thing to do. Six months earlier, a newspaper owner in Chicago had offered me four hundred and fifty thousand dollars for the film. I thanked him and kindly declined his offer. In retrospect, probably not the best idea, but it had taken me so long to get the film back into the family; I couldn't bear to part with it. It was an important piece of history that my grandfather had taken and I wanted to keep it for my family. I didn't want it for the money, I wanted it for history.

My father disagreed.

I called the man in Chicago to see if he was still interested in buying the film. He had just learned he had terminal cancer and was unwilling to make the purchase. I understood. I quickly called some of the more influential people I know in finance to see if they knew of anyone who would want to buy the film. Time was of the essence and I didn't have enough of it to find a buyer before the owner rescinded the offer on the home my Mother dearly loved.

I had only one choice.

We 'donated' the film to the Sixth Floor Museum against my wishes. I called my one-time friend Gary Mack and begged him to explain to the then director, Jeff West, how very valuable the film was and that the amount they were offering would indeed be what my family needed to purchase the home, but wasn't fair or equitable. He told me he couldn't help me and hung up. I was crushed. I thought of Gary as a friend. That was the last time I would talk to him until I began to write this book in 2013. As the 'go-to' person for worldwide researchers as well as the media, I will probably be blacklisted by the Sixth Floor Museum for writing about my experiences. It is the risk I must take in the name of truth.

Silverberg, against my wishes but with my father's blessing, negotiated the deal with the Sixth Floor Museum for less than a third of what the Zapruder family received from *Life* magazine in 1963. Little did I or the public know that at the same time Silverberg, and a team of lawyers, were negotiating a donation for the Nix film with the Sixth Floor Museum, he was also negotiating with the U.S. government to pay the Zapruder family over $16.5 million dollars. After this deal, I fired him. The Sixth Floor Museum then employed him.

I questioned my judgement. Could this be coincidence? Bad business on our part? Having faith that people will do the right thing? How could I have been so trusting? How could I have allowed what happened to my grandfather happen again but this time to me? I became disheartened with the whole "take advantage while you can" mindset that seemed to contaminate everyone I had trusted or known. I truly knew how my grandfather felt.

Furthermore, it wasn't just people within the community. It was my family as well. My mother passed away in 2001 after only living for two years in her dream home. My father spiraled into the depths of grief and depression; a grief that still rears its ugly head from time to time today. He lives with me and my family. When I contacted the Sixth Floor Museum about using frames of my grandfather's film for the book, Gary Mack said I would have to license it for a fee. *I, the granddaughter of Orville Nix would have to license my grandfather's film. Time/Life* had sold the Zapruder family the rights back to their film for one dollar. That was after years of giving half of all the royalties *Life* received to the Zapruder family as well. Yet I was told I would have to pay for the rights to use the Nix film in my book. I asked Gary to send me the contract, as I remembered making a stipulation that if the original was ever found, it would belong to me. I also wanted to reread it as to what I could or couldn't say. I was not allowed to disclose how much my family was paid for our "donation."

Surprisingly, another two contracts were sent to me in July of 2013. Both were between my father and the Museum; one dated 2002 the other 2004. Unbeknownst to me, the 2002 contract was for all the letters, correspondence and research I had kept after my grandfather died and all the letters and research I had accrued through my search for the original film and in its return to my family. My father had every right to donate my grandfather's letters as an only child heir, but he had no right to donate my research and letters. The Sixth Floor Museum took it all anyway, though half of the letters and research were addressed to me: Gayle Nix Jackson. How they could legally enter into a contract like that is a mystery to me, though I know that my father was grieving during that time and was obviously not thinking with a clear mind. The Sixth Floor, Gary Mack, and the late Jeff West (who was later fired from his position there) took full advantage of the situation. They were to me what Burt Reinhardt and Maurice Schonfeld were to my grandfather. My father had never taken a big interest in finding out the truth about my grandfather's film, and after my disgust in dealing with Gary Mack, he must have felt I wouldn't mind that he took my personal work and sold it to the Museum. It makes me wonder how many other people this has happened to during the Sixth Floor's tenure. I am appalled it happened to me, but it did and short of suing the father I love but was very upset with, I forgave him. It took me months to do so.

The 2004 contract was for the camera my grandfather used, a donation my father had told me he was going to make. During that meeting with Gary Mack and the Sixth Floor, my father gave him all the home movies of vacations, family trips, and more that my grandfather had taken until he died. Gary promised to transfer them all digitally for my father (as of this writing it hasn't been done since 2004) and then told my father that he had a lead on the original film. He told my father that seeing the other films might help him determine if the lead, a woman in South Texas, had the original film or not. He never told my father whether or not the lead was real and still has all my grandfather's personal film reels. Of course my father never called Gary and asked about the lead. He, as I mentioned, has never had the interest I had and shared with his dad, my grandfather, about the Nix film.

Again, with the transparency I would like to see the media and our government practice, I will admit that if there was any way I could get the Nix film copyright back from the Sixth Floor Museum I would do so. The Nix film has been used more times than one can count and the Museum has made more money from it than my family or my grandfather ever made. Furthermore, I am dismayed by the stance they now take in regards to those who don't believe the "official record" of the JFK assassination. To not take a stance is to take one. To not elaborate on both sides of the story with equal vigor is also taking a stance. I would recommend that the Museum not take any stance at all and curate with truth, not agenda. Though I have tried, it does seem that some circles can't be broken. It is up to those individuals, like you the reader, who will find the truth as to what really happened on November 22, 1963. Reread the words of Jones Harris. Look at the pictures in this book of the photographic work done on the Nix film by Rick Needham. Go to the JFK Assassination Forum and see his work as well as the work of Martin Hinrichs. In seeing those, how can you not question the existence of another gunman?

For posterity, for the past, for our history, don't allow the powers that be ignore your questions. Demand answers while we have the ability to ask questions. The circle of historical lies, misinformation and disinformation must be broken.

Now is the time.

ABOUT THE AUTHOR

Gayle Nix Jackson describes herself as a "one time goddess who had a reality check." To the rest of the world, she's that woman that loves the Texas Rangers and knows more about baseball than household cleaning.

Gayle holds an undergraduate degree in English and Business from Dallas Baptist University and an MA in English and Rhetoric from Texas Woman's University. While beginning her PhD studies, she found she was pregnant with her and her husband Darryl's first child, Taylor, after being told by physicians for twelve years she would never have children. Three years later, she became pregnant with her son, Chance. She has been married for 30 years.

Gayle was in downtown Dallas on November 22, 1963 the day her grandfather, Orville Nix, took the famous Nix film of the assassination. In 1988, twenty-five years after he sold his film to UPI, she negotiated with the now defunct company to have the film returned to the Nix family. It was then she discovered the camera original Nix film is missing.

She has been searching for it ever since.

Oliver Stone used a copy of the film in his blockbuster *JFK* and she appeared on several national television shows including *Geraldo, Montel Williams,* and *Entertainment Tonight* pleading for its return. John Barbour, the godfather of reality TV, included an interview with her in his award-winning documentary, *The Garrison Tapes.*

Orville Nix: The Missing JFK Assassination Film is Nix-Jackson's first of three books regarding the horrific events of November 22, 1963. She hopes her readers will educate their children and others as to the mishandling of the JFK assassination investigation and the loss of key evidence, like the original Nix film.

Gayle is currently working on her next JFK book.

Read Gayle's blog and get updates at: **www.gaylenixjackson.com**

Facebook: **www.facebook.com/gayle.nixjackson**

Twitter: **@gaylejack**

INDEX

A

B

C

D

E

F

G

H

I

J

K

L

M

N

O

P

R

S

T

U

V

W

Y

Z

BIBLIOGRAPHY

"A Permanent Record of What we Watched on Television from November 22 to 25, 1963." *TV Guide 12 (4)* 25 January 1964: 24-40

Adamson, Bruce C. de Mohrenschildt and Zapruder. Interview with the Author, January, 2014

Agee, Philip. *Inside the Company: CIA diary*. New York: Stonehill Publishing, 1975

Aguilar, Gary. "Is Vincent Bugliosi Right that Neutron Activation Analysis Proves Oswald's Guilt?" n.d. *Mary Ferrell Foundation.* 9 September 2013. <http://www.maryferrell.org/wiki/index.php/Essay_-_Is_Vincent_Bugliosi_Right_that_Neutron_Activation_Analysis_Proves_Oswalds_Guilt>

Airport, JFK. "History of JFK Airport." n.d. *JFK Airport.* 19 August 2013. <http://jfkairport.co/jfk-history.html>

Anderson, Jack. " American Expose: Who Murdered JFK?" *Journal Graphics* (1988). Transcript

Andrew, Christopher. *The Sword and the Shield: The Mitrokhin Archive and the Secret History of the KGB*. Basic Books, 1999

Armstrong, John. *The Harvey and Lee Page*. 1999-2013. <http://www.harveyandlee.net/>

Art, Amon Carter Museum of. *Hotel Texas: An Art Exhibition for the President and Mrs. John F. Kennedy*. n.d. <http://www.cartermuseum.org/exhibitions/hotel-texas-an-art-exhibition-for-the-president-and-mrs-john-f-kennedy>

Assassinations, The House Select Committee on. "Forrest Sorrels Testimony." 1974. *Mary Ferrell Foundation.* Report. 2 August 2013

Atlantic, The. *Castro /CIA Plot: Inside the Department of Dirty Tricks*. August 1979. <http://www.theatlantic.com/magazine/archive/1979/08/inside-the-department-of-dirty-tricks/305460/3/>

Backes, Joseph. "Why JFK Went to Texas." 1999. *Fair Play.* 2 September 2013. <http://www.acorn.net/jfkplace/09/fp.back_issues/32nd_Issue/jfk_texas.html>

Bacon, Francis. "Quote." n.d. 12 July 2013. <http://www.brainyquote.com/quotes/authors/f/francis_bacon_3.html>

Beran, Michael Knox. "Fifty Years After Dallas." *National Review Online.* 11 November 2013. web. <http://nationalreview.com/article/364483/fifty-years-after-dallas-michael-knox-beran/page/0/1>

Bernstein, Carl. "The CIA & the Media." *Rolling Stone* 20 October 1977

Bible, The King James. *Through a Glass Darkly 1 Corinthians 13:12*. n.d.

Birnbaum, Bernard. "Your Grandfather, Orville Nix ." June 1967

Bradford, Clint. "List of Films and Movies Taken at Dealey Plaza on 11/22/63." n.d. *Clint Bradfords JFK Info Website.* Ed. Berkley Enterprises Inc. From Computers and Animation. 2 November 2013. <http://www.jfk-info.com/photos1.htm>

—. "Zapruder's WFAA-TV Transcript." n.d. *JFKinfo.Com.* 26 August 2013. <http://www.jfk-info.com/wfaa-tv.htm>

Bradford, Rex. "The Fourteen Minute Gap: Update." 8 September 2002. *History Matters.* 16 September 2013. <http://www.history-matters.com/essays/frameup/FourteenMinuteGap_Update/FourteenMinuteGap_Update.htm>

Bryant, John "Birdman". *The John Birch Society -- Exposed!* n.d. Web. 4 September 2013. <http://www.thebirdman.org/Index/NetLoss/NetLoss-Oliver.html>

Buchan, John (Lord) Tweedsmuir. *Pilgrim's Way: An Essay in Recollection.* New York: Houghton-Mifflin, 1940

Buchanan, Thomas. *Who Killed Kennedy?* Putnam, 1964

Bugliosi, Vincent. *Reclaiming History: The Assassination of President John F. Kennedy*. W. W. Norton & Company, 2007

Burnham, Gregory. *The Amazing Web of Abraham Zapruder: The Man Who Filmed the JFK Assassination.* n.d. 18 August 2013. <http://www.john-f-kennedy.net/amazingwebofabrahamzapruder.htm>

Calculator, Consumer Price Index. 2013. web. July 22 2013. <http://www.calculatorpro.com/calculator/cpi-calculator/>

Camera, Keystone. "Keystone K-810 Instruction Manual." Boston: Hallet Square, May 1963

Camper, Frank. *The MK:ULTRA Secret.* n.d.

Canfield, Michael and Alan J. Weberman. *Coup d'etat in America: The CIA and the Assassination of John F. Kennedy.* 1975

Carlisle, Randy. "Photo of Austin's Barbecue Restaurant." n.d.

Caro, Robert A. *The Passage of Power: The Lyndon Johnson Years Vol. 4.* New York: Knopf, 2012

Cartoon. *The Dallas Morning News.* Dallas, 22 November 1963

Castleman, Dr. Kenneth "Telephone Interview Regarding the Jet Propulsion Laboratory and CalTech Studies of the Nix film commissioned by UPI and Maurice Schonfeld." April 11, 2014. Telephone

Central Intelligence Agency. *CIA/Cold War History.* n.d. <http://www.coldwar.org/articles/40s/CentralIntelligenceAgencyCIA.asp>

—. "Truman and Inception of the CIA." *Center for the Study of Intelligence.* n.d. <https://www.cia.gov/library/center-for-the-study-of-intelligence/kent-csi/vol20no1/html/v20ila02p_0001.htm>

Chalk, Phillip. "Rather: Wrong from the Beginning." 14 March 2005. *JFK Murder.com.* 5 September 2013. <http://jfkmurder.com/rather.html>

Church, George J. "Crawling with Bugs." *Time* 20 April 1987: 14-24

Clarke, Thurston. "J.F.K.'s Last Hundred Days: The Transformation of a Man and the Emergence of a Great President." *Vanity Fair* 2013. 11 August 2013. <http://www.vanityfair.com/politics/2013/07/icebergs-jfk-jackie-death-patrick>

Cody, John, Dallas Police Department. Interview. Nightline. 1994

Committee, Church. "Destruction of the Hosty Note." Vers. Church Committee Book V. n.d. *Mary Ferrell Foundation.* Electronic Web Page. 2 November 2013. <http://www.maryferrell.org/mffweb/archive/viewer/showDoc.do?absPageId=150555>

Congress, US. "House Select Committee on Assassinations." *Report together with additional and supplemental views, of the Select Committee on Assassinations*. U.S. Govt. Printing Office, 1976

Considered, NPR All Things. *Walter Cronkite on the Assassination of President Kennedy*. 22 November 1963. 22 November 2013. <http://www.npr.org/2013/11/22/246628793/walter-cronkite-on-the-assassination-of-john-f-kennedy>

Conway, Debra. *The Running Woman: Toni Foster*. Dallas, 2000

Corn, David. *Blond Ghost: Ted Shackley and the CIA's Crusades*. New York: Simon & Schuster, 1994

Corsi, Jerome. *Did JFK Seal his Fate with Plan to Dump LBJ?* 11 November 2013. 30 November 2013. <http://mobile.wnd.com/2013/11/did-jfk-seal-his-fate-with-plan-to-dump-lbj/>

Dallas Texas Hats, 1963. November 2013. 23 November 2013. <http://www.thefedoralounge.com/archive/index.php/t-43371.html>

Dallas, The Ultimate. *History of Dallas the Series*. n.d. <http://www.ultimatedallas.com/bigd/>

Department, Dallas Police. "Photo of Jim Leavelle." n.d.

—. "Texas Supplemental Report on the Assassination of President John F. Kennedy and the Serious Wounding of Governor John B. Connally." *Texas Portal to History*. Report. Dallas: Dallas Police Department, 1964 5 October. Digital Images. <http://texashistory.unt.edu/ark:/67531/metapth338634/>

Donald, Mark. "Good Time Charlie." 23 12 1999. *The Dallas Observer Online*. web. 28 December 2013. <http://www.dallasobserver.com/1999-12-23/news/good-time-charlie/full/>

Douglass, James. *JFK and the Unspeakable: Why he Died and Why it Matters*. Orbis, 2008

"DPD Homicide and Oswald." n.d. <http://whatreallyhappened.com/RANCHO/POLITICS/JFK/oswald3.jpg>

Dunkel, Gerda. "The Muchmore Film Enhanced." 2013. <https://www.youtube.com/watch?v=yKqWozXc4KY>

Edisen, Adele. "Honest Joe's Pawn Shop." *Vehicle on the Grassy Knoll*. Ed. Deep Politics Forum. 3 October 2008. Deep Politics Forum Website. 28 October 2013. <Adele Edisen: Forum Post on https://deeppoliticsforum.com/forums/showthread.php?66-The-Vehicle-on-the-Grassy-Knoll 10/03/2008>

Epstein, Edward Jay. *Inquest*. New York: Viking, 1967

—. "Legend: The Secret World of Lee Harvey Oswald." *Reader's Digest* 1978: 109

Ferrell, Mary. *Picture of Comrade Kostin letter from Oswald*. n.d. 14 August 2013. <http://www.maryferrell.org/mffweb/archive/viewers/showDoc.do?absPageId=131701>

Ficknel, Herc. "Dallas Morning News Cartoon." *Hunting Cartoon*. Dallas: Dallas Morning News, 22 November 1963. Newspaper

Fonzi, Gaeton. *The Last Investigation: What Insiders Know about the Assassination of JFK*. Thunders Mouth Press, 1993

Forum, The JFK Assassination. 2009-2013

—. *J.D. Tippit*. 2009-2013. Web Forum. 2 September 2013. <http://www.jfkassassinationforum.com/index.php?action=search2>

—. *Jack Ruby*. 2009-2013. Web Forum, Multiple threads. 12 September 2013. <http://www.jfkassassinationforum.com/index.php?action=search2>

—. *Jerry Belknap*. Ed. Duncan MacRae. June 2010. web forum. 29 August 2013. <http://www.jfkassassinationforum.com/index.php/topic,2680.0.html>

—. *LHO, Ruby and the DPD*. Ed. Duncan MacRae. 15 November 2013. 16 November 2013. <http://www.jfkassassinationforum.com/index.php/topic,9364.msg273265.html#msg273265>

—. *Malcolm Summers*. Ed. Duncan MacRae. 2010. 24 August 2013. <http://www.jfkassassinationforum.com/index.php?topic=2553.0>

—. *Okay LNer's Convince Me*. 12 September 2013. 16 September 2013. <http://www.jfkassassinationforum.com/index.php/topic,6986.0.html>

—. *Was it a Mauser, a Carcano, or both?* 2009-2013. Web Forum. 2013 2 October. <http://www.jfkassassinationforum.com/index.php/topic,2664.0.html>

—. *Witness Intimidation-Wilma Tice*. 2009-2013. 3 October 2013. <http://www.jfkassassinationforum.com/index.php/topic,2995.msg55737.html#msg55737>

Frontline. "G. Robert Blakey Interview." *PBS*. 2003. <http://www.pbs.org/wgbh/pages/frontline/biographies/oswald/interview-g-robert-blakey/#addendum>

Gallagher, Mary Barelli. *My Life with Jacqueline Kennedy*. New York: D. McKay Company, 1969

Garrison, Jim. *On the Trail of the Assassins*. n.d.

Gibson, Donald. "The Creation of the Warren Commission." *Probe* 1996, 4 ed.

Gibson, Lois. "Sketch of Authority Malcolm Summers Saw on the Knoll." n.d.

Goggins, William M. "James Tague: Unintended Victim in Dealey Plaza." n.d. *Kennedy Assassination*. 29 October 2013. <http://mcadams.posc.mu.edu/tague.htm>

Grier, Peter. "John F. Kennedy: Why Books Were a Big Part of His Life." 23 November 2013. *DC Decoder*. 23 November 2013. <http://www.csmonitor.com/USA/DC-Decoder/Decoder-Wire/2013/1123/John-F.-Kennedy-Why-books-were-a-big-part-of-his-life-video>

Griggs, Ian. "DPD Structure, 1963." 1998. 7 October 2013. <http://the-puzzle-palace.com/dpd1963.html>

Groden, Robert and Diane Allen. *The Killing of a President*. New York: Viking Studio Books, 1993

Gun, The Smoking. "Dark Day in Dallas." 2013. *Turner SI digital Network.*<http://www.thesmokinggun.com/file/police-notes-oswald-interrogation>

Harris, Jones. *Honest Joe's Pawn Shop* Gayle Nix-Jackson. 29 October 2013

Harris, Jones. *The Grassy Knoll and UPI* Gayle Nix-Jackson. 14 November 2013

Henelly, Robert and Jerry Policoff. "How the Media Assassinated the Real Story." n.d. *Citizens for the Truth About the Kennedy Assassination*. 8 August 2013. <http://www.ctka.net/cbs/policoff.html>

Hepburn, James (pseudonym). *Farewell America*. Lichenstein: Frontiers Press, 1968

Herman, Edward and Noam Chomsky. *Manufacturing Consent: The Political Economy of the Mass Media*. Pantheon, 1988

Hersh, Seymour. *The Dark Side of Camelot*. n.d.

Hinrichs, Martin. "Orville Nix Film Importance." 2013

—. "The Nix Film Closeup." n.d. *The JFK Assassination Forum*. 2013. <http://www.jfkassassinationforum.com/index.php/topic,8696.msg255621.html#msg255621>

Hoover, J. Edgar. "Memo concerning control of the Warren Commission and LHO acted Alone." 1964. *JFK Lancer.* 2 November 2013. <http://www.jfklancer.com/Hoover.html>

House Select Committee, on Assassinations. "Oswald in Mexico City aka Lopez Report." n.d. *Mary Ferrell Foundation.* 12 September 2013. <http://www.maryferrell.org/mffweb/archive/viewer/showDoc.do?mode=searchResult&absPageId=68651>

House Select Committee, On Assassinations. "Politics and Presidential Protection: The Motorcade." 1979. *Mary Ferrell Foundation.* web. 12 September 2013

House Select, Committee on Assassinations. *The Secret Service*. U.S. Government, n.d.

Hunt, John. "Beverly Oliver's Photos." n.d. 11 September 2013. <http://mcadams.posc.mu.edu/huntpost.txt>

Hurt, Henry. *Reasonable Doubt: An Investigation Into The Assassination Of John F. Kennedy*. New York: Holt, Rinehart, and Winston, 1985

Israel, Lee. *Kilgallen*. n.d.

"JFK Assassination on Television." 27 October 2013. *Los Angeles Times.* 2 November 2013. <http://www.latimes.com/entertainment/tv/showtracker/la-et-st-jfk-assassination-tv-20131027,0,296954.story#axzz2ihkUMVng>

"JFK Parade Route." *The Dallas Morning News* 22 November 1963. Newspaper

JFK. Dir. Oliver Stone. Perf. Joe Pesci. 1991

"JFK: Clean Bill for CIA." *Newsweek* 23 June 1976: 21

Jones, Penn. "Forgive My Grief." *Midlothian Mirror* 1966

Katzenbach, N. "Memo to Bill Moyers." *NARA*. Washington DC, 25 November 1963. 9 September 2013. <Memo from Katzenbach to Moyers of 11/25, attachNARA RIF #124-10085-10080>

Kennedy, John F. "Ask Not What Your Country Can Do For You." *John F. Kennedy's Inaugural Address*. 20 January 1961

—. "Commencement Address at Yale University." *Commencement Speech at Yale*. New Haven, 11 June 1962

—. *National Security Action Memorandum Number 55*. Washington, DC, 1961. document. <http://www.jfklibrary.org/Asset-Viewer/sjtthyMxu06GMct7OymAvw.aspx>

—. "Personal Remark." 1960

—. "Public Address on Civil Rights." 11 June 1963

—. "Quote." *John F. Kennedy Quotes*. Brainy Quotes, n.d. 6 July 2013. <http://www.brainyquote.com/quotes/authors/j/john_f_kennedy.html>

—. "Quote from Inaugural Speech." January 1961

—. "Quote from Prayer Breakfast." 7 Feb 1963

—. "Quote, Space Speech." *Joint Session of Congress Speech about Space*. 25 May 1961

—. "Quote, Speech." *Presidential Proclamation 3560 : Thanksgiving Day*. 5 November 1963

—. "Quote, Speech." *Speech by Senator John F. Kennedy, Convention Hall, Philadelphia, PA*. Philadelphia, 31 October 1961

—. "Recorded Remarks for Broadcast." *Recorded for the Opening of a USIA Transmitter*. Greenville, NC, 8 February 1963

—. "Remarks at Loyola College." 1958

—. "Remarks on personal safety to Pierre Salinger." n.d.

—. "Remarks to the American Legion." *Speech*. 1961

—. "Speech in New York City before the American Newspapers Publisher's Association." New York, April 1961

—. "Speech Quote in North Dakota." *University of North Dakota Address by President John F. Kennedy*. September 1963

—. *When England Slept*. 1940

Kennedy, President's Commission on the Assassination of President. "Report of the President's Commission on the Assassination of President Kennedy." 1964. *Mary Ferrell Foundation*

Kennedy, Robert F. "Quote." *One Man*. n.d. <http://www.lionheartautographs.com/autograph/17889-KENNEDY,-JACQUELINE-ALS:-'I-think-of-what-Bobby-said-about-JFK---he-believed-that-'one-man-can-make-a-difference-and-every-man-should-try''>

Kerr, James. *The National Tattler* 1974

Kilgallen, Dorothy. *Murder One*. New York: Random House, 1967

Kos, The Daily. *Adlai Stevenson in Dallas in 1963*. 22 November 2010. website. 3 August 2013. <http://www.dailykos.com/story/2010/11/22/922161/-The-far-right-in-Dallas-in-November-1963>

Krock, Arthur. "Intra-Administration War in Vietnam." 1963. *JFK Lancer*. 28 October 2013. <http://www.jfklancer.com/Krock.html>

Kross, Peter. *Oswald: The CIA and the Warren Commission: The Unanswered Questions*. Bridger House Publishing, 2012

Lane, M. Duke. "Freeway Man." n.d. <http://mcadams.posc.mu.edu/FreeWayman.htm>

Lane, Mark. "Defense Brief for Oswald." *National Guardian* 19 December 1963

Lawson, Winston. "Winston Lawson Testimony to Warren Commission." Vers. Hearings & Exhibits Vol. IV. n.d. *History Matters Archive*. 26 July 2013. < http://www.history-matters.com/archive/jfk/wc/wcvols/wh4/html/WC_Vol4_0168b.htm>

Lestrud, Walter. *Jack Puterbaugh Interview*. 10 October 2013. 11 October 2013. <http://stillwatergazette.com/2013/10/19/scene-jfk-assassination-chaos/>

Levin, Marvin. *Honest Joe's* Gayle Nix Jackson. 13 December 2013. telephone

Lewis, Jonathan. *Spy Capitalism: ITEK and the CIA*. Yale University Press, 2002

Library, LBJ. "Nicholas Katzenbach Oral History Transcript." n.d. *LBJ Library*. Ed. Univ. of Texas. 5 October 2013. <http://www.lbjlib.utexas.edu/johnson/archives.hom/oralhistory.hom/katzenbach/katzenb1.pdf>

Lifton, David. Fetzer, Jim. *The Great Zapruder Film Hoax: Deceit and Deception in the Death of Jfk*. Ed. James Fetzer. Open Court Publishing Co, Reprint edition (15 Sep 2003)

—. "Pig on a Leash." 3 January 2013. email to author

Lifton, David S. *Best Evidence: Disguise and Deception in the Assassination of John F. Kennedy*. 1981

Lincoln, Evelyn. *Kennedy and Johnson*. New York: Holt, Rinehart & Winston, 1968

Luce, Henry. *Henry R. Luce, recorded interview by John L. Steele*. Prod. John F. Kennedy Library Oral History Program. 11 November 1965. Oral Interview

MacFarlane, Robert. "Zapruder Film." 10 August 1999. *Los Angeles Times*. web. 3 August 2013

Mack, Gary. "Answer to email about Officers with Zapruder." 2013

—. "The Man Who Named the Grassy Knoll." 1998. *The Kennedy Assassination Page.* Ed. John McAdams. 5 August 2013. <http://mcadams.posc.mu.edu/gk_name.htm>

MacRae, Duncan. *The Nix Parking Lot RE: Rick Needham's GIF--A Second Car?* 17 April 2009. 19 August 2013. <http://www.jfkassassinationforum.com/index.php/topic,626.0.html>

Marrs, Jim. *Crossfire: The Plot that Killed Kennedy.* New York: Carroll & Graf, Inc., 1989. Book

Marshall, Bruce. "Orville Nix Film Evidence Quote." 2013

McAdams, John. *The Kennedy Assassination.* n.d. 2013. <http://mcadams.posc.mu.edu/home.htm>

McElvaine, Robert. *Huffington Post.* 22 11 2011. 12 August 2013. <http://www.huffingtonpost.com/robert-s-mcelvaine/jfk-killed-right-wing-extremism_b_1106354.html>

McKnight, Gerald. *Breach of Trust* . University of Kansas Press, 2005

McMillian, Peter. *Spartacus Educational.* n.d. 2013. <http://www.spartacus.schoolnet.co.uk/JFKSinvestCIA.htm>

Meagher, Sylvia. *Accessories After the Fact.* Skyhorse Publishing, 2013

—. "Notes for a new investigation." *Esquire* December 1966

—. *Subject Index to the Warren Report and Hearings and Exhibits*. New York: Scarecrow Press, 1966

Millican, A.J. "Testimony of A.J. Millican by DPD." 1963

Minnis, Jack and Staughton Lynd. "Seeds of Doubt: Some Questions about the Assassination." *The New Republic* 21 December 1963: 14-20

Minutaglio, Bill and Steven L. Davis. *1963.* Twelve, 2013

Morley, Jefferson. *How Henry Wade, DA of Dallas, ran afoul of the FBI and CIA.* 10 July 2013. 11 August 2013. <http://jfkfacts.org/assassination/news/how-henry-wade-da-of-dallas-ran-afoul-of-j-edgar-hoover/>

—. *Jefferson Morley Biography.* n.d. web. 30 October 2013. <http://jeffersonmorley.com/Bio.html>

—. *JFK Facts.* October 2012. 2013. <http://jfkfacts.org/>

—. "Unanswered Questions Still About the CIA Still Surround JFK's Death." n.d. *U.S. News.com.* 23 October 2013. <http://www.usnews.com/debate-club/was-

jfks-assassination-a-conspiracy/unanswered-questions-about-the-cia-still-surround-jfks-death>

Morrissette, Denis. *The Jfk Assassination Files*. n.d. 28 November 2013. <http://jfkassassinationfiles.com/>

Museum, The Sixth Floor. *Orville Nix Film Overview and Timeline*. n.d. web. 3 October 2013. <http://www.jfk.org/go/collections/about/orville-nix-film-interview>

—. *The Zapruder Interview*. n.d. 11 September 2013. <http://www.jfk.org/go/collections/about/abraham-zapruder-interview-transcript>

—. *Zapruder Film Timeline*. n.d. <http://www.jfk.org/go/collections/about/zapruder-film-chronology>

Myers, Dale K. "Badgeman." 2004. 31 October 2013. <http://www.jfkfiles.com/jfk/html/badgeman.htm>

"Myth Makers;Mysterious Deaths of People Involved in the Case." *Time* 11 November 1966: 33-34

Nasaw, David. *The Patriarch: The Remarkable Life and Turbulent Times of Joseph P. Kennedy*. Penguin, 2012

Needham, Rick. "Dealey Plaza Map Showing Witnesses Seen in the Nix Film." 7 January 2014

—. "Movement from behind the fence, from the Nix film" 6 February 2009. *The JFK Assassination Forum.* 12 August 2013. <http://www.jfkassassinationforum.com/index.php/topic,356.0.html>

—. "Nix Film Enhanced." 2009-2013 <http://www.mejuba.com/albums/Rick1960/119522/9562192/show/original>

—. "Nix Frame Enhancement." *Frames 79-94*. n.d.

NEWS, CBS. *$16 Million Dollars for Zapruder Film*. 1999. web. 6 August 2013. <http://www.cbsnews.com/news/16-million-for-zapruder-film/>

News, Dallas Morning. "Rubin Goldstein Obituary." *Newspaper*. n.d.

Nix, Orville. "Keystone Camera Letter." 1965

—. "The Nix Film." *The Nix Film*. Dallas, 22 November 1963. Film

Nix-Jackson, Gayle. "Missing Nix Film Research." 2 February 1988

NPR. "Eddie Barker on the Kennedy Assassination." November

O'Neill, Tip. *Man of the House:The Life and Political Memoirs of Speaker Tip O'Neill* . St. Martins Press, 1988

Organ, Jerry. "The Zapruder Film." 2000. *The Kennedy Assassination Page.* 16 August 2013. <http://mcadams.posc.mu.edu/organ2.htm>

Palamara, Vince. *A Fact Sheet on Inconsistencies*. 1998. 28 August 2013. <http://www.jfk-assassination.net/palamara/factsheet_vmp.html>

—. *Biography*. 2013. web. 28 12 2013. <http://vincepalamara.com/about/>

—. *Survivor's Guilt: The Secret Service and the Failure to Protect President Kennedy*. Trine Day, 2013. Book

Parr, Joshua. "Rubin Goldstein: Honest Joe's Leaves Legacy in Deep Ellum." *SMU Campus Daily* November 2009

Payne, Darwin. "The Press Corps and the Kennedy Assassination." *Association for Education in Journalism* (1970)

Perry, Dave. "Who Speaks for Roscoe White?" n.d. 3 October 2013

Photo. "11/22/1963 Front Page Headline." *Dallas Morning News*. n.d.

—. "1957 Plymouth Fury like Orville Nix owned." n.d.

—. "Abraham Zapruder" n.d.

—. *Abraham Zapruder's Bell&Howell Camera*. n.d.

—. "Actress Jennifer Jones." n.d.

—. "Artwork donated for JFK Hotel Texas Visit." n.d.

—. "Cedar Crest Movie Theater." n.d.

—. "Charles and Beatrice Hester." n.d.

—. "Dallas Terminal Annex Building." n.d.

—. "Dallas Times Herald, 11/21/1963." *Presidential Parade Route Map*. n.d.

—. "Eames Chairs Custom designed for *Time/Life*." n.d.

—. "FBI Building in Dallas ." 1963

—. "Griff's Burgers in Oak Cliff" n.d.

—. "Hertz Clock above the TSBD." n.d.

—. "Honest Joe's Vehicle." n.d.

—. "Hotel Texas November, 1963." n.d.

—. "Jacqueline Kennedy Mannequin." n.d.

—. "JFK Presidential Parade Route." *Dallas Morning News*. 1963

—. "JFK: Wanted for Treason." 1963

—. "Kennedy Slain On Dallas Street." *Dallas Morning News*. Dallas, 23 November 1963

—. "Keystone K-810 Camera." n.d.

—. "Lee Harvey Oswald in Black Sweater." November 1963

—. "Orville Nix" n.d.

—. "Pamela Turnure, Jackie Kennedy's Press Secretary and friend of Jones Harris." n.d.

—. "Red Pegasus Horse in Dallas." n.d.

—. "Rick Needham Enhancement of the Nix Film." n.d.

—. "Ruth Gordon, mother of Jones Harris." n.d.

—. "Serpentine sidewalks in front of *Time/Life* Bldg." n.d.

—. "Signs Welcoming JFK." n.d.

—. "The Carousel Club." n.d.

—. "Walgreens Store on Main St. Dallas." 1963

—. "Welcome to Dallas Mr. Kennedy." n.d.

—. "White Valiant like Orville Nix Jr. drove." n.d.

—. "Wyatt's Cafeteria." n.d.

Plato. "Quote." (427-347 BC)

Plaza, The Sixth Floor Museum at Dealey. "Filming Kennedy: Home Movies from Dallas." n.d. *The Sixth Floor Museum at Dealey Plaza.* 1 August 2013. <http://www.jfk.org/go/exhibits/home-movies/orville-nix>

Poole, Robert. "In Memoriam: Barry Goldwater." *Reason Magazine (Obituary)* August-September 1998

Post, The Washington. *High Court to Rule on Warrantless Wire-Tapping.* Washington, 20 October 2013. <http://www.washingtonpost.com/opinions/high-court-to-rule-on-warrantless-wiretapping/2013/10/20/37bbc808-377f-11e3-8a0e-4e2cf80831fc_story.html>

Preparata, Guido Giacamo. *The Ideology of Tyranny: The Use of Neo-Gnostic Myth in American Politics*. n.d. 2 October 2013

Price, J.C. “Dallas Sheriff's Report.” Dallas, November 1963

Processing, Dynacolor Film. Dallas, 1 December 1963

Reeves, Thomas. *A Question of Character: A Life of John F. Kennedy*. New York: The Free Press, 1991

Report, The Warren. “The Warren Report.” Vol. XI. Washington, D.C.: U.S. Governmental Printing Office, n.d. XXVI vols. 598

RetroNewser. *Bossa Nova Baby' by Elvis Presley peaks at #8 in USA 50 years ago today*. 16 November 2013. 18 November 2013. <Bossa Nova Baby' by Elvis Presley peaks at #8 in USA 50 years ago today (1963)>

Robinson, Gaille. “Art review: ‘Hotel Texas at the Amon Carter Museum of American Art.” 11 October 2013. *Ft. Worth Starpp-Telegram*. 25 October 2013. <http://www.star-telegram.com/2013/10/10/5236254/art-review-hotel-texas-at-the.html>

Rosenbaum, Marcus. “Inconsistencies Haunt Official Record.” 10 November 2013. *NPR*. 10 November 2013. <http://www.npr.org/2013/11/10/243981006/inconsistencies-haunt-official-record-of-kennedys-death>

Rush to Judgement. Dir. Mark Lane. Perf. Orville Nix. 1967. Documentary

Russell, Richard. “Telephone Conversation No. 184.” *Recordings and Transcripts of Telephone Conversations*. Washington, DC, 29 November 1963. transcript. 13 November 2013. <http://www.transition.lbjlibrary/org/items/67483>

—. “Telephone Conversation, No. 185.” *Recordings and Transcripts of Telephone Conversations*. Washington: LBJ Presidential Library, 29 November 1963. Transcript. 13 November 2013. <http://www.transition.libjlibrary.org/items/show/67483>

Salandria, Vincent J. *The JFK Assassination: A False Mystery Concerning State Crimes*. Dallas, 20 November 1998. Speech given at COPA

—. “The Warren Report?” *Liberation* March 1965: 14-32

Salinger's JFK-Cuban Cigar Stories. Perf. Pierre Salinger. n.d. YouTube Video. <http://www.youtube.com/watch?v=dHazLBTZUEs>

Sanders, Craig and Laurie E. Jasinski. “HUNT, LAMAR.” n.d. *Handbook of Texas Online*. 15 October 2013. <http://www.tshaonline.org/handbook/online/articles/fhu99>

“Sanger Harris Advertisement.” *The Dallas Morning News* 22 November 1963. Newspaper

Scally, Chris. "TABULAR ZAPRUDER FILM CHRONOLOGY 2010." 2010. *JFK Lancer.* 22 August 2013. http://jfklancer.com/zapruder/Tabular_Z%20Film_Chronology.html

—."NIX FILM CHRONOLOGY 2014." 2014.

—. "Personal Letter from Dr. Alan Gillespie," Jet Propulsion Laboratory, Califonia Institute of Technology, October 15, 1976.

Scheim, David. *The Mafia Killed President Kennedy*. London: Virgin Books, 1988

Schlesinger, Arthur M., Jr. *A Thousand Days: John F. Kennedy in the White House*. Boston: Hougton Mifflin, 1965 rpt; 2002

Schonfeld, Maurice. *Me and Ted Against the World : The Unauthorized Story of the Founding of CNN*. HarperBusiness, 2001

—. "Nix Custodial Memories." *Telephone Conversation with Gayle Nix Jackson.* DeSoto, 18 February 1990. telephone

Schonfeld, Maurice W. "The Shadow of a Gunman." *Columbia Journalism Review* (1975): 46-50

Schonfeld, Reese. "The Shadow of a Gunman." *Columbia Journalism Review* November 2011

Shackleford, Martin and Debra Conway. "Stolley and the Zapruder Film." n.d. *Who Killed JFK.* 2 November 2013

"Shadow on a Grassy Knoll: Photographic-analysis Shows no New Evidence." *Time* May 1967

Shafer, Jack. "The Time and Life Acid Trip." June 2010. *Slate.*<http://wwwsalte.com/articles/news_and_politics/press_box/2010/06/the_time_and_life_acid_trip.html>

Shanklin, Gordon J. "Letter to Orville Nix." 1964

Shropshire, Mike. "No Holds Barred." *D Magazine* 1981. <http://www.wrestling-titles.com/us/tx/noholdsbarred.html>

Siff, Steven. "Henry Luce's Strange Trip: Coverage of LSD in Time and Life, 1954-1968." *Journalism History* 34.3 (2008)

Simkin, John. *James Wagenvoord.* 2009. web. 2 11 2013

—. "Jeanne de Mohrenschildt." n.d. *Spartacus Educational.*<http://www.spartacus.schoolnet.co.uk/JFKmohrenschiltJ.htm>

—. *Lee Harvey Oswald.* n.d. 8 September 2013. <http://www.spartacus.schoolnet.co.uk/JFKoswald.htm>

—. *Penn Jones*. n.d.

—. *Suite 8F*. 1997-2013. 26 October 2013. <http://www.spartacus.schoolnet.co.uk/JFKgroup8F.htm>

—. *The Republic Bank*. 2006. <http://educationforum.ipbhost.com/index.php?showtopic=7641>

—. *The Zapruder Film*. 2009-2013. 14 September 2013

"Skillern's Drugstore Advertisement." *The Dallas Morning News* 22 November 1963. Newspaper

Sorrels, Forrest. "Warren Commission Testimony." 1964. 9 August 2013. <http://www.jmasland.com/wctestimony/secret%20service/sorels1.htm>

Speer, Pat. *A New Perspective on the Kennedy Assassination*. n.d. Web Book. 15 September 2013

Sprague, Richard E. "Excerpts from his Investigations: The Taking of America 1-2-3." 1977. 24 August 2013

—. "The American News Media and the Assassination of President John F. Kennedy: Accessories After the Fact-- Conclusion." *Computers and Automation* 22 (1973): 31-38

Stolley, Richard B. " What Happened Next; Film of John Kennedy's Assassination ." *Esquire* November 1973: 134-135. 262-263

Stone, Roger. *The Man Who Killed Kennedy: The Case Against LBJ* . Skyhorse Publishing, 2013

Summers, Anthony. *Conspiracy*. London: Fontana Paperbacks, 1980

—. *Official and Confidential*. n.d.

Texas, The University of North. *Radio Traffic Transcript from President John F. Kennedy's arrival to Lee Harvey Oswald's Arrest*. 22 November 1963. 18 November 2013. <Dallas (Tex.). Police Dept.. , Report, November 22, 1963; digital images, (http://texashistory.unt.edu/ark:/67531/metapth337556/ : accessed November 18, 2013)>

The Day the Dream Died. Dir. Plumley. 1988

The JFK Assassination: The Jim Garrison Tapes. Dir. John Barbour. 1992. Film, Documentary

The President's Assassination Records Review Board. "Final Report of the Assassination Records Review Board." 1998. <http://www.fas.org/sgp/advisory/arrb98/part03.htm>

Thomas, Donald B. *Hear No Evil: Social Constructivism and the Forensic Evidence in the Kennedy Assassination*. Skyhorse Publishing, 2013

Thompson, Josiah. *Six Seconds in Dallas*. New York: Random House, 1967

Times, New York. *E.K. Thompson, 89, Editor Who Helped Shape Life Magazine*. 9 October 1996. 7 September 2013. <http://www.nytimes.com/1996/10/09/arts/e-k-thompson-89-editor-who-helped-shape-life-magazine.html>

Times, The New York. *Izvestia Interview with Kim Philby*. n.d.

"Transcript, Nicholas Katzenbach Oral History Interview (Interview Number), (Date of Interview), by (Name of Interviewer), (page number), LBJ Library. Online: <web address of cited transcript>. ." n.d.

Trask, Richard. *Pictures of the Pain*. Yeoman Press, 1994

Twyman, Noel. *Bloody Treason*. Ramcho Santa Fe: Laurel Publishing, 1997

U.S. House of Representatives. *Report of the Select Committee on Assassinations 95th congress, 2nd session*. Report No. 95-1828 (HSCA Report). Washington, D.C.: Government Printing Office, 1979. Government Report

—. "The Evolution and Implications of the CIA-Sponsored Assassination Conspiracies Against Fidel Castro." *Appendix to Hearings Before the Select Committee on Assassinations*. Washington, D.C., 1979. 147

U.S. Senate. *Final Report of the Select Committee to Study Government Operations with Respect to Intelligence Activities*. Church Committee. Washington, D.C.: Government Printing Office, 1976

Unger, Robin. *JFK Assassination and Research Photo Gallery*. n.d. <http://www.jfkassassinationgallery.com/>

—. "Orville Nix Email." 2013

University, Baylor. "Penn Jones." n.d. *Baylor University W. R. Poage Legislative Library*. 9 October 2013. <http://www.baylor.edu/lib/poage/jones/index.php?id=57477>

Wagenvoord, James. "Telephone Interview Regarding *Life* Magazine Meeting with Orville Nix." 31 December 2013. Telephone

Warren Commission. "Interview with DPD Officer J.M. Smith." 1964. *Mary Ferrell Foundation*

Warren, Commission. "Orville Nix FBI Testimony." January 1964. *History Matters*. U.S. Government. 5 August 2013. <http://www.history-matters.com/archive/jfk/wc/wcvols/wh24/html/WH_Vol24_0279a.htm>

—. "Report on LHO Death Threats." n.d. *History Matters.* 29 November 2013. <http://historymatters.com/archive/jfk/wc/wr/html/WCReport_0117a.htm>

—. "Testimony of Lyndal Shaneyfelt, FBI." 1964. *Mary Ferrell Foundation*

—. "Warren Commission Interview with Fritz and Curry regarding threats on LHO's life." 1964. *Mary Ferrell Foundation*

—. "Warren Commission Testimony of D.V. Harkness, Vol. VI, pg 312." 1964. *Mary Ferrell Foundation*

—. "Warren Commission Testimony of Postal Inspector Harry Holmes Vol. VII." 1964. *Mary Ferrell.* web. 28 July 2013

Weisberg, Harold. *White Wash: The Report on the Warren Report.* Hyattstown, 1965

White, Jack. "JFK White Collection." Waco, Texas: Poage Library, Baylor University, n.d. Document. 15 October 2013. < http://digitalcollections.baylor.edu/cdm/compoundobject/collection/po-jfkwhite/id/2438/rec/4>

Whitmey, Peter. "Jean Hill: Lady in Red." n.d. *Clint Bradford's JFK Info Website.* 3 November 2013. <http://www.jfk-info.com/whimteyl.htm>

—. "The First Dissenting Witness: Mary Woodward." n.d. 11 October 2013. <http://www.karws.gso.uri.edu/JFK/the_critics/Whitmey/Witness.html>

Wilkes, Donald E. "Destiny Betrayed: The CIA, Oswald and the JFK Assassination." *Flagpole Magazine* 7 December 1975: 8. web

—. "The CIA, Oswald and the JFK Assassination." *Flagpole Magazine* 7 December 1975: 8

Wise, Wes. *Remembrances of Orville Nix* Gayle Nix Jackson. 14 October 2013. telephone

Work, How Things. *12 WPA Projects That Still Exists.* 20 August 2013. <http://people.howstuffworks.com/12-wpa-projects-that-still-exist.htm>

Wrone, David R. *The Zapruder Film – Reframing JFK's Assassination.* University Press of Kansas, 2003

CITATION NOTES

HSCA: House Select Committee on Assassinations

WC: The Warren Commission

CR: The Church Report

ARRB: Assassination Records Review Board

---

[1] .... Kennedy, John F. Quote from Speech in New York City before the American Newspapers Publishers Association. April, 1961

[2] .... Nix-Jackson, Gayle letters referencing attempt to find the original Nix film

[3] .... McFarlane, Robert. Zapruder Film. August 10, 1999. *Los Angeles Times*

[4] .... Lifton, David. *"Pig on a Leash—Addendum"*. Email attachment to author

[5] .... Bradford, Clint. List of Films and Movies Taken at Dealey Plaza on November 22, 1963

[6] .... Sixth Floor Museum at Dealey Plaza, *The Nix Film* description

[7] .... Francis Bacon Quote

[8] .... Kennedy, John F. Quote from Prayer Breakfast Speech, Feb 7, 1963

[9] .... The Daily Kos, *Adlai Stevenson in Dallas in 1963*. November 22, 2010

[10] .... Minutaglio, Bill and Steven L. Davis, *Dallas 1963,* 92

[11] .... Photo of Wyatt's Cafeteria

[12] .... Photo of Keystone K-810 model camera

[13] .... Photo of Terminal Annex Building

[14] .... Photo of Cedar Crest Movie Theater

[15]..........*Dallas Times Herald*, November 21, 1963. Map of parade route

[16]..........Simkin, John. *Abraham Zapruder Biography*, Spartacus Educational. Web

[17]..........Simkin, D. Harold Byrd Biography. Spartacus Educational. Web

[18]..........Photo of Jennifer Jones and reference to Zapruder's naming

[19]..........Simkin, George de Morhenschildt. *Relation to Zapruder. Coincidence?* Spartacus Educational. See Bruce C. Adamson

[20]..........Schlesinger, Arthur. *A Thousand Days: John F. Kennedy in the White House.* 9

[21]..........Simkin, John. *Jeanne LeGon DeMohrenschildt*

[22]..........Photo of Jackie Kennedy mannequin

[23]..........Warren Commission XII. The testimony of Forrest V. Sorrels was taken at 9:45 A.M. on May 7, 1964, at 200 Maryland Avenue NE., Washington, D.C. by Mr. Samuel A. Stern, assistant counsel of the President's Commission. Mr. David W. Belin, assistant counsel for the President's Commission, and Mr. Fred B. Smith, Deputy General Counsel, U.S. Treasury Department were present. 336

[24]..........Sheraton Hotel where the Secret Service team stayed

[25]..........The Hotel Texas in Ft. Worth

[26]..........Image of Henry Moore Three Points Sculpture: http://dallasmuseumofart.org/View/FutureExhibitions/dma_496179

[27]..........Robinson, Gaille. *Hotel Texas Art Review at the Amon Carter.* Ft Worth Star-Telegram

[28]..........Photos of art in each room of Hotel Texas in Ft. Worth

[29]..........Clarke, Thurston. *JFK's Last Hundred Days: The Transformation of a Man and the Emergence of a Great President.* Jackie Kennedy's favorite flower, periwinkle iris from Thurston Clarke

[30]..........President John F. Kennedy's favorite Cuban cigar was a Cuban H. Upmann. From a YouTube interview with Pierre Salinger, JFK's press secretary

[31]..........McElvaine, Robert. *Huffington Post,* Kennedy Quote. After seeing the John Birch Society ad in the *Dallas Morning News*

[32]..........Photo of Orville Nix

[33]..........*Dallas Morning News* Front page, November 22, 1963, Morning edition

[34]..........Hersh, Seymour. *Dark Side of Camelot.* 406-407

[35]..........Parade Route Map, *Dallas Morning News*. Morning edition

[36]..........Hunting Cartoon in the *Dallas Morning News,* November 22, 1963

[37] .... Photo of Welcome to Dallas Mr. Kennedy

[38] .... HSCA,Vol.11, pg. 149 Sorrels Testimony

[39] .... WC Hearings and Exhibits Testimony of Win Lawson regarding Lumpkin and Industrial Blvd:, Vol. IV, 328

[40] .... Lestrud, Walter. Puterbaugh Interview October 10, 2013. Web

[41] .... Kennedy. Quote from the University of North Dakota Address, September, 1963

[42] .... Needham, Rick. Map of where Orville stood in Dealey Plaza along with witness locations during the assassination sequence of the Nix film

[43] .... Keystone K-810 Camera manual

[44] .... Photos of welcoming crowds

[45] .... How Things Work Website: *12 WPA projects That Still Exist—Dealey Plaza, 2013.* Web

[46] .... Mack, Gary. *The Man Who Named the Grassy Knoll.* John McAdams. Web

[47] .... Photo of Zapruder's Bell & Howell Camera

[48] .... Marrs, Jim. *Crossfire*, 265

[49] .... Wagenvoord, James. Telephone Interview with author. Billie Sol Estes and Bobby Baker Scandals were to be the *Life* magazine cover before the assassination

[50] .... Palamara, Vince. *Survivor's Guilt: The Secret Service and the Failure to Protect the President.* This article discusses the directions to remove bubble-top given at Love Field Airport

[51] .... Garrison, Jim. *On the Trail of the Assassins*, xiii

[52] .... Kennedy, Quote from Remarks made to Press Secretary Pierre Salinger on his personal safety. 1963

[53] .... Photo of Carousel Club

[54] .... Photo of Walgreen's on Main Street in Dallas, 1963

[55] .... Photo of Wanted for Treason handbill advertised in the *Dallas Morning News* on November 22, 1963

[56] .... Organ, Jerry. *"The Zapruder Film."* Organ discusses Zapruder's vertigo and the need for Sitzman to steady him as he took the film. 2000. Web

[57] .... Photo of Charles and Beatrice Hester taken from a frame in the Zapruder film. Beatrice was Zapruder's payroll clerk and her husband Charles had met her that day to view the parade together

[58]..........JFK Assassination Forum. *Jerry Belknap Topic*. Various threads. Web Forum. Belknap was the man identified as having a "fainting spell" or "epileptic seizure". He worked part-time in the *Dallas Morning News* mail room. You can also find out more about him in Warren Commission Document 1245: FBI Gemberling Report. July 2, 1964

[59]..........See the Nix Film

[60]..........Kennedy, Quote from Inaugural Address, January 20, 1961

[61]..........Retronewswer: *Bossa Nova Baby* by Elvis Presley standings on the Billboard Charts. November, 1963

[62]..........Museum, Sixth Floor: *Zapruder Film Timeline.* Harry McCormick and Zapruder

[63]..........Scally, Chris. *Tabular Zapruder Film Chronology*. 2010. Phone calls from Zapruder to Schwartz and the DPD

[64]..........Sixth Floor Museum, *Oral History: Darwin Payne*

[65]..........Sixth Floor Museum *Zapruder Film Chronology*

[66]..........WC, Forrest Sorrels, Vol VII, 352

[67]..........National Public Radio Program: *All Things Considered. Cronkite's National Announcement of Kennedy's Death on CBS.* Web

[68]..........Mack, Gary. DPD Officers Osburn and Jones drive Zapruder. Email to author

[69]..........Museum, Sixth Floor. *Zapruder Film Timeline*. Jay Watson, WFAA

[70]..........Ibid, Bert Shipp, WFAA

[71]..........Museum, Sixth Floor. *Zapruder WFAA Interview Transcript*

[72]..........Wrone, David. *The Zapruder Film: Reframing JFK's Assassination*. 150-155

[73]..........Warren Commission, Vol. VII. Sorrels called back to Dallas after LHO is arrested. 350

[74]..........Wrone. 151

[75]..........Backes, Joseph, *"Why JFK Went to Texas"*. 1999. Web

[76]..........Simkin, *Republic Bank Tower Meetings*

[77]..........Scally, Chris. *Tabular Zapruder Chronology*. 2010

[78]..........Consumer Price Calculator. Web

[79]..........Kennedy. Quote from Campaign Speech by Senator John F. Kennedy. Convention Hall, Philadelphia, PA. October 31, 1960

[80]..........Photo of 1957 Plymouth Fury

[81]..........Photo of a White Valiant Automobile

82 .... Keystone K-810 Camera Operating Manual. 1963

83 .... The Sixth Floor Museum. "*Abraham Zapruder WFAA Interview Transcript*". Web

84 .... Ibid

85 .... Photo of Hertz clock atop Texas School Book Depository removed in 1979

86 .... Nix-Jackson, Gayle. My great-uncle, Dr. Eual Dipprey was the physician for the owner of Lee Harvey Oswald's Rental Home at 1026 Beckley. Her name was Gladys Johnson

87 .... JFK Assassination Forum. *J.D. Tippit Topic*, Various threads. Web Forum

88 .... Donald, Mark. *Good Time Charlie. The Dallas Observer Online.* 1999. The "Decker Hold" was named after Dallas County Sheriff Bill Decker and meant that the prisoner could receive no visitors, sheriff's orders

89 .... Poole, Robert. "In Memoriam: Barry Goldwater." *Reason Magazine (Obituary),* 1998

90 .... Kennedy. Quote from the speech given in New York City before the American Newspapers Publisher's Association. April, 1961

91 .... Bryant, John "Birdman." *The John Birch Society—Exposed!* Web. Article on the history of the John Birch Society

92 .... Photo of Headlines in *Dallas Morning News* November 23, 1963

93 .... JFK Assassination Forum. *Was it a Mauser or Carcano or both?* Various Threads. Web Forum. Mauser rifle first identified as weapon by the DPD

94 .... *The Nix Film.* See the segment filmed on Saturday November 23, 1963

95 .... Stolley, Richard. *What Happened Next: Film of John F. Kennedy's Assassination. Esquire* 134

96 .... Ibid

97 .... Stolley, 135

98 .... Simkin, *The Zapruder Film*

99 .... Kennedy. Quote from the speech made before the Joint Session of Congress about space. May 25, 1961

100 .... Photo of Austin's Barbecue Restaurant

101 .... Photo of Austin's Barbecue Drink Cup

102 .... Katzenbach, Nicholas. Memo to Bill Moyers. NARA. November 25, 1963

103 .... Gibson, Donald. *The Creation of the Warren Commission. Probe,* 1966, 4 Ed

[104] ....Photo of Jim Leavelle. White Resistol hats distinguished investigators from other DPD officers

[105] ....Warren Report: *Report of the President's Commission on the Assassination of President John F. Kennedy.* United States Government Printing Office, 912 pages. No tape recorders were used during LHO interview

[106] ....*The Smoking Gun: Dark Day in Dallas.* 2013. Questions about handwritten notes taken by Fritz, Curry and others in Oswald's interview. *Turner Online.* Web

[107] ....JFK Assassination Forum: *Which rifle? A Mauser or a Mannlicher-Carcano.* Various threads. Web Forum

[108] ....Chalk, Phillip. *Rather: Wrong from the Beginning.* Eddie Barker chastises Dan Rather's embellishments of Dallas schoolchildren clapping as if happy the President was assassinated. They were happy because they were going home early

[109] ....WC. Interview with Fritz and Curry regarding threats on Oswald's life. During the night, between 2:30 and 3 A.M., the local office of the FBI and the Sheriff's office received telephone calls from an unidentified man who warned that a committee had decided "to kill the man who had killed the President." Shortly after, an FBI agent notified the Dallas police of the anonymous threat. The Police department and ultimately Chief Curry were informed of both threats. 209 See also: htttp://historymatters.com/archive/jfk/wc/wr/html/WCReport_0117a.htm

[110] ....Morley, Jefferson. *How Henry Wade, Dallas DA, Ran Afoul of the FBI and CIA.* July 10, 2013. Web

[111] ....JFK Assassination Forum. *Plans to Escort Oswald to Dallas County Jail.* Various Threads. Web Forum

[112] ....Warren Commission interview of Oswald by Postal Inspector Holmes

[113] ....Dallas Hats Forum. *White Resistol San Antone Hats worn by DPD Homicide Investigators*

[114] ....Photo of sweater Oswald requested

[115] ....Griggs, Ian. *DPD Structure, 1963.* 1998. Web

[116] ....Ibid

[117] ....JFK Assassination Forum: *Jack Ruby.* Various Threads. 2009-2013. Though Ruby professed to be a huge Kennedy admirer, he wasn't watching the motorcade at all. He was at the Dallas Morning News placing an ad for his club.

[118] ....Simkin, *Lamar Hotel group—Suite 8f.* Spartacus Educational

[119]........ Kennedy. Quote from Proclamation 3560 Thanksgiving day speech. November 5, 1963

[120]........ Warren Commission. Testimony of Forrest Sorrels and his thoughts that shots came from the grassy knoll area. Vol.VI. 1964

[121]........ Kennedy. Quote from speech given at prayer breakfast. February 2, 1963

[122]........ Shropshire, Mike. "No Holds Barred." *D Magazine.* Midget wrestling televised from the Sportatorium in Dallas. 1988

[123]........ *The Nix Film*

[124]........ Dynacolor Film Processing Lab in Dallas was on Halifax St. in Dallas. It no longer exists

[125]........ Warren Commission. Testimony of Lyndal Shaneyfelt of the FBI. The FBI had issued an edict to all film processing plants that any film containing assassination footage must be handed over immediately. Vol V. 1964

[126]........ *The Nix Film*

[127]........ Conway, Debra. *The Running Woman.* Toni Foster. 2009

[128]........ These men seen on the stairs in the Nix film are Emmet Hudson, and two men who have never been definitively identified. Some believe the man in the red shirt is Francis Lee Mudd

[129]........ JFK Assassination Forum, *Malcolm Summers.* Various threads

[130]........ Kennedy quote from his Public Address on Civil Rights. June 11, 1963

[131]........ Photo of Santa Fe Building where FBI was housed in 1963

[132]........ Nix-Jackson. Letter from J. Gordon Shanklin of Dallas FBI

[133]........ Nix-Jackson. Letter from Joe Abernathy of FBI Dallas

[134]........ Nix-Jackson. *Life* magazine offer to buy film. Interview with James Wagenvoord

[135]........ Shackleford, Martin. Updated by Debra Conway. *A History of the Zapruder Film.* The public was told Zapruder was only paid $25,000 and that he donated it to J.D. Tippet's widow. Only later was the public told Zapruder was paid $150,000. James Wagenvoord later told the author that the Tippit widow didn't receive any of Zapruder's funds; they went to a Police Benevolence Fund. This would mean Zapruder perjured himself during his Garrison testimony

[136]........ JFK Airport. *History of JFK Airport*

[137]........ Cody, John. Interview on *Nightline* regarding Dallas Police Department. *Dallas called City of Hate.* 1994

[138]........ Sanders, Craig and Laurie E. Jasinski. *Lamar Hunt: The Texas Handbook Online.* Lamar Hunt coins term Super Bowl. Web

[139] ....*History of Dallas: the Series*. From the Ultimate Dallas website

[140] ....Photo of Pegasus Horse atop Magnolia Hotel

[141] ....Photo of Serpentine design of sidewalk into *Time/Life* lobby

[142] ....Nix-Jackson. Interview with Maurice Schonfeld regarding the meeting of Orville Nix, Orville Nix, Jr., Reinhardt and Schonfeld in New York at UPI, 1990. Schonfeld, in a later article, erroneously describes the author as Orville Nix's niece as well as stating Orville Nix was given a "Stetson Hat"

[143] ....Obituary of Edward K. Thompson of *Life* in the *New York Times*. October 9, 1996

[144] ....Photo of Eames chair

[145] ....Nix-Jackson, Gayle. Telephone Interview with James Wagenvoord regarding *Time/Life* in New York. 2013

[146] ....Photo of Griff's burgers in Dallas. 1963

[147] ....Schonfeld, Maurice. *Shadow of a Gunman.* 1975. 46-50

[148] ....Nix-Jackson, Gayle. Interview with Orville Nix regarding Handshake contract with UPI

[149] ....Sixth Floor Museum at Dealey Plaza. *Orville Nix Overview and Timeline.* Nix contract broken by UPI by showing Fox Movietone news in theaters

[150] ....Morley, Jefferson. Morley names important files in CIA's undisclosed files 2017. Jfkfacts.org. Web

[151] ....Kennedy Quote from the Yale Commencement Address. June 11, 1962

[152] ....Baylor University W.R. Poage Legislative Library, *Penn Jones Biography.* Web

[153] ....Ibid

[154] ....Ibid

[155] ....Lane, Mark. *Defense Brief for Oswald.* 1969

[156] ....Minnis & Staughton Article on Conspiracy: "Seeds of Doubt: Some Questions About the Assassination". *The New Guardian.* 1963. 14-20

[157] ....Douglass, James. *Who Killed Kennedy*? 478

[158] ....Buchanan, Thomas. *Who Killed Kennedy?* 178

[159] ....Hepburn, James (pseudonym) *Farewell, America.* 1968

[160] ....Simkin. *Suite 8F*

[161] ....Siff, Steven. *Henry Luce's Strange Trip: Coverage of LSD in Time and Life.* 1954-1968. 2008

[162] ....Shafer, Jack. "The Time and Life Acid Trip". *Slate.* June, 2010. Web

[163]........ Siff. Vol. 34.3

[164]........ Preparata, Guido Giacamo. *The Ideology of Tyranny: The Use of Neo-Gnostic Myth in American Politics.* Web. Chapter seven discusses the philosophy of Derrida and Foucault

[165]........ Krock, Arthur. Kennedy quote from *Intra-Administration War in Vietnam.* JFK Lancer website. This article attributes the quote to "a very high (ranking) U.S. Official who has spent much of his life in the service of democracy." Web

[166]........ Reeves, Thomas. *A Question of Character: A Life of John F. Kennedy.* NY. 1991

[167]........ Beran, Michael Knox. "Fifty Years after Dallas." *National Review Online.* JFK letter to Paul Fay November 21, 2013. Web

[168]........ Nasaw, David. *The Patriarch: the Remarkable Life and Turbulent Times of Joseph P. Kennedy.* 79

[169]........ Ibid. 83

[170]........ Kennedy, John F. *Why England Slept.* 1940

[171]........ Luce, Henry. Recorded interview at the JFK Presidential Library. Luce and Joseph Kennedy. 1965

[172]........ Caro, Robert. *The Passage of Power. The Lyndon Johnson Years Volume 4.* New York. 2012. 65

[173]........ Ibid

[174]........ Twyman, Noel. *Bloody Treason.* 831

[175]........ Summer, Anthony. *Official and Confidential.* 272

[176]........ Simkin. *Suite 8F.* Texas oilmen were worried that JFK would repeal the oil depletion tax, costing them millions of dollars

[177]........ Central Intelligence Agency Website. *The CIA and the Cold War.* Truman quote about the CIA. Web

[178]........ Ibid

[179]........ Ibid

[180]........ Wilkes, Donald E. "Destiny Betrayed: Oswald, the CIA and the JFK Assassination" *Flagpole Magazine* 1975

[181]........ Douglass, James. *JFK and the Unspeakable: Why he Died and Why it Matters.* 331-332

[182]........ Agee, Phillip. *Inside the Company: CIA Diary.* New York. Allan Lane. 1975. Pages regarding the many CIA coups. 573-583

[183]........ CIA website. *CIA History.* 2013. Web

[184] ....CIA website. *Current Events.* NSA accused of wiretapping. Web. 2013

[185] ....Greir Peter. *"John F. Kennedy: Why Books Were a Big Part of his Life."* Kennedy advises Allen Dulles to read Ian Fleming novels. JFK loves espionage

[186] ....HSCA Findings on assassination attempts on Castro. 1979

[187] ....Canfield, Michael and Alan Weberman. *Coup d'état in America: The CIA and the Assassination of JFK.* 1975. Allen Dulles fall guy for Bay of Pigs. 115

[188] ....Kennedy. NSA55 Memorandum number 55 on National Security

[189] ....Simkin, Jeanne DeMohrenschildt

[190] ....Morley, Jefferson. *Oswald and the DRE.* jfk-info.org

[191] ....Morley. *George Joannides.* jfk-info.org

[192] ....Armstrong, John. *The Harvey and Lee Page.* 2009-2013. Web

[193] ....Bradford, Rex. *The Fourteen Minute Gap.* LBJ and JEH on Oswald in Mexico City

[194] ....Ferrell, Mary. Comrade Kostin letter by Oswald

[195] ....Morley. JFK Facts Website. Warren Commission never told about CIA activities

[196] ....Morley. JFK Facts Website. *What are in the CIA withheld documents?*

[197] ....Fonzi, Gaeton. *The Last Investigation.* 154

[198] ....Agee, Phillip. *Inside the Company: CIA Diary.* Operation Mongoose. 67

[199] ....Camper, Frank. *The MK: ULTRA Secret.* 2013. Web

[200] ....Krock, Arthur. *Intra-Administration War in Vietnam.* JFK Lancer.com. 1963

[201] ....Kennedy quote from speech for the American Newspaper Publishers Association. New York. 1961

[202] ....Simkin. *Penn Jones Biography*

[203] ....Jones, Penn. *Excuse my Grief.* Online at the W.R.Poage Collection at Baylor University. 2013. Web

[204] ....Schonfeld, David Wolper, *Four Day in November.* UPI book of Nix and Muchmore Films

[205] ....Bernstein. *CIA and the Media.* News Organizations fronts for the CIA

[206] ....Ibid

[207] ....Simkin, John. Wagenvoord email regarding his knowledge of the Baker/Estes scandal pushed back as the *Life* front page

[208]........ Wagenvoord interview with author. December 31, 2013

[209]........ Henelly and Policoff. *How the Media Assassinated the Real Story.* Nix and CBS

[210]........ Stolley, Richard. C.D Jackson at *Time/Life* orders for Zapruder film

[211]........ Schonfeld, M. *Shadow of a Gunman.* Marie Muchmore's film also shows the grassy knoll and was purchased by UPITN. 1975

[212]........ Ibid

[213]........ Ibid

[214]........ Henelly and Pollicoff. *How the Media Assassinated the Real Story*

[215]........ Photo of Ruth Gordon, Jones Harris's mother

[216]........ Photo of Pamela Turnure

[217]........ Phone conversation with Jones Harris. October 13, 2013

[218]........ Honest Joe's Gun and Pawn Shop

[219]........ Jones Harris telephone conversation. November 9, 2013

[220]........ Schonfeld, Reese. *Shadow of a Gunman.* 1975

[221]........ Sixth Floor Museum Oral History Interview with Eddie Goldstein. 2013

[222]........ Levin, Marvin. Telephone Interview. 2013

[223]........ Ibid

[224]........ Schonfeld, Maurice. *Shadow of a Gunman.* 2013

[225]........ Ibid

[226]........ Ibid

[227]........ Kennedy quote from speech to the American Newspaper Publishers Association. New York. 1961

[228]........ LBJ Library. Nicholas Katzenbach Oral History. Transcript. Online. LBJ and Katzenbach

[229]........ Ferrell, Mary. Katzenbach memo to Bill Moyers. 1963. Web

[230]........ Kerr, James. *The National Tattler.* Texas Court of Inquiry. 1974

[231]........ Gibson, Donald. "The Creation of the Warren Commission." *Probe.* Political Committees to investigate assassination. 1966

[232]........ Dallas Police Department. Texas Court of Inquiry from Portal to Texas History Online. Web

[233]........ Kerr. *The National Tattler.* Waggoner Carr. 1974

[234]........ Russell, Richard. Telephone conversation No. 184. *Recordings and Transcripts of Telephone Conversations.* Earl Warren reluctantly becomes head of Commission

235 ....Ibid

236 ....Kerr, James. *The National Tattler.* Waggoner Carr discusses his treatment by Katzenbach and the Warren Commission

237 ....Nix-Jackson, Gayle. FOIA reports later names this man as Joe Abernathy of the Dallas FBI

238 ....Nix-Jackson. Letter from J. Gordon Shanklin

239 ....Nix-Jackson. Letter from FBI to pick up the film

240 ....Nix-Jackson. Receipt for return of the Keystone Camera to Orville Nix

241 ....Photo of Keystone Capri K-27 Camera

242 ....Kennedy quote from recorded remarks for broadcast. 1963

243 ....Price, J.C. *Dallas Sheriff's Report.* 1963

244 ....Whitmey, Peter. *The First Dissenting Witness: Mary Woodward.* List of witnesses not asked to testify

245 ....Hurt, Henry. *Reasonable Doubt: An Investigation into the Assassination of John F. Kennedy.* New York. 1985. 266

246 ....King James Bible: 1 Corinthians 13:12 "...through a glass darkly"

247 ....Kennedy, Robert F. Quote from *One Man* as related by Jackie Kennedy

248 ....WC: Testimony of Forrest Sorrels. Seating arrangement in lead car of motorcade

249 ....WC: Testimony of Forrest Sorrels. Curry radios to the Trade Mart

250 ....WC: Testimony of Forrest Sorrels

251 ....JFK Assassination Forum. *Witness Intimidation—Wilma Tice.* Various Threads. Jean Hill and other witnesses intimidated by DPD and authorities. Web

252 ....WC: Testimony of Forrest Sorrels. Where he thought gunshots came from

253 ....Ibid

254 ....Ibid

255 ....Parr. *The Mayor of Elm Street.* Rubin Goldstein Biography

256 ....Levin, Marvin. Telephone interview with author about Honest Joe's customer who pawned his prosthetic arm whenever he needed extra money

257 ....Parr, Joshua. *The Mayor of Elm Street.* Rubin Goldstein Obituary

258 ....Levin, Marvin. Interview with the author explains how his law partner helped draft the Texas Blue Law to remedy Rubin Goldstein's sales problem on Sundays

[259]........ Levin, Marvin. Interview with the author. Truthful Joe's inception, Levin law firm

[260]........ Jones Harris telephone interview. October 22, 2013

[261]........ Warren Commission findings on Jack Ruby's Mafia connections

[262]........ HSCA on Ruby Mafia Connections

[263]........ Jones Harris telephonic conversation with the author. October 19, 2013

[264]........ Lewis, Jonathan. ITEK connections to CIA. 3

[265]........ Plato quote

[266]........ Whitmey, Peter. *Lady in Red.* From Clint Bradford's JFK Assassination Information website

[267]........ Jones Harris telephone conversation with the author. October 22, 2013

[268]........ Summers, Anthony. *Conspiracy.* 92

[269]........ Hill, Jean. Interview *Dallas Morning News.* 1991

[270]........ Parr. *The Mayor of Elm Street.* Honest Joe, Rubin Goldstein

[271]........ Levin, Marvin. Phone interview with the author. December 13, 2013

[272]........ *Dallas Morning News.* Rubin Goldstein's Obituary

[273]........ Photo of Honest Joe's Edsel

[274]........ See *The Bell Film* of the Assassination

[275]........ Jones Harris conversation with author November 11, 2013

[276]........ Schonfeld, Maurice. *Shadow of a Gunman.* 1975

[277]........ Lewis explains ITEK inception and background. 2

[278]........ Ibid

[279]........ Ibid

[280]........ Lewis., 3

[281]........ Schonfeld *Shadow of a Gunman.* Discusses how he found the Frank Lindsay and Kim Philby connection. 2013

[282]........ *The New York Times.* Izvestia interview with Kim Philby

[283]........ Schonfeld. *Shadow of a Gunman.* 2013

[284]........ *Four Days in November.* David Wolper video

[285]........ Schonfeld. *Me and Ted Against the World: The Unauthorized Story of the Founding of CNN.* 2001

[286]........ Sprague, Richard. Excerpts from *Taking of America 1-2-3.* Chapter Nine

[287]........ Jones Harris phone conversation. October 19, 2013

[288]........ Schonfeld. *Memories of the Nix Film.* Interview with the author. 1990

[289] ....Warren Commission testimony of J.M. Smith. Vol. XII. 535

[290] ....Ibid

[291] ....Warren Commission testimony of D.V.Harkness. Vol. VI. 312

[292] ....Scheim, David. *The Mafia Killed President Kennedy.* 1988. On Mafia placement of men on the knoll. 30-31

[293] ....Anderson, Jack. *American Expose: Who Murdered JFK?* New York: Journal Graphics' Transcript. 1988. 14

[294] ....Photo of the sketch made by Lois Gibson of the man Malcom Summers saw on the grassy knoll

[295] ....Nix-Jackson. Letter to Keystone about Nix Camera and advertising

[296] ....Lane, Mark. *Rush to Judgment.* Video. 1967

[297] ....Kennedy note to mother in hospital the day his infant son Patrick died. Per Thurston Clarke

[298] ....White, Jack. Biography at Baylor Library Online. Web

[299] ....Myers, Dale. *Badgeman.* 2004 Article on Gary Mack and Jack White's search for Badgeman in the Moorman photograph

[300] ....White, Jack. Post on the Education Forum http://educationforum.ipbhost.com/index.php?showforum=126

[301] ....*Warren Commission Report* Testimony of JM White about woman saying she saw a gunmanin the bushes. Vol. XII. 535

[302] ....Thompson, Josiah. *Six Seconds in Dallas.* 207

[303] ...."Shadow on the Grassy Knoll: Photographic Analysis Shows No New Evidence" *Time.* HSCA Findings from ITEK regarding the Classic Gunman image. Bernie Hoffman stated that this report was the kind of report written to disprove a gunman, not find one. May, 1967

[304] ....Plumley, UK Film. *The Day the Dream Died.* Video

[305] ....Jones Harris phone conversation. October, 2013

[306] ....Ibid

[307] ....Ibid

[308] ....Hunt, John. *Beverly Oliver's Photos.* 1991. Web

[309] ....Edisen, Adele. *Honest Joe's Pawn Shop.* Deep Politics Forum. 2008. Web

[310] ....Hunt. Beverly Oliver's Photos. 1991. Web

[311] ....Perry, Dave. *Who Speaks for Roscoe White?* Web

[312] ....Marrs, Jim. *Crossfire.* 1989. 88

[313] ....Lane, M. Duke. *Freeway Man.* Web

[314]........ Goggins, William M. *James Tague: Unintended Victim in Dealey Plaza.* Web

[315]........ HSCA Final Report. Acoustic evidence of second gunman. 1979. 491

[316]........ Andrew, Christopher. *The Sword and the Shield: The Mitrokhin Archive and the Secret History of the KGB.* Basic Books. 1999. Mr. Hunt note from Oswald. 298

[317]........ Hunt. Beverly Oliver. *Found film is Nix Film*

[318]........ The motorcade route remained the same from November 18th until the 22nd

[319]........ Bernstein, Carl. "The CIA and the Media." *Rolling Stone Magazine.* October. 1977

[320]........ Camper, Frank. *The MK: ULTRA Secret.* Article on CIA Mind Conditioning accessed. 2013. Web

[321]........ The Assassination Records Review Board Final Report. CIA withheld information from JFK committees and tax records still have not been released. 1998

[322]........ HSCA. *Oswald, the CIA and Mexico City aka the Lopez Report.* Oswald was definitely in Mexico as can be attested to by Marina, the FBI and the CIA. Web

[323]........ Dunkel, Gerda. See the Muchmore film of the limousine brake lights on YouTube

[324]........ Church Committee: Final Report of the Select Committee to Study Government Operations with Respect to Intelligence Activities. 1976. The destruction of evidence from Hosty's notes to autopsy notes

[325]........ Kross, Peter. *Oswald: The CIA and the Warren Commission: The Unanswered Questions.* Bridger House Publishing. 2012. Splinter the CIA quote. 382

[326]........ Grier, Peter. *John F. Kennedy: Why Books Were a Big Part of His Life.* DC De-Coder Online. Kennedy's favorite of the Ian Fleming James Bond series was *From Russia with Love.* November 22, 2013. Web

[327]........ Buchan, Lord John Tweedmuir. *Pilgrim's Way: An Essay in Recollection.* New York. Houghton-Mifflin. 1940. Grier states Kennedy loved the book *Pilgrim's Way* and even gave Jacqueline Bouvier a copy of it while they were courting so she would better understand him. November22, 2013. Web

[328]........ Kennedy. Quote from the speech given to the American Newspaper Publishers Association in New York. April, 1961

[329]........ Reeves, Thomas. *A Question of Character: The Life of John F. Kennedy.* New York. The Free Press. 1991. 84

[330] ....Herman, Edward and Chomsky, Noam. *Manufacturing Consent: The Political Economy of the Mass Media.* Pantheon. 1988. 306

[331] ....Bernstein. "The CIA and the Media" *Rolling Stone Magazine.* October 10, 1977. Operation Mockingbird was a secret campaign by the CIA to influence the media

[332] ....Morley, Jefferson. *Joannides funds DRE.* www.jfkinfo.org

[333] ....CBS Four part televised program. *The Warren Commission.* June, 1967

[334] ....Henelly, Robert and Jerry Pollicoff. *How the Media Assassinated the Real Story.* Bernard Birnbaum. CBS. Web

[335] ....Nix-Jackson. Letters from Birnbaum

[336] ....Eddie Barker interview on National Public Radio regarding the Kennedy Assassination

[337] ....O'Neill, Tip. *Man of the House.* 178

[338] ....Barbour, John. *The JFK Assassination: The Jim Garrison Tapes Video.* 1992

[339] ....See Moses Weitzman testimony before the Assassinations Records Review Board. There is a tape recording as well as a transcript on the Mary Ferrell site. More of his responses can be found in my transcripts of our conversations.

[340] ....The letter to Chris Scally from Dr. Alan Gillespie is dated October 15, 1976 and reads, "Under our agreement with Mr. Schonfeld we cannot supply you with a copy of that (requested) report. However, we feel it is impossible to use the Nix film to resolve the question conclusively either way, especially to support the grassy knoll assassin theory. Furthermore, there are other places on the grassy knoll, either obscured by geometry or underexposed in the Nix film, where persons might hide. Thus the Nix film cannot rule out grassy knoll assassins.

[341] ....In speaking with Dr. Kenneth Castleman, he stated that he indeed remembered working on the Nix film but was not allowed to do so by the Jet Propulsion Laboratory. He was forced to pass the work to one of his students at the California Institute of Technology, James Lattimer, to study the work. He also said that the copy he had was a color copy and he was asked to study the area behind the concrete pergola, not the picket fence area.

[342] ....Nix-Jackson. Letter from UPI's Frank Kane

[343] ....Ibid

[344] ....Nix-Jackson. G. Robert Blakey correspondence

[345] ....G. Robert Blakey interview with PBS *Frontline*

[346]........ Nix-Jackson. Letter from Alexander Boch of UPI

[347]........ Nix-Jackson. My appearances on national television shows including *Geraldo, Entertainment Tonight, Montel Williams*

[348]........ Hennelly, Pollicoff

[349]........ Wise, Wes. Telephone interview discussing bothun photo. September 12, 2013

[350]........ Wise. Telephone interview about Orville Nix. October, 2013

[351]........ Morley, Jefferson. *Biography.* www.jeffersonmorley.com

[352]........ Vince Palamara Biography

[353]........ Stone, Roger. *The Man Who Killed Kennedy: The Case Against LBJ*

[354]........ Kennedy. Quote from Speech made at the American Legion. 1961

[355]........ The JFK Assassination Forum. www.jfkassassinationforum.com

[356]........ The JFK Assassination Forum. YouTube Channel

[357]........ Robin Unger's JFK Photo Gallery. http://jfkassassinationgallery.com/

[358]........ Needham, Rick. Study of Hughes Film finds Orville Nix

[359]........ Needham. Nix Study on JFK Assassination Forum

[360]........ Photo of Nix Film Frame by Rick Needham

[361]........ Carvalho, Craig. Quote on Needham's findings in the Nix Film

[362]........ Frame from the Nix Film by Rick Needham

[363]........ Thompson, Josiah. *Six Seconds in Dallas.* 153

[364]........ Needham. Photo of image in Nix Film

[365]........ MacRae, Duncan. JFK Assassination Forum

[366]........ HSCA Report and Findings

[367]........ Hinrichs, Martin. JFK Assassination Forum

[368]........ Morrissette, Denis. http://jfkassassinationfiles.com

[369]........ Unger, Robin. JFK Assassination Forum

[370]........ Unger, Robin. Quote

[371]........ Hinrichs, Martin. Quote from email correspondence with author

[372]........ Marshall, Bruce. Quote from email correspondence with author

[373]........ Marrs, Jim. *Crossfire: The Plot that Killed Kennedy.* 580

[374]........ Kennedy. Quote from speech at Loyola

[375]........ The Church Committee. Destruction of Oswald Note

[376]........ Oliver Stone's Movie *JFK*. Quote by Joe Pesci's character, David Ferrie